THE WISDOM *of*
the LOTUS SUTRA

THE WISDOM OF THE

LOTUS SUTRA

A DISCUSSION

VOLUME III

EXAMINING CHAPTERS 11–15:

THE EMERGENCE OF THE TREASURE TOWER · DEVADATTA

ENCOURAGING DEVOTION · PEACEFUL PRACTICES

EMERGING FROM THE EARTH

Daisaku Ikeda

Katsuji Saito • Takanori Endo • Haruo Suda

World Tribune
—Press—

Published by
World Tribune Press
606 Wilshire Blvd.
Santa Monica, CA 90401

ISBN: 978-0-915678-71-6

Design by Gopa & Ted2, Inc.
Cover image © Photodisc

10 9 8 7 6

Library of Congress Cataloging-in-Publication Data

The Wisdom of the Lotus Sutra : a discussion : /
    Daisaku Ikeda… [et al].
        p. cm.
        Includes index.
        ISBN: 0-915678-71-3 (v. 2 : alk.paper)

        1. Tripitaka. Sutrapitaka.
Saddharmapundarikasutra — Criticism.
interpretation, etc. I. Ikeda, Daisaku.

BQ2057.W57 2000   294.3'85—dc21
                    00-011670

Table of Contents

Editor's Note

This book is a series of discussions among SGI President Daisaku Ikeda, Soka Gakkai Study Department Chief Katsuji Saito and vice chiefs Takanori Endo and Haruo Suda. It was first serialized in English starting with the April 1995 issue of *Seikyo Times* (now *Living Buddhism*).

The citations most commonly used in this book have been abbreviated as follows:

+ GZ, page number(s) refers to the *Gosho zenshu*, the Japanese-language compilation of letters, treatises, essays and oral teachings of Nichiren Daishonin.

+ LSOC, page number(s) refers to *The Lotus Sutra and Its Opening and Closing Sutras*, translated by Burton Watson (Tokyo: Soka Gakkai, 2009).

+ OTT, page number(s) refers to *The Record of the Orally Transmitted Teachings*, translated by Burton Watson (Tokyo: Soka Gakkai, 2004).

+ WND, page number(s) refers to *The Writings of Nichiren Daishonin*, vol. 1 (WND-1) (Tokyo, Soka Gakkai, 1999) and vol. 2 (WND-2) (Tokyo: Soka Gakkai, 2006).

PART I:

"The Emergence of the Treasure Tower" Chapter

1 One's Life
Is Itself the Treasure Tower

Ikeda: Dr. David W. Chappell[1] once suggested to me that dialogue based on the spirit of the Lotus Sutra — on a sense of respect and appreciation for the infinite worth of each person's life — would hold the key to the future of humankind. Such respect for life is in fact the message of the Lotus Sutra and of the "Treasure Tower" chapter. The rich soil of such mutual respect can sustain fruitful dialogue and friendship, and the flourishing of peace. He also expressed the belief that military force is no match for the strength of human friendship.

Saito: As you suggest, the Lotus Sutra — Buddhism — is certainly not remote or far removed from our daily lives. For it to have any real meaning, it has to become manifest in our immediate actions.

Endo: The American mythologist Joseph Campbell writes, "I think of compassion as the fundamental religious experience and, unless that is there, you have nothing."[2]

Ikeda: Buddhism lies close at hand in the here and now. It exists in daily life, in human existence, in society. To present Buddhism as belonging to some realm removed from life and reality is a deception.

Saito: Priests of later times often shrouded Buddhism in mystical terms in order to appropriate authority for themselves, so for many, Buddhism has an aura of the esoteric hanging over it.

Endo: They've taken what the Buddha went to great lengths to explain as clearly and simply as possible and added layers of obfuscation and obscurity.

Ikeda: Since ancient times, a great many interpretations have been given to the chapter we will be studying, "The Emergence of the Treasure Tower." In some cases, such interpretations meant a great deal to the people to whom they were articulated. Nichiren Daishonin, however, points to its ultimate significance when he plainly says that the teaching of the treasure tower refers to "our individual bodies" (OTT, 91). In the same vein, comparing the appearance of the treasure tower to one's emergence at birth, he says: "The Treasure Purity World is the wombs of our mothers" (OTT, 91); and, "the process of emerging from these wombs is called 'coming forth and appearing'" (OTT, 228).

Our lives are dignified treasure towers. Yet this truth eludes us. To realize that this truth is indeed our lives is in fact "seeing the treasure tower." The ceremony that takes place in the "Treasure Tower" chapter is a mirror that reveals the true aspect of our lives. The Gohonzon that Nichiren established, based on the ceremony in the "Treasure Tower" chapter, is the "clear mirror" in which we can perceive our true selves.

Buddhism is close at hand; it is concerned with the reality of our lives. This should be our basic stance as we try to come to terms with the teachings of the Lotus Sutra.

THE APPEARANCE OF THE TREASURE TOWER

At that time in the Buddha's presence there was a tower adorned with the seven treasures, five hundred yojanas in height and two hundred and fifty yojanas in width and depth, that rose up out of the earth and stood suspended in the air. Various kinds of precious objects adorned it. It had five thousand railings, a thousand, ten thousand rooms, and numberless streamers and banners decorated it. Festoons of jewels hung down and ten thousand million jeweled bells were suspended from it. All four sides emitted a fragrance of tamala leaves and sandalwood that pervaded the whole world. Its banners and canopies were made of the seven treasures, namely, gold, silver, lapis lazuli, seashell, agate, pearl, and carnelian, and it was so high it reached to the heavenly palaces of the four heavenly kings. (LSOC, 209)

Endo: This chapter opens with the appearance of the treasure tower, an enormous tower that suddenly emerges from the earth and suspends itself in midair. Then, quite without warning, a great voice is heard issuing from within the tower:

> "Excellent, excellent! Shakyamuni, World-Honored One, that you can take … the Lotus Sutra of the Wonderful Law, and preach it for the sake of the great assembly! It is as you say, as you say. Shakyamuni, World-Honored One, all that you have expounded is the truth!" (LSOC, 209–10)

Hearing such words of praise leaves those in the assembly with great doubt. Someone asks: "World-Honored One, for what reason has this treasure tower risen up out of the earth? And why does this voice issue from its midst?" (LSOC, 210).

Shakyamuni explains that in the treasure tower there is a Buddha named Many Treasures, and that this Buddha once made the following great vow: "If, after I have become a Buddha and entered extinction, in the lands in the ten directions there is any place where the Lotus Sutra is preached, then my funerary tower … will come forth and appear in that spot to testify to the sutra and praise its excellence" (LSOC, 210).

Suda: The bodhisattva questioning Shakyamuni persists: "World-Honored One, we wish to see the body of this Buddha" (LSOC, 211).

Endo: But there is a condition. In order for Many Treasures Buddha to show himself, Shakyamuni must first gather all of the Buddhas who, as his emanations, are expounding the Law in the ten directions of the universe. To cause these Buddhas to gather, Shakyamuni purifies the *saha* world three times, enlarges it by the addition of many other worlds, and combines all of these worlds into one magnificent Buddha land. This is what is meant by "three transformations of the land."

When Shakyamuni opens the treasure tower after all the Buddhas have gathered, Many Treasures Buddha is seen solemnly seated within.

Suda: Reading the description in the sutra, you can almost hear the people catch their breath at the incredible sight before them.

Endo: Many Treasures Buddha reiterates his praise for Shakyamuni's preaching of the Lotus Sutra, saying, "Excellent, excellent, Shakyamuni Buddha!" (LSOC, 214). He then moves over and invites Shakyamuni to join him on his seat.

Suda: Shakyamuni and Many Treasures Buddha thus seated together within the treasure tower is the origin of the term *two Buddhas seated side by side.*

Endo: Now the people are gazing up at the Buddhas in the tower high above them. At this point, Shakyamuni lifts the entire assembly into the air. That is the beginning of the Ceremony in the Air.

Shakyamuni calls to them: "Who is capable of broadly preaching the Lotus Sutra of the Wonderful Law in this saha world? Now is the time to do so, for before long the Thus Come One will enter nirvana. The Buddha wishes to entrust this Lotus Sutra of the Wonderful Law to someone so that it may be preserved" (LSOC,

215). Next he explains that the tower of Many Treasures Buddha has appeared and the Buddhas from the ten directions have gathered in this place, at this time, to "make certain the Law will long endure" (LSOC, 217).

Suda: In other words, this is the vow they make to ensure that the Law will never perish.

Endo: Shakyamuni explains (by describing the "six difficult and nine easy acts") just how difficult it will be to embrace and spread the Lotus Sutra in the world after his passing, compared with the difficulty of embracing and spreading other sutras. He urges those in the assembly to arouse a strong desire and vow to accomplish this very difficult task, saying that those who do will attain the unsurpassed Way of the Buddha. This is the basic outline of the "Treasure Tower" chapter.

Saito: I guess the high point would be the appearance of the magnificent and grand treasure tower, beautifully adorned with the seven treasures, which include gold, silver, lapis lazuli and agate.

Ikeda: The appearance of the great tower dramatically marks the beginning of the Ceremony in the Air. The Daishonin says that what then takes place is "no ordinary ceremony" (WND-1, 437).

Endo: It certainly is by no means "ordinary." The appearance of the treasure tower, the testimony of Many Treasures Buddha, the three transformations of the land, the gathering of Shakyamuni's emanations from throughout the universe, the two Buddhas Shakyamuni and Many Treasures sitting side by side—here we have a succession of extraordinary and entirely unprecedented events.

Suda: The extraordinary size of the treasure tower is itself remarkable. Measuring five hundred *yojanas* in height and two hundred and fifty *yojanas* in width and depth, it is enormous.

A *yojana* was a unit of measure used in ancient India. It indicated the distance that the royal army could travel in a day. According to one explanation, it corresponds to forty Chinese *ri* (a *ri* being about one-third of a mile). There are a number of other definitions, but even calculated conservatively five hundred *yojanas* would be equal to one-third the diameter of the Earth. A distance so great must have been all but incomprehensible to the people of the day.

Ikeda: They're not the only ones who would have difficulty imagining something that enormous. We cannot fathom a tower of such dimensions without thinking in astronomical terms. The fact that it is adorned with seven kinds of treasures is also extraordinary.

Endo: Several points are hard to visualize. For example, the sutra says that Many Treasures Buddha is within the treasure tower, but where would he have been within such an enormous edifice? Shakyamuni opens the treasure tower with his right hand and sits down alongside Many Treasures, but is the door large or small? And where in the treasure tower is the door located?

Ikeda: That's why there is nothing surprising about Abutsu-bo[3] asking Nichiren Daishonin to explain the meaning of the treasure tower.

Saito: The shape of the treasure tower isn't clearly explained either. We are told that it is "high," but is it rectangular? Is it cylindrical? Is it shaped like a cone or a pyramid? Is it dome shaped? None of this is clear.

Ikeda: Maybe the people of India at the time had a certain image of its shape. But it seems to me that what a tower symbolized to them is more important than its precise shape.

Suda: Well, "tower" (Jpn *to*) comes from the Chinese translation of the Sanskrit term *stupa*. Indian stupas are said to have had extraordinarily rich symbolism. Incidentally, the Japanese words *sotoba* and *toba* (memorial tablets) are transliterations of stupa.

The term *stupa* appears in ancient Vedic (i.e., Hindu) texts. Its meanings include "axis connecting heaven and earth" and "top of the fulcrum." Certain Vedic texts say that the entire universe is like a tree; the crown, or top-most portion, of this tree is called the stupa. It seems this portion was also taken to symbolize the entire universe.

Ikeda: Given that cultural background, it may be that the sutra's description of the treasure tower conjured up an image of some cosmic entity in the minds of the ancient Indians.

Endo: It's interesting that both *toba* and the treasure tower are stupas. Corrupt priests will badger people to make *toba* offerings [i.e., pay a fee to have a memorial tablet inscribed for a deceased person] simply to make money. But they never bother erecting the treasure tower in their own lives.

Suda: Originally, stupas were often in the shape of a dome, and these were called "eggs" (Skt *anda*). Not only did they resemble eggs in their shape, but the term alludes to a golden egg that is mentioned in a Vedic creation myth. The egg, it seems, symbolized the universal creative power or principle.

Endo: In terms of ancient Indian cosmology, there also appears to be a connection with Mount Sumeru, which was supposed to stand at the center of the world. The people of India seem to have regarded the lofty peaks of the Himalayas and other mountains as a kind of ideal land. These mountains seem to have held great meaning for them, perhaps because they were the source of water — something very important for a land as arid as India.

Stupas often contained symbols of various kinds representing Mount Sumeru as an ideal land. Also in Buddhist texts are many statements suggesting that stupas were identified with Mount Sumeru.

Ikeda: The Himalayas, which I saw when I visited Nepal, are certainly a majestic sight. They struck me as having the imposing dignity of a treasure tower connecting heaven and earth.

It seems to me that a common thread in everything that has been said so far is that stupas symbolize the center of the world and of the universe. I think that the treasure tower in the Lotus Sutra, which is astronomically large, also carries this significance.

In the "Treasure Tower" chapter, Shakyamuni purifies the world three times to cause the Buddhas throughout the universe who are his emanations to gather, and he unifies a vast number of lands—the figure given is "410 thousand million *nayutas*"[4] of lands—into one Buddha land.

Countless Buddhas assemble, emitting enough brilliance to illuminate the darkness of night. The lapis lazuli ground is covered with countless jewels and flowers. Jeweled trees grow lush. It is a scene of dizzying golden brilliance. And at the center of everything stands the treasure tower.

The treasure tower is at the center of the universe. In brilliance it is like a gathering of all the jewels in the universe. Its magnificence metaphorically indicates that the life of each person is a cluster of jewels. Its immense size illustrates the truth that each person's life is as vast as the universe.

Saito: Because the treasure tower floats in the air, it would indeed have the appearance of an axis connecting heaven and earth.

Ikeda: Nichiren Daishonin says, "[In terms of Myoho-renge-kyo] the air represents *renge*, earth represents *kyo*, and heaven represents *myoho*" (OTT, 95). In other words, the treasure tower floating in midair between heaven and earth indicates that heaven, air and earth are in their entirety Myoho-renge-kyo.

The universe in its entirety, as signified by heaven and earth, is

Myoho-renge-kyo. Our lives are Myoho-renge-kyo. And the treasure tower is also Myoho-renge-kyo. This points to the grand truth that our lives and the universe are one.

In terms of the doctrine of the three truths, the identification of the universe with the entity of the Mystic Law is the truth of nonsubstantiality. And the identification of one's body with the Mystic Law is the truth of temporary existence.

Saito: Each living entity is the temporary unification of the five components (i.e., form, perception, conception, volition and consciousness). This is what the truth of temporary existence means.

The Record of the Orally Transmitted Teachings says, regarding the chapter's title, "The Emergence of the Treasure Tower": "The word 'treasure' stands for the five components of life, form, perception, conception, volition, and consciousness. The word 'tower' stands for the harmony and combination of the five components. The five components functioning in harmony is designated a treasure tower. The harmony of the five components emerges or is seen in the five characters Myoho-renge-kyo. This is the meaning of the word *ken*, to emerge or to be seen" (OTT, 89).

In other words, when we perceive that our lives are Myoho-renge-kyo, we are seeing the treasure tower. This is the truth of temporary existence.

Ikeda: You've explained the truth of nonsubstantiality and the truth of temporary existence. The treasure tower's emergence, then, must correspond to Myoho-renge-kyo, which is the truth of the Middle Way. In the mirror of the treasure tower (i.e., the Gohonzon) we see the treasure tower within ourselves. We perceive that we ourselves are the treasure tower.

Saito: The treasure tower, in other words, is none other than the lives of people who believe in the Mystic Law and chant Nam-myoho-renge-kyo. This is what Nichiren Daishonin repeatedly emphasizes.

Endo: In one place, for example, the Daishonin says, "the 'Treasure Tower' chapter exists within the body of Nichinyo" (WND-1, 915–16). He also says:

> In the Latter Day of the Law, no treasure tower exists other than the figures of the men and women who embrace the Lotus Sutra. It follows, therefore, that whether eminent or humble, high or low, those who chant Nam-myoho-renge-kyo are themselves the treasure tower, and, likewise, are themselves the Thus Come One Many Treasures . . .
>
> At present the entire body of the Honorable Abutsu is composed of the five elements of earth, water, fire, wind, and space. These five elements are also the five characters of the daimoku. Abutsu-bo is therefore the treasure tower itself, and the treasure tower is Abutsu-bo himself. No other knowledge is purposeful. (WND-1, 299)

Ikeda: Abutsu-bo wanted to learn the significance of the treasure tower. The Daishonin explained to him simply: The treasure tower is none other than you yourself. And, adding, "No other knowledge is purposeful," he indicates that this is the main point to grasp. In other words, there is nothing to be gained from trying to understand other theories or doctrines.

Once we understand that we who pray to the Gohonzon are ourselves the tower of many treasures, what need do we have of further doctrinal understanding? We are studying the Lotus Sutra in this manner to confirm our understanding of its essential meaning and to deepen our faith and be able to talk about the Lotus Sutra with others. Knowledge that strays from this fundamental objective is of no value for the purpose of attaining Buddhahood.

Based on that, why don't we draw out the main points about the treasure tower as it is described in the Lotus Sutra?

THE TREASURE TOWER IS NONE OTHER
THAN MYOHO-RENGE-KYO

Saito: The "Treasure Tower" chapter explains the origins of the treasure tower. Based on both the Sanskrit text and Kumarajiva's Chinese translation, we know the following:

(1) In the past, Many Treasures Buddha, living in a world called Treasure Purity in the eastern part of the universe, heard the doctrine of Myoho-renge (termed "White Lotus" in the Sanskrit text) and attained Buddhahood. (2) When he was about to enter extinction, Many Treasures entrusted people with the task of building an immense treasure tower for the enshrinement of the "body of the Thus Come One." (3) Because of the strength of his vow (referred to earlier), this treasure tower appears wherever and whenever the doctrine of Myoho-renge is taught. (4) The reason for the treasure tower's appearance is to hear the doctrine of Myoho-renge being expounded and to testify to its truth. (5) In order for the treasure tower to open and the "body of the Thus Come One" to be revealed, the Buddha, expounding the doctrine of Myoho-renge, must gather all his emanations from the worlds in the ten directions.

What stands out in these descriptions is the frequent reference to the doctrine of Myoho-renge. In Kumarajiva's Chinese translation, this is rendered variously as "the Lotus Sutra" or "this sutra," though it is not repeated as many times, making it less conspicuous. But in the Sanskrit text, the expression *doctrine of the White Lotus* is stressed repeatedly. Also, in the entire Lotus Sutra, this term appears most frequently in the "Treasure Tower" chapter.

Ikeda: The treasure tower bears a close relationship to the five characters of Myoho-renge-kyo. Or, more precisely, as the Daishonin said, the treasure tower is itself Myoho-renge-kyo.

Saito: It is particularly important to note that the treasure tower is meant to appear wherever the doctrine of Myoho-renge is being expounded. This is indicative of the relationship between the treasure tower and Myoho-renge-kyo.

Plants, for instance, bloom in response to the external causes or stimuli of sunlight and water. Similarly, the treasure tower appears in response to the Lotus Sutra being expounded. We could say the treasure tower in its entirety is the essential manifestation of the Law of Myoho-renge-kyo.

Suda: In the sutra, the treasure tower certainly does appear in response to the preaching of the Lotus Sutra, just as a lotus flower blossoms when struck by the rays of the sun. I can imagine that's how it must have seemed to those gathered in the assembly.

Ikeda: The treasure tower of Myoho-renge-kyo does indeed appear in response to the preaching of Myoho-renge-kyo. When we chant the Mystic Law and practice for our own happiness, as well as that of others, our lives become the treasure tower. Put another way, the treasure tower emerges in our lives. The Law that we chant is Myoho-renge-kyo. And Myoho-renge-kyo is also the entity of our lives.

Josei Toda said:

> I once asked a scholar who had become a priest: "The Lotus Sutra says that the treasure tower appears where the Lotus Sutra is being expounded. But Nichiren Daishonin expounded the Lotus Sutra and no treasure tower appeared. Why is this?" The man looked very perplexed.
>
> When Abutsu-bo asked the Daishonin about the treasure tower, the Daishonin told him, "Abutsu-bo is the treasure tower itself, and the treasure tower is Abutsu-bo himself." Your body is itself the treasure tower. Within that treasure tower, within your life, are seated the two Buddhas Shakyamuni and Many Treasures. And they have called forth Bodhisattva Superior Practices.[5]

Suda: This is a real pitfall for scholars who tend to understand Buddhism only in terms of theory. They think of the treasure tower as existing some place far away.

Ikeda: President Toda also said:

> The mystic life of the world of Buddhahood is an intrinsic part of our own lives. The power and condition of this life of Buddhahood exceeds the reach of one's imagination and defies description in words. But we can concretely manifest it in the entity of our own lives. The ceremony in the "Treasure Tower" chapter explains that we can in fact manifest in our lives the inherent world of Buddhahood. In the ceremony of the "Treasure Tower" chapter, Shakyamuni reveals the principles of the "mutual possession of the Ten Worlds" and "three thousand realms in a single moment of life" within his own life.[6]

The ceremony in the "Treasure Tower" chapter explains the sanctity of the world of Buddhahood, which all beings inherently possess. Why, then, does Myoho-renge-kyo need to be expressed in concrete form as the treasure tower? Because this is the teaching for the age after the Buddha's passing; it's to ensure that the Law will long endure.

Up to this point, it has been explained that those who hear the Lotus Sutra and believe in and understand it can definitely attain Buddhahood. I think the appearance of the treasure tower is actual proof of the Lotus Sutra's power.

From "Treasure Tower" on, Shakyamuni teaches in terms of life in this world what he had explained only theoretically in preceding chapters. This, in other words, is the essential teaching. The preparatory section[7] of the essential teaching (or latter half of the Lotus Sutra) begins with the "Treasure Tower" chapter.

The testimony of Many Treasures Buddha goes beyond his

utterances of "Excellent, excellent!" from within the treasure tower attesting to the veracity of the Lotus Sutra. Rather, the appearance of Many Treasures Buddha and of the treasure tower, each in its own way, serves as actual proof of the truth of Myoho-renge-kyo.

The title of the chapter, "The Emergence of the Treasure Tower," means perceiving Myoho-renge-kyo through the appearance of the treasure tower. Its appearance could be thought of as the direct experience of Myoho-renge-kyo. In other words, the treasure tower teaches that our lives are Myoho-renge-kyo. In that sense, the Daishonin calls the "Treasure Tower" chapter a "bright mirror."

Endo: He says: "Now when Nichiren and his followers chant Nam-myoho-renge-kyo, they see and understand the ten thousand phenomena as though these were reflected in a bright mirror. This bright mirror is the Lotus Sutra. And in particular it is the 'Treasure Tower' chapter" (OTT, 149). He also says, "The five bodily sections, or the five elements that make up the bodies of living beings such as us, are reflections of Myoho-renge-kyo, and therefore we should learn to use the 'Treasure Tower' chapter as our mirror" (OTT, 51–52).

Ikeda: The "tower adorned with the seven treasures" is the grand and dignified original form of our lives. The treasure tower expounded in the Lotus Sutra is indeed an accurate response to Socrates's philosophical dictum "Know thyself."

The treasure tower that those in the assembly see when lifted up in the air must be the entity of their own lives. They no doubt saw an unshakable self, solemn and towering. That's why it's called a "bright mirror."

Meaning is also connected to the fact that the treasure tower emerges from the earth. Here the earth symbolizes the reality of the nine worlds, of people's lives. The treasure tower is more than a mere expression of the life of Buddhahood; its emergence from the earth indicates that people can choose to construct the treasure tower within their own lives. The nine worlds themselves contain the world of Buddhahood. That's why the treasure tower emerges from the earth.

The Fusion of Reality and Wisdom

Saito: Nichiren Daishonin says that the two Buddhas Shakyamuni and Many Treasures indicate the two principles of reality and wisdom, and the two seated side by side therefore signifies the fusion of reality and wisdom. Many Treasures represents reality, and Shakyamuni, the wisdom to correctly perceive it. How should we understand this?

Ikeda: President Toda said that "reality" means the objective world, and "wisdom," the subjective world. He was not using these terms in a Western, dualistic sense. Rather, his comment assumes the essential unity of the subjective and objective realms.

Suda: Nichiren Daishonin says, "Reality means the true nature of all phenomena, and wisdom means the illuminating and manifesting of this true nature" (WND-1, 746).

Ikeda: That's right. In fact, President Toda often said, "If being a grocer is your 'reality,' then working hard to make your business prosper is manifesting the 'fusion of reality and wisdom.'"

Of course, whatever our occupation—whether fishmonger or corporate employee—we each have a mission to fulfill and a path in life. That is our "reality." It is the light of wisdom that causes this reality to shine. Effecting the perfect fusion of reality and wisdom in our lives means becoming indispensable wherever we are.

This is not limited to human beings. Cherry trees sense the changing of the seasons, and when spring comes they all at once burst into bloom. This also illustrates the fusion of reality and wisdom. It could be said that the wisdom of cherry trees lies in their innate sense of spring's arrival.

Suda: It would indeed be astonishing if they were to bloom in summer.

Ikeda: In essence, everyone is a Buddha. That is our "reality." It is the light of wisdom that causes the world of Buddhahood in our lives to shine. Our Buddhahood starts shining when we develop the wisdom to realize we are Buddhas. This is the fusion of reality and wisdom. From our standpoint, according to the Buddhist principle of "substituting faith for wisdom," wisdom means faith. That we possess the world of Buddhahood is the objective truth, the reality, of our lives. Faith causes this reality to shine in actuality.

Shakyamuni and Many Treasures represent ordinary people who cause the original world of Buddhahood in their lives—usually covered over by the soot of earthly desires—to shine. The Thus Come One is an ordinary person, a human being. Nichiren Daishonin says, "Shakyamuni, Many Treasures, and the Buddhas of the ten directions represent the world of Buddhahood within ourselves" (WND-1, 365).

Again, Many Treasures corresponds to reality because he always appears where the Lotus Sutra is being expounded. In other words, he represents eternal truth. And Shakyamuni causes this eternal truth to manifest here and now.

Put another way, something eternal manifests in the here and now as a result of the two Buddhas sitting side by side, that is, through the fusion of reality and wisdom. In fact, it is only in the here and now that something eternal can appear. Anything else is just an illusion.

Shakyamuni represents wisdom, or the subjective entity. The Mystic Law manifests in our lives only when we wage a great struggle on our own initiative. We experience the fusion of reality and wisdom when we work to carry out our mission burning with the conviction: "I am a Bodhisattva of the Earth! I am a Buddha!"

Saito: And Nam-myoho-renge-kyo is the expression of this fusion of reality and wisdom.

Ikeda: That's right. "Reality" means the reality of the Mystic Law, and "wisdom," the wisdom of the Mystic Law. This is what the Daishonin teaches when he writes: "What then are these two elements of reality and wisdom? They are simply the five characters of Nam-myoho-renge-kyo" (WND-1, 746).

Reality and wisdom are not separate; they are a single entity. Reality gives rise to wisdom, and wisdom illuminates reality. That is their relation. Thinking about this in terms of the sun may make it easier to grasp. The substance of the sun is its "reality." Just as the sun emits light and thereby illuminates and causes itself to appear, reality produces wisdom.

Suda: The two Buddhas Shakyamuni and Many Treasures are functions of the Law of Nam-myoho-renge-kyo. Shakyamuni and Many Treasures express the Law of Nam-myoho-renge-kyo embodying the oneness of reality and wisdom.

Ikeda: Nichiren Daishonin says: "Therefore, the two Buddhas, Shakyamuni and Many Treasures, are Buddhas who are functions [of Myoho-renge-kyo]. It is Myoho-renge-kyo that is the true Buddha" (WND-1, 384).

THE GOHONZON AND THE CEREMONY IN THE AIR

Endo: In terms of the Gohonzon inscribed by Nichiren Daishonin, this passage clarifies why the Law of Nam-myoho-renge-kyo appears prominently down the center, and Shakyamuni and Many Treasures are positioned on either side.

Saito: The two Buddhas seated side by side also express the principle of the true aspect of all phenomena; Many Treasures represents all phenomena, and Shakyamuni, the true aspect. They also express the oneness of life and death; Many Treasures represents death, and Shakyamuni, life.

Suda: The Daishonin inscribed the Gohonzon based on the ceremony that takes place in the "Treasure Tower" chapter, incorpo-
rating such elements as the two Buddhas seated side by side.

The Daishonin says that only he is qualified to "give concrete
form to the ceremony of the two Buddhas seated side by side in
the treasure tower" (WND-1, 383). He also declares: "This mandala
is in no way my invention. It is the object of devotion that depicts
Shakyamuni Buddha, the World-Honored One, seated in the treasure tower of Many Treasures Buddha, and the Buddhas who were
Shakyamuni's emanations as perfectly as a print matches its wood-
block" (WND-1, 831).

Ikeda: In explaining the significance of the "Treasure Tower" chapter to Abutsu-bo, the Daishonin prefaced his remarks by saying that
this matter "is of great importance" (WND-1, 299). That is because
the Ceremony in the Air is a fundamental issue relating to the
Gohonzon.

Saito: In a letter to Shijo Kingo, he says [regarding the significance
of Shakyamuni and Many Treasures in the treasure tower as representing reality and wisdom], "These are teachings of prime
importance" (WND-1, 318).

Ikeda: The Great Teacher T'ien-t'ai of China explains that the
appearance of the treasure tower has two distinct functions: one
is to lend credence to the preceding chapters and the other is to
pave the way for the revelation to come.

Suda: That's mentioned in the *Words and Phrases of the Lotus Sutra.*[8]
That the treasure tower lends credence to the preceding chapters
means that it certifies the truth of Shakyamuni's words in the earlier chapters. Thus the great voice of Many Treasures Buddha
issues from within the treasure tower asserting that Shakyamuni's
words are true.

Ikeda: By his voice and his appearance, Many Treasures testifies to the truth of the Mystic Law. This is the function of Many Treasures Buddha. In the Soka Gakkai today, this is in a sense the function of the members of the Many Treasures Group.

Endo: I now see the significance of forming the Many Treasures Group as a way to honor longtime members who have rich experiences in life and in faith.

Ikeda: These are people who have dedicated their lives to the noble mission of proving the truth of the Mystic Law. Each of them is literally a treasure of the Soka Gakkai, of kosen-rufu and of society.

I hope all members will live long lives. The longer we live, the greater the victory of kosen-rufu. Also, I hope members who are advanced in years, as Many Treasures Buddhas of kosen-rufu, will always be ready to warmly praise their juniors with a sense of "Excellent, excellent!"

Endo: By lending credence to the preceding chapters, the "Treasure Tower" also paves the way for the revelation to come; that is, it sets the stage for the teaching that follows. Shakyamuni's gathering of the Buddhas of the ten directions is his starting point to expound the "Life Span" chapter. The fact that he has so many emanations suggests that Shakyamuni has been instructing others as a Buddha for an extremely long time.

Ikeda: From a literal standpoint, "preceding chapters" (in "lend credence to the preceding chapters") refers to the first half of the Lotus Sutra (or theoretical teaching). And "the revelation to come" means the Lotus Sutra's second half (or essential teaching). The emergence of the treasure tower is the starting point to preach the essential teaching that follows.

In terms of the Nichiren Buddhism, however, the treasure tower's appearance paves the way for Nichiren Daishonin's essential teaching. The preaching in the "Treasure Tower" chapter becomes the starting point for the Daishonin's establishment of the Gohonzon. From this standpoint, "the revelation to come" means the Daishonin's revelation of the object of devotion for the Latter Day of the Law. That's why Nichiren Daishonin calls the object of devotion he has inscribed the treasure tower.

The Gohonzon is the Daishonin's very life, the life of the Buddha inherently endowed with the three enlightened properties, or "three bodies."[9] It is the treasure tower of Nam-myoho-renge-kyo.

As was mentioned, the two Buddhas Shakyamuni and Many Treasures represent reality and wisdom. In terms of the Buddha's three bodies, Many Treasures Buddha, representing reality, signifies the "Dharma body," or property of the Law. Shakyamuni, representing wisdom, signifies the "reward body," or property of wisdom. And the Buddhas of the ten directions, representing the compassion that arises through the fusion of reality and wisdom, signify the "manifested body," or property of action. The appearance of these three Buddhas — Shakyamuni, Many Treasures and the Buddhas of the ten directions — expresses the state of life inherently endowed with the three bodies that the Daishonin himself revealed.

Let us discuss the three bodies in detail on another occasion. The important point here is that the Daishonin opened a path whereby all people of the Latter Day can themselves actualize these three enlightened properties now and naturally endow their lives. And that is the path of believing in and upholding the Gohonzon.

Saito: This is what is meant by "The eternally endowed three bodies . . . are gained through a single word. And that single word is faith" (OTT, 125).

Ikeda: Nichiren Daishonin says that those who believe in the Lotus Sutra "can enter the treasure tower of the Gohonzon" (WND-1, 832), indicating that they can construct a treasure tower within their lives.

Because of the principle of the oneness of life and its environment, when we open up the treasure tower in our lives, the world in which we live also becomes the treasure tower; and so we "enter the treasure tower." Then, while dwelling in the world of the original Buddha, we can freely take action. Our bodies, which amount to barely a speck in the larger scheme of things, are adorned with the seven treasures, and our state of life limitlessly expands approaching the vastness of the universe. Nothing is more wondrous than this transformation of our lives.

While in prison (during World War II for his refusal to compromise his religious beliefs), President Toda made an in-depth study of the Lotus Sutra. He realized that its essence is to be found in the Gohonzon that Nichiren Daishonin inscribed. He understood, in other words, that there is not the slightest deviation between the words and phrases of the Lotus Sutra and the teaching of the Daishonin. And at this realization he shed tears of joy.

Saito: You describe that scene in the first volume of *The Human Revolution.* You wrote that, right after his release from prison, Mr. Toda examined the Gohonzon in his home, scrutinizing every character. And then he said: "'It was just like this. No mistake. Exactly, just as I saw it....' Murmuring silently, he satisfied himself that the solemn and mysterious Ceremony in the Air he had witnessed in his cell was indeed inscribed on the Gohonzon. Profound delight surged through him and tears streamed down his face" (p. 20).

Endo: Today we can only imagine the joy he must have felt. At that point, he became all the more confident of the truth of what he had realized while in prison.

Ikeda: Because of President Toda's conviction in this, faith in the Gohonzon became firmly established in the Soka Gakkai. This is the origin of the Soka Gakkai's great development.

President Toda saw everything with perfect clarity. It was impossible to put something over on him. The only way to approach him was with complete honesty and forthrightness. To people who approached him in that way, he responded in kind without fail. Over time, I have come to appreciate even more keenly President Toda's greatness. It's something I feel with my entire being.

An example that comes to mind has to do with the practice of making pilgrimages to holy sites. Many religions revere places associated with their founders as special. Sites with strong connections to Nichiren Daishonin include the Izu Peninsula and Sado Island, where the Daishonin was sent into exile; Tatsunokuchi and Komatsubara, where he encountered severe persecution; Kamakura, where he was active for many years; his birthplace, Kominato; Mount Minobu, where he spent his final years; and Ikegami, where he died. But President Toda did not treat these places as holy sites. Rather, he taught that we should always base ourselves on the Gohonzon. In this we can see his profound insight.

When we pray to the Gohonzon with strong faith, then that place, wherever it may be, becomes the holiest of lands. It becomes the site of the Ceremony in the Air. It becomes Eagle Peak. There, the treasure tower emerges.

Suda: I understand that many of the world's religions designate specific sites as being particularly relevant. In most cases their believers have the choice to visit them or not. But to require adherents to visit such sites, in my view, limits a religion's universality and can certainly diminish the scope of its appeal.

Ikeda: You're quite right. We, on the other hand, can attend the eternal Ceremony in the Air here and now. We can cause the treasure tower to shine in our lives, our daily existence, our homes. That is the greatness of faith in the Gohonzon. It is always close at hand and always reflected in our immediate reality.

The Ceremony in the Air, in contrast to the ceremonies at Eagle Peak that precede and follow it, takes place in a realm that transcends time and space. It does not occur in a specific historical time or place. For precisely this reason, we can attend the Ceremony in the Air at any time and in any place.

When we pray to the Gohonzon, which depicts the Ceremony in the Air, we become one with the eternal and universal life in the present moment; and, right where we are, we manifest the vast state of life from which we can survey the entire universe.

In that sense, our daily practice of gongyo and chanting daimoku is a journey of life of an even grander scale than that of an astronaut looking down on Earth from outer space.

THE SEVEN TREASURES ADORN THE SELF

Endo: Then the seven treasures that adorn the treasure tower must exist within our own lives.

Ikeda: Yes. They exist nowhere but within our lives.

Saito: Nichiren Daishonin reveals to Abutsu-bo that the seven treasures indicate "hearing the correct teaching, believing it, keeping the precepts, engaging in meditation, practicing assiduously, renouncing one's attachments, and reflecting on oneself" (WND-1, 299).

Ikeda: These are treasures within our lives. In contrast to what people commonly regard as treasures, the gold, silver and other treasures adorning the treasure tower indicate treasures in the realm of faith; they are the treasures, for example, of "listening to the teaching" and "believing it." They are the only treasures we can take with us after our death. They are eternal wealth.

Endo: These seven treasures, also referred to as the "seven riches of the Law," are indispensable elements of Buddhist practice.

Suda: President Ikeda, I recall an explanation you once gave of the concept of the seven treasures. "Listening to the true teaching," you explained, means a seeking spirit to hear about Buddhism. You said Buddhist practice begins with "listening." "Believing it" means the power of belief. According to the principle of "substituting faith for wisdom," wisdom arises from faith. You also said, it is the power of faith that forges bonds between people. "Keeping the precept," which originally carried the meaning of "stemming injustice and eradicating evil," indicates advancing straight ahead along the correct path of Buddhism. This could also be termed a spirit of self-regulation or deep sense of justice. "Attaining peace of mind" means meditation — pacifying the mind, banishing rambling thoughts, and entering a state of calm and stability. "Peace of mind" could be thought of as a quiet and unwavering spirit or conviction. "Practicing assiduously" means to exercise tireless diligence. It refers to the spirit to advance toward attaining Buddhahood in this lifetime and realizing kosen-rufu. "Unselfishly devoting oneself" means discarding attachments. This implies having the courage to break free of the lesser self or ego, and the spirit to realize great ideals. "Forever seeking self-improvement" means having the humility to reflect on oneself.

Ikeda: All of these are encompassed in the word *faith.* They are all included in SGI activities. We work with the sun during the daytime and reflect on ourselves in the light of the moon at night, ever seeking to advance — all based on the Mystic Law. When we practice with this spirit of "faith manifesting itself in daily life," our lives are adorned with the seven treasures. This is the way to accumulate true and eternal wealth.

Saito: Not only do these treasures apply to faith, they are conditions of humanity that are prized universally.

Ikeda: Practicing faith means to lead the most correct life. Acquiring wisdom means attaining the most profound understanding of human nature.

The treasure tower exists in human life. To understand it in these terms is to see beyond our apparent differences and perceive the sanctity of life itself. The reason for this is that on the most essential level of life, there is no such thing as superior and inferior. Everyone alike possesses life. On the level of life there are no differences of gender, skin color or ethnicity. There is no discrimination on the basis of wealth or social status. Everyone is equal.

To base oneself on the treasure tower, therefore, is to establish the view of the sanctity and equality of human life. It is true humanism.

Endo: "Irrespective of social status," as the Daishonin says to Abutsu-bo, means that all beings alike are infinitely worthy of respect.

Ikeda: Those who discriminate against others violate the sanctity of their own lives. On the other hand, when we treasure the lives of others, the treasure tower within us shines.

Suda: That's the spirit of the "oneness of self and others."

Saito: It sounds like we're approaching the theme of the "Bodhisattva Never Disparaging" chapter.

Endo: Let's not get too far ahead.

Ikeda: This is in fact an important theme that runs generally through the entire Lotus Sutra. I expect we'll have the chance to discuss it in detail on another occasion.

True Democracy

Endo: Isn't respecting other people as treasures in fact the spirit of democracy? I recall Walt Whitman, the great poet of democracy, expressing the view that "at the core of democracy, finally, is the religious element."[10] Dr. Chappell, similarly, has suggested that in the twenty-first century religion will, of necessity, play an increasingly important role in people's lives.

Suda: I have also read Whitman's description of democracy. He writes that he assumes democracy "to be at present in its embryo condition, and that the only large and satisfactory justification of it resides in the future, mainly through the copious production of perfect characters among the people, and through the advent of a sane and pervading religiousness."[11]

Saito: In a lecture on democracy and religion at the Boston Research Center for the 21st Century, Professor Vincent Harding of the University of Denver,[12] a close friend of the late civil rights leader Dr. Martin Luther King Jr., argued that American democracy is still highly imperfect. Touching on the achievements of Dr. King, he emphasized that to make democracy live up to its promise, there is a great need for leaders with roots in religion who can truly sympathize with the people.

Ikeda: Respect for the individual is the very soul of democracy. Democracy's success hinges on whether people can recognize the lives of all as equally sacred. Everything depends on this.

Suda: Many Japanese think our nation has fully achieved democracy. But it seems to me that Whitman's comment, made 130 years ago, that democracy was still in an embryonic stage, and Dr. Harding's insight are all the truer today.

Ikeda: That's because, ultimately, democracy is a manner of living. In the words of Tomas Masaryk, the founding father of Czechoslovakia, "Democracy is not only a form of government, it is not only what is written in constitutions; democracy is a view of life, rests on faith in men, in humanity and in human nature."[13]

Democracy, in other words, means trusting people as noble and eternal entities in and of themselves, not viewing them as a means to some end. When we believe in ourselves and trust others in this way, then, according to Masaryk, it will not be possible for one person, whose life is eternal and infinite, to regard another person, whose life is equally eternal and infinite, with indifference: "The eternal to the eternal cannot be indifferent, the eternal cannot misuse the eternal, it cannot exploit and violate it."[14] In other words, it is impossible for someone who is aware of the eternal nature of his being to maliciously exploit or violently repress another person whose being he recognizes as equally eternal.

Nichiren Daishonin says, "The treasure towers are none other than all living beings, and all living beings are none other than the complete entities of Nam-myoho-renge-kyo" (OTT, 230). This is the perspective of the "The Emergence of the Treasure Tower" chapter.

We perceive the treasure tower in our own lives, and we perceive the treasure tower in the lives of others. And we are working to sanctify the places where we live and the entire world with forests of treasure towers. Let us construct "treasure towers of kosen-rufu" in our communities. Let us each leave behind an eternal golden monument of personal achievement. Let us adorn our lives by challenging ourselves with the spirit, "This is where I will build my treasure tower."

Shakyamuni expounded the Lotus Sutra as the crowning achievement of his life of great struggle. And the treasure tower first appeared in response to Shakyamuni's tireless efforts to widely propagate the Mystic Law. Many Treasures Buddha appeared to support him, and Shakyamuni's emanations, the Buddhas in the ten directions of the universe, gathered around him. Behind all of this were Shakyamuni's tireless efforts and deep determination for kosen-rufu.

When we take action for kosen-rufu, the treasure tower appears. This is not a matter of theory; it comes down to a hands-on struggle with reality, an earnest win-or-lose effort to overcome great difficulties. Through waging such a struggle, our lives shine with the seven treasures of "listening to the true teaching, believing it, keeping the precept, attaining peace of mind, practicing assiduously, unselfishly devoting oneself, and forever seeking self-improvement." Nichiren Daishonin, likewise, amid great difficulties, established the treasure tower of the Gohonzon.

From that standpoint, it is no coincidence that the "Treasure Tower" chapter uses the principle of the six difficult and nine easy acts to explain the difficulty of propagating the Mystic Law in the Latter Day. Let's take up this concept in the next chapter.

NOTES

1. Dr. Chappell was director of the Center for Buddhist Studies of the University of Hawaii at Manoa and is currently professor of comparative religions at Soka University of America. He is a member of the International Association of Buddhist Studies and the Society for the Study of Chinese Religions.

2. Joseph Campbell with Bill Moyers, *The Power of Myth*, ed. Betty Sue Flowers (New York: Doubleday, 1988), p. 212.

3. Abutsu-bo: A follower of the Daishonin on Sado Island.

4. *Nayuta*: An Indian numerical unit corresponding to 100,000,000,000.

5. Josei Toda, *Toda Josei zenshu* (Collected Works of Josei Toda), vol. 7, pp. 455–56.

6. Ibid., vol. 6, p. 275.

7. Preparatory section: The first of the three divisions of a sutra (preparation, revelation and transmission), a format often used in interpreting sutras thought to have been formulated by the Great Teacher T'ien-t'ai of China. Preparation indicates the introductory section, revelation contains the main teaching, and transmission is the concluding part. In the case of the Lotus Sutra, in addition to the entire sutra having these divisions, each half may be further analyzed into three sections.

8. T'ien-t'ai, *The Words and Phrases of the Lotus Sutra*, vol. 8.

9. Three bodies: Three kinds of body a Buddha may possess. A concept set forth in Mahayana Buddhism to organize different views of the Buddha appearing in the sutras. The three bodies are: (1) The Dharma body, or body of the Law. This is the fundamental truth, or Law, to which a Buddha is enlightened. (2) The reward body, obtained as the reward of completing bodhisattva practices and acquiring the Buddha wisdom. Unlike the Dharma body, which is immaterial, the reward body is thought of as an actual body, although one that is transcendent and imperceptible to ordinary people. (3) The manifested body, or the physical form that a Buddha assumes in this world in order to save the people. Generally, a Buddha was held to possess one of the three bodies, and the three bodies represented three different types of Buddhas. On the basis of the Lotus Sutra, however, the Great Teacher T'ien-t'ai taught that these are not separate bodies but represent three integral aspects of a single Buddha. From this point of view, the Dharma body indicates the essential property of a Buddha, which is the truth or Law to which the Buddha is enlightened. The reward body indicates the spiritual property, or the wisdom that enables the Buddha to perceive the truth. It is called reward body because such wisdom was seen as the reward of ceaseless effort and discipline. The manifested body indicates compassionate actions, or the physical property of a Buddha. It is the body with which a Buddha carries out compassionate actions to lead people to enlightenment, or those actions themselves. Nichiren Daishonin taught that these three bodies or properties are "uncreated," or eternally inherent, in all people's lives.

10. Walt Whitman, *Democratic Vistas and Other Papers* (London: The Walter Scott Publishing Co., Ltd., 1888; reprint, Michigan: Scholarly Press, 1970), p. 27.

11. Ibid., p. 40.

12. Dr. Harding is professor of religion and social transformation at the Iliff School of Theology, University of Denver.

13. Karel Capek, *Masaryk on Thought and Life: Conversations with Karel Capek*, trans. M. & R. Weatherall (New York: The Macmillan Company, 1938), p. 191.

14. Ibid., p. 190.

2 Recognizing the Infinite Value of Each Person's Life

Saito: The more I think about the treasure tower, the more strongly I sense that it teaches us today something of fundamental importance. Symbolically, it proclaims that the human being is not insignificant and powerless.

People today, by and large, are satisfied neither with their lives nor with the state of the world. A feeling of powerlessness seems to predominate. People are asking themselves, "But what can I possibly do to change things?" Futility and despair cast a dark shadow over their inner lives and over society. Isn't this, perhaps, the basic dilemma of the modern era?

Ikeda: You've raised a vital issue. The problem is particularly acute in the so-called developed countries. In the United States, for example, there are signs that young people increasingly are suffering because of low self-esteem. In many cases, these young people so despise themselves that, in order to escape their pain, they resort to drug use.

Endo: They don't realize their inherent worth. And if people cannot treasure themselves, how can they ever treasure others?

Ikeda: It is a great tragedy to see one's life and the lives of others as inconsequential. In our society, everything has been magnified to colossal proportions. The human spirit, laboring under the immense weight of society, seems to groan in despair. As early as the 1960s, Norman Cousins, who was known as the conscience of America, wrote about this.

In one place, he writes: "In traveling around the United States, I have been made aware of a melancholy tension. The questions people ask are not related to their personal incomes or the need to find better ways to amuse themselves. They want to know how to overcome their sense of personal futility on the big issues."[1]

Suda: The possibility of nuclear war and ensuing feelings of vulnerability must have weighed heavily on people's spirits at that time.

Ikeda: The nuclear threat was only one source of people's insecurity.

In the past, the world that people were aware of was circumscribed. When a problem arose in their city or village, they could readily grasp it, directly express their views on the matter and influence the outcome of events. But now people have become anonymous citizens of vast countries. They are more and more aware that their destiny is inextricably linked with the destiny of the entire human race. While people worry about the direction in which their country and humankind as a whole are heading, they are uncertain how to express their personal views on such matters or what action to take to influence outcomes. And even where they find they can do something, they are not confident their efforts will truly help improve things. This is the predicament people find themselves in today.

Dr. Cousins argues, "There can be no more important education today than education for personal effectiveness and a sense of connection with big events."[2] This of course applies to the education one receives in school, but that is not all. I regard the popular movement we in the SGI are developing as social education in a broad sense. It is a movement to empower people by showing them that, through their efforts, they can definitely change the world. And it is a movement to develop solidarity among people who aim to do this.

Saito: That's a good example of what we call "actual three thousand realms in a single moment of life."[3] Nichiren Daishonin said, "From this single element of mind spring all the various lands and environmental conditions" (WND-2, 843). In other words, he teaches that it is within the power of each of us to change the world in which we live.

The treasure tower symbolizes the greatness of each person's life. The individual is a microcosm living in exquisite harmony with the macrocosm. Surely there is no greater joy than realizing that our lives exist in a state of indivisibility with the vast universe.

Ikeda: Speaking of the microcosm, we know that the human body is made up of the same chemical elements as the universe. Similarly, when you examine the constituent elements of the seven treasures that adorn the treasure tower, you'll find that each one also exists in our bodies.

Endo: That's right. I did a little research on the seven treasures. In the Buddhist scholar Kumarajiva's Chinese translation of the sutra, the seven treasures are gold, silver, lapis lazuli, seashell, agate, pearl and carnelian. Of these, gold, silver, agate and pearl are well-known gems and precious metals. Lapis lazuli is a semiprecious stone with a deep azure color. "Seashell" means the shell of a giant clam. Carnelian is a translucent quartz; Chinese carnelian, by the way, is said to be very rare.

Saito: The list varies from text to text. For example, in the Sanskrit text of the Lotus Sutra, the seven treasures include coral, amber and crystal.

Endo: Nonetheless, of the seven treasures, the basic component of lapis lazuli, agate and carnelian is silicon. Silicon is absolutely essential for the development of the human body; it is needed for the formation and growth of the skeletal system. And the main component of pearl and agate is calcium, which we know plays a very important role in building bones and teeth.

I also discovered that agate shows a variety of different hues depending on the kind of metal in which it is set. In iron, it has a reddish hue; in cobalt, it is blue; and in chrome, it appears green. These metals are all indispensable for the proper maintenance of our bodies: iron for carrying oxygen in the blood, cobalt for building blood cells, and chrome for the metabolism of sugar and fat.

Other metals required by our bodies include copper, zinc, tin, manganese and nickel. And our bodies may also require gold, mercury and some other metals.

Ikeda: That's fascinating. You are right when you say our lives are literally treasures.

Hydrogen, oxygen, carbon and nitrogen are the most common elements in the human body. The metals that you mentioned, maintained in precise equilibrium, support the microcosm of our lives.

Suda: I understand that the total length of blood vessels in the human body is an astounding sixty thousand miles. That's two-and-a-half times the circumference of the Earth. It's hard to believe that such a great distance is contained within one's body.

Ikeda: In "The Unanimous Declaration by the Buddhas,"[4] Nichiren Daishonin elaborates on the statement by the Great Teacher Miao-lo of China, "This body of ours is modeled after heaven and earth." He says, for example, "The veins like the rivers and streams" (WND-2, 848 and 849). Our lives, in other words, mirror the natural world.

Saito: Buddhism is truly universal in scope. The Daishonin also said, "The eyes correspond to the sun and moon, and their opening and closing correspond to day and night" (WND-2, 848–49).

Ikeda: "The eyes correspond to the sun and the moon." While this might at first seem far-fetched, if we stop to think about it we can see the reasoning. Referring to an ancient saying, Goethe writes: "Were they not sun-akin, our eyes, / To sunlight's glory they'd be blind."[5] He further observes, "Nothing's outside that's not within."[6]

Nichiren Daishonin, in discussing the words of Miao-lo that I just mentioned, explains that to know oneself is to know all things in the universe. When you change, your environment changes, too. When your inner resolve changes, everything is transformed. This is the principle of three thousand realms in a single moment of life. This principle is summed up by Goethe's maxim, "Nothing's outside that's not within."

Suda: Buddhism explains that a law or principle pervades all life and the entire universe. Scientists, influenced in part by Goethe, have considered this from the standpoint of the physical manifestation of life. Goethe observed that plant parts are all helical or spiral shaped. He noted, for example, the way in which bindweed twists around the plants among which it grows, and how the white birch tree rotates around its central axis.

The same spiral pattern is evident in the shell of a shellfish, the horns of sheep and oxen, and in elephant tusks. Blood vessels are also woven from spiral-shaped fibers. In the submicroscopic world, DNA, which carries our genetic information, has the structure of a double helix. And in the macrosphere, a similar spiral or "whirlpool" shape can be seen in tornadoes and typhoons, as well as many galaxies.

Endo: The same pattern is found in whirlpools created by tidal currents. Since ancient times, the spiral seems to have symbolized life force, growth and evolution. One researcher propounds the view that the spiral, because it is produced by the repetition of similar phenomena, is an expression of rhythm.[7]

Ikeda: There certainly is rhythm in the universe, and the rhythm of the life of an individual pulsates in perfect harmony with it. It seems to me that life, in essence, is an expression of a sympathetic resonance between the macrocosm of the universe and the microcosm of our lives.

The universe itself produces a kind of cosmic rhythm. It is a compassionate rhythm that enables all living things to grow and advance. You might even call it a "wavelength" of compassion. Living beings are "receivers" that can intercept this wavelength. No matter where we are, when we tune in to the "frequency" of Buddhahood, our lives are embraced in this compassionate melody, infusing us with the spirit to realize growth in our lives and help others do the same.

We could also use the image of a tuning fork to describe this phenomenon. If you have two tuning forks of the same pitch and you ring one, then the other tuning fork, even if it is some distance from the first, will start ringing.

Saito: What you've described is the acoustical phenomenon of resonance.

Ikeda: Yes. To continue the analogy, when the tuning fork of our lives begins to ring with compassion, then, even if at first we are all alone, other "tuning forks" will start to ring with the same compassion. And though at first perhaps only two or three will catch the rhythm, others will definitely follow. Compassion has a certain "wavelength"; but some person has to be the first to emit it. A tuning fork will not ring if it is left lying on its side, however; to produce a sound, it must stand upright. The same is true of our lives.

In the "Treasure Tower" chapter, the gathering of the Buddhas in the ten directions is like so many tuning forks starting to ring in unison in response to the reverberations of the tuning fork of Shakyamuni's spirit to "make certain the Law will long endure" (LSOC, 217). This is a grand illustration of the principle of sympathetic resonance.

THE THREE TRANSFORMATIONS OF THE LAND

> *Shakyamuni Buddha, in order to provide seats for all the Bud-*
> *dhas that were arriving, once more transformed two hundred ten*
> *thousand million nayutas*[8] *of lands in each of the eight direc-*
> *tions, making them all clean and pure and without hells, hun-*
> *gry spirits, beasts or asuras. He also moved all the heavenly and*
> *human beings to another region . . . the whole area comprising*
> *a single Buddha land, a jeweled region level and smooth.*
> (LSOC, 213)

Saito: That's a wonderful image. To cause his emanations who were
preaching the Law in the worlds of the ten directions to return
and gather together in one place, Shakyamuni transforms and
purifies the strife-ridden *saha* world[9] three times. This is the origin of the term "the three transformations of the land." The term
expresses the transformation of the realm of the environment. The
first transformation is when Shakyamuni changes and then purifies
the *saha* world. As he does so, he moves all the human and heavenly beings dwelling there to another region, with the exception
of those in the assembly where the Lotus Sutra is being
expounded.

But the number of the Buddha's emanations in the ten directions is so great that they cannot all fit in the *saha* world. To accom-
modate them, Shakyamuni next transforms and purifies 210
thousand million *nayutas* of other lands in each of the eight directions,[10] and moves the heavenly and human beings living there to
another world. He then joins these several lands together to form
a single Buddha land. This is the second transformation. The third
transformation occurs when Shakyamuni transforms and purifies
an additional 210 thousand million *nayutas* of lands in the eight
directions, removing the heavenly and human beings in those lands
to another region. He also made each of those worlds part of the
one great Buddha land.

When the transformations were complete, the Buddhas of the ten directions filled the 420 thousand million *nayutas* of lands that Shakyamuni had purified and consolidated into one land. This is the three transformations of the land.

Ikeda: It's interesting that he moves the heavenly and human beings in these lands to other regions. I would imagine that various interpretations of this are possible.

Suda: One interpretation is that those heavenly and human beings are among the beings of the six paths.[11] Because beings transmigrating in the six paths are deluded, they cannot see the Buddha land that Shakyamuni created when he transformed and purified the *saha* world. This, perhaps, is what is meant when the text says they were "moved to another region." Unless you yourself change, things won't look any different.

Endo: Similarly, although the world is changing rapidly in the post-Cold War era, many people, particularly here in Japan, it would seem, are still caught up in outmoded ways of thinking reminiscent of the Cold War.

Saito: In *Words and Phrases of the Lotus Sutra*,[12] the Great Teacher T'ien-t'ai of China says that Shakyamuni effects the three purifications through *samadhi*.

Ikeda: The Sanskrit word *samadhi* means to settle and focus the mind; in other words, to meditate. From our standpoint, *samadhi* means establishing an imperturbable state of life; constructing a sound and stable inner realm that nothing can disturb. In that sense, the principle of the three transformations not only speaks to the transformation of the land; it also addresses the transformation of one's inner state of life.

RESTORING PEOPLE'S AILING LIVES TO HEALTH

Saito: I recall that in the "War and Reconciliation" chapter of the fifth volume of *The Human Revolution*, you explained the principle of the three transformations through a very familiar example.

You presented the hypothetical case of two families that had been closely related for many generations. Let's call them the Saitos and the Endos. The two families were next-door neighbors, but their ancestors had quarreled, so for many years they didn't speak to one another. In the meantime, the Endo family became very good friends with another family — let's call them the Sudas — who lived a thousand miles away.

In time, the Saito and Endo families' memory of their ancestors' animosity faded, and gradually they felt the desire to forgive and forget. The Endo family, however, out of fear of offending their new friends the Sudas, simply could not find it in themselves to reach out to the Saitos in friendship. Naturally this upset the Saitos very much.

Now what would have happened, you asked, if at this point the neighboring Saitos and the Endos had simply let bygones be bygones and embraced one another in friendship? Everything would have changed completely, and the three families could have begun a harmonious relationship. Such a change, you explained, illustrates the principle of the transformation of the land. This is the basic outline.

Endo: You suggested that Japan and China were in the same predicament as the neighboring families, and that the United States was like Japan's new friend from afar. You were making the case that Japan should develop friendly relations with China. At the time when you wrote this, Japan and China on the one hand, and China and the United States on the other, were in great conflict. I recall how truly inspired I felt when I read your words.

Ikeda: Even in international relations, human beings are the key. Countries are gatherings of people, and they are created by people.

It is impossible, therefore, that people could be unable to change them. Moreover, one must realize that the state exists for the sake of the people, not the other way around.

People have lost sight of this simple and clear fact. Enthralled by self-righteous ideologies, by concern over petty profit and loss, by emotionalism, by erroneous ideas and prejudice and, fundamentally, by ignorance about human nature and life itself, people shut themselves up in their own narrow worlds.

Only when we cut the chains of these attachments can we respect other people as human beings and begin to conduct truly humanistic dialogue.

Saito: When you visited the Soviet Union at the height of the Cold War, President Ikeda, many people criticized you. Undaunted, you said, "I will go there, because there are people there." And you set to work building a bridge of friendship.

At the time, it seemed as though the conflict between China and the Soviet Union would continue indefinitely. As a matter of fact, I heard that your visit to the Soviet Union drew criticism from the Chinese, too. Still, you maintained your conviction, asserting that China and the Soviet Union would definitely mend their relations. Things turned out exactly as you said.

I think it's about changing mistrust into trust. This is easy to say, but extremely difficult to put into practice.

Ikeda: If you consistently take action in the arenas of power based on humanism, you are certain to encounter difficulties. This is an example of the principle of "the six difficult and nine easy acts," which we find in the "Treasure Tower" chapter.

Ricardo Díez-Hochleitner, president of the Club of Rome, has suggested that while we may say that the Earth is sick, the real problem is that the human beings who inhabit the earth are sick. The three transformations indicates making the world healthy by restoring the ailing lives of its people to health.

The Three Categories of Illusion

Suda: In *Words and Phrases of the Lotus Sutra*, T'ien-t'ai correlates the three transformations of the land with the three categories of illusion, which are illusions of thought and desire, illusions as innumerable as particles of dust and sand, and illusions about the true nature of existence. The three transformations of the land in effect eradicate the three illusions.

Illusions of thought, by the way, are mistaken views, while illusions of desire arise from the three poisons, namely, greed, anger and foolishness.

Endo: Blaming sufferings on someone or something outside oneself is an example of an illusion of thought. When we realize that the causes for everything that happens to us are within our own lives, we have defeated this illusion of thought.

Saito: Broadly speaking, feeling prejudice toward others or judging people on the basis of social class can also be considered an illusion of thought.

Ikeda: Indeed. When we view people in this way, we indiscriminately accept images that other people over time have intentionally created. When we readily rely on images without trying to open our hearts and discern the truth for ourselves, we quickly succumb to prejudice. Once we become biased, it is human nature to become attached to those biases and be reluctant to surrender them. This is another type of illusion of thought.

Suda: By contrast, it could be said that illusions of desire are impurities nesting still more deeply in life. These illusions cloud our eyes to the truth.

Ikeda: These illusions could be described as distortions of life itself.

They distort the mirror of the heart in which other people are reflected, giving us a skewed image of others.

Needless to say, the poisons of greed, anger and foolishness destroy human relations, and they have a similarly deleterious effect on relations between countries. Ultimately, illusions of thought and desire produce nothing but prejudice and hatred. In such a frame of mind, you cannot conduct openhearted dialogue with anyone, nor will others approach you with open hearts.

Saito: The second transformation of the land signifies the purification of the illusions as innumerable as particles of dust and sand. These illusions afflict bodhisattvas. They are the countless worries that arise when bodhisattvas struggle to help others become happy.

Ikeda: That's right. This is something SGI members all experience. Before taking faith, we struggle earnestly just to overcome our own worries and sufferings. After taking faith, however, we increasingly come to worry about the well-being of others. For example, we may worry about how to encourage someone who is sick. These are noble worries.

Endo: There are even instances where, for example, in trying to intervene in a marital dispute, it may happen that, ironically, we end up suffering while the couple becomes happy.

Ikeda: For people who embrace the Mystic Law, to worry about friends and pray for their happiness comes naturally. We should not forget just how noble such efforts are. Without hesitation, SGI members dive right into the reality of the *saha* world, with all its conflict, to come to the aid of people who are suffering.

The sutra says that in the second and third transformations Shakyamuni purifies 210 thousand million *nayutas* of lands in the eight directions. This is the very image of the expansion of kosen-rufu.

SGI members dare to take on this most difficult work for those who are struggling the hardest. By their actions, they are constructing "cities of tranquil light" in all parts of the world. As a result of their encouragement, friends who had been in the depths of suffering stand up and enact a drama of revitalization based on the Mystic Law. This itself is the splendid transformation of an "impure land" filled with suffering into a "pure land" pervaded with joy.

Saito: Each person's human revolution can fundamentally transform the destiny of an entire country.

Ikeda: Put into words, the transformation of the land may sound static; but since it comes about through individuals earnestly grappling with reality, it is actually a highly dynamic principle. As the sutra indicates where it says, "The saha world thereupon immediately changed into a place of cleanness and purity" (LSOC, 212), the pure land is not to be found in some other world. Rather, this world itself becomes the Land of Tranquil Light.

Put succinctly, the Buddha's land is a place where many human treasure towers are constructed, where everyone shines. The appearance of forests of these treasure towers creates the Buddha land.

Endo: The third transformation represents the eradication of illusion about the true nature of existence.

Ikeda: Illusion about the true nature of existence is literally illusion about the nature of one's own life. This is the fundamental source of all illusions. If we are ignorant about the nature of our own existence, then we will be ignorant about the nature of other people's lives, too.

On the other hand, when our lives are free of illusion, we can perceive the treasure tower that shines resplendent in all people, in all beings. Such an open heart is the nature of enlightenment.

The closed heart that prevents us from seeing the treasure tower is ignorance about the nature of life, or darkness. This is the crux of the problem.

In the future I hope we can discuss darkness and enlightenment from various angles. For the time being, why don't we consider their relation to the six difficult and nine easy acts in light of the "Treasure Tower" chapter?

Since propagating the Lotus Sutra is ultimately a struggle to overcome the fundamental darkness in our own lives, it is the most difficult of all tasks. And since this is also a struggle against the devil king of the sixth heaven, in carrying out this work we are sure to meet with obstacles.

THE SIX DIFFICULT AND NINE EASY ACTS

The other sutras
number as many as Ganges sands,
but though you expound those sutras,
that is not worth regarding as difficult.
If you were to seize Mount Sumeru
and fling it far off
to the measureless Buddha lands,
that too would not be difficult.
If you used the toe of your foot
to move the major world system,
booting it far away to other lands,
that too would not be difficult.
If you stood in the Summit of Being heaven
and for the sake of the assembly
preached countless other sutras,
that too would not be difficult.
But if after the Buddha has entered extinction,
in the time of evil,
you can preach this sutra,
that will be difficult indeed! (LSOC, 218)

Suda: To begin with, the principle of the six difficult and nine easy acts indicates just how difficult it will be to propagate the Mystic Law after Shakyamuni's death.

Saito: In his writings, Nichiren Daishonin repeatedly cites the sutra passage describing the six difficult and nine easy acts and indicates that it has special relevance to himself.

Ikeda: In "The Opening of the Eyes," the Daishonin goes so far as to say, "If a person fulfills the teaching of 'the six difficult and nine easy acts' of the Lotus Sutra, then, even though he may not have read the entire body of sutras, all should follow him" (WND-1, 268). He indicates that just as all the "river gods" follow the "lord of ocean," and as all "mountain gods" follow the "lord of Mount Sumeru," all Buddhas and bodhisattvas follow the Daishonin, who read the teaching of the six difficult and nine easy acts with his entire being and thereby attained mastery of all sutras.

The Lotus Sutra is the king of all sutras, and the essence of its practice lies in the teaching of the six difficult and nine easy acts. One who internalizes this teaching therefore walks the supreme path in life.

Saito: Why don't we consider the six difficult and nine easy acts in terms of the flow of the "Treasure Tower" chapter? The three transformations have taken place, and all of the Buddhas have assembled. Shakyamuni and Many Treasures Buddha have taken their places within the treasure tower, and all beings in the assembly have been raised into the air. The stage has been set, and the Ceremony in the Air at last begins.

Shakyamuni says: "Who is capable of broadly preaching the Lotus Sutra of the Wonderful Law in this saha world? Now is the time to do so, for before long the Thus Come One will enter nirvana. The Buddha wishes to entrust this Lotus Sutra of the Wonderful Law to someone so that it may be preserved" (LSOC, 215).

Endo: Starting with this first exhortation, Shakyamuni calls out three times to the bodhisattvas urging them to spread the teaching after his death.

Ikeda: In "The Opening of the Eyes," Nichiren Daishonin refers to this as the "three pronouncements."

Suda: In the second pronouncement, Shakyamuni clarifies that the reason why Many Treasures Buddha has appeared and Shakyamuni's emanations in the ten directions have gathered is to "make certain the Law will long endure" (LSOC, 217). And the third time, he issues his exhortation after revealing the extreme difficulty of propagating the Lotus Sutra in the future by describing the six difficult and nine easy acts.

Ikeda: In this light, it is plain that the Ceremony in the Air is "for the time after the Buddha's passing." Shakyamuni, Many Treasures and the Buddhas of the ten directions unanimously urge that the true teaching be spread in the future. That is the purpose for the creation of such a magnificent stage.

Endo: The nine easy acts are as follows: (1) to teach innumerable sutras other than the Lotus Sutra; (2) to take up Mount Sumeru and hurl it to the measureless Buddha lands; (3) to kick the entire major world system (thousand-millionfold world) into another quarter with one's toe; (4) to stand in the highest heaven and preach innumerable sutras other than the Lotus Sutra; (5) to grasp the sky with one's hand and travel around with it; (6) to place the earth on one's toenail and ascend to the Brahma heaven; (7) to walk across a burning prairie carrying a bundle of dry grass on one's back without being burned; (8) to preach eighty-four thousand teachings and enable one's listeners to obtain the six transcendental powers; and (9) to enable innumerable people to reach the stage of *arhat* and acquire the six supernatural powers.

Suda: One tends to wonder just what is easy about these things; or if it's perhaps not some kind of mistake, and that these are actually supposed to be the "nine difficult acts."

Saito: We can classify these nine into two groups: "physical" and "doctrinal." The second, third, fifth, sixth and seventh are physical tasks, and the first, fourth, eighth, and ninth are primarily doctrinal. The point is that they are all "easy" compared to the six difficult acts.

Ikeda: The reason for their inclusion is of course to illustrate by contrast the great challenge of the six difficult acts. Even so, it cannot be said that they are subjective or exaggerated. I think this formulation carries profound meaning.

Endo: The six difficult acts are as follows: (1) to preach the Lotus Sutra, (2) to write out and embrace it and cause others to write it out, (3) to read this sutra even for a little while, (4) to embrace this sutra and expound it to even one person, (5) to listen to and accept this sutra and ask about its meaning, and (6) to honor and embrace faith in it after the Buddha's death.

In short, it is extremely difficult to carry out the practice of the Lotus Sutra for oneself and others in the Latter Day of the Law.

Ikeda: Do you know why this is?

It's partly because the Lotus Sutra of the Latter Day of the Law is the Great Pure Law of Nam-myoho-renge-kyo. There is also an important distinction when it comes to spreading the Law; only Bodhisattvas of the Earth can carry out the practice of the Mystic Law. Furthermore, those who practice the Lotus Sutra are certain to encounter great difficulties. That's probably the key point.

In *The Record of the Orally Transmitted Teachings,* Nichiren Daishonin, addressing Shakyamuni's statement in "Treasure Tower" that "This sutra is hard to uphold" (LSOC, 220), says "One who upholds this Lotus Sutra should uphold it with the understanding that one will encounter difficulties" (OTT, 97).

Saito: "This Lotus Sutra" means the Gohonzon of Nam-myoho-renge-kyo, which is the Lotus Sutra of the Latter Day. And "uphold" means to devote one's life to the widespread propagation of the Mystic Law.

Endo: Only those who endure persecution on behalf of the Law and persevere in its propagation truly "uphold the Mystic Law." If people merely read the sutra, while failing to spread the teaching and running away from difficulties, they are not upholding the Lotus Sutra.

Saito: In that sense, SGI members are genuinely carrying out the extremely difficult practice of embracing the Lotus Sutra in the modern age, after the example of Tsunesaburo Makiguchi, the founding president, who died upholding the teaching.

Conquering Fundamental Darkness

Ikeda: In light of the six difficult and nine easy acts, we understand just how terrifically challenging it is to dedicate one's life to kosen-rufu.

Without relying on power, authority or wealth, SGI members have, by their own efforts, spread the great teaching that can enable all people to attain enlightenment to 163 countries and territories around the world. Nichiren Daishonin no doubt praises this most highly. Shakyamuni, Many Treasures and the Buddhas of the ten directions surely all send their applause.

Suda: Because these acts are so difficult, immediately after Shakyamuni attained enlightenment he hesitated, unsure of whether to expound the Law. The Daishonin also describes feeling some uncertainty before establishing his teaching.

The Daishonin says he realized that if he uttered so much as a word about the fundamental cause of human misery, then without a doubt not only he himself but his parents, siblings and even his mentor would suffer persecution at the hands of the ruler. On the other hand, he knew that if he failed to do so he would be lacking in compassion.

The Daishonin worried about whether he should speak out or hold his tongue. He realized, in light of passages in the Lotus Sutra and the Nirvana Sutra, that if he did not tell people the truth, then, while he might not suffer any negative consequences in his present life, in the future he would be certain to fall into the hell of incessant suffering. On the other hand, if he spoke out, then the three obstacles and four devils would attack him. Taking these considerations into account, the Daishonin resolved to propagate his teaching.

He knew that if he lacked the fortitude to follow through when persecuted by the ruler, then he would be better off not saying anything from the start. It is said that the Daishonin recollected the principle of the six difficult and nine easy acts in the "Treasure Tower" chapter.

Endo: With the six difficult and nine easy acts in mind, Nichiren Daishonin made his great determination. He says, "I vowed to summon up a powerful and unconquerable desire for the salvation of all beings and never to falter in my efforts" (WND-1, 240). The question here is why difficulties arise when someone spreads the Lotus Sutra.

Suda: There are two reasons: the Lotus Sutra is the "sutra of propagation," and it is the teaching expounded in accord with the Buddha's own mind. In other words, in the Lotus Sutra, the Buddha expresses his enlightenment just as it is, without modifying his explanation or accommodating it to the understanding or capacity of others. In that sense, it's only natural that this teaching should provoke a strong reaction.

Saito: It is certainly true, as the saying goes, that good medicine is bitter. History offers countless examples of instances where speaking the truth has invited strong condemnation. Many pioneering individuals, including scientists such as Galileo, encountered persecution. In some cases, it even cost them their lives.

Endo: Those in power will deny and fiercely react against even the plainest truth if it threatens to destroy the status quo.

Suda: There is a famous story about how Galileo, upon being sentenced to life in prison by the Inquisition, mumbled under his breath, "But it [the Earth] does move."[13] In addition to the Catholic Church, proponents of Scholasticism were also eager to crush his assertions. In Scholasticism, philosophy was forced into reconcilability with Church doctrine, providing the ideological moorings of society.

Ikeda: When we talk about ideology, it sounds very complex. But the truth is that any society and any age have a worldview and a set of values that form people's consciousness. When something contradicts this worldview or system of values, there will be an opposing reaction. We find examples of this in both present and past, East and West.

Suda: This is something Descartes, who challenged the metaphysical view of the universe associated with Scholasticism, also encountered. When he wrote *The World*, he feared he would be punished just as Galileo had because it contained Copernican theory. So he did not make it public.

Ikeda: That's normal. Everyone prizes his or her own life. But the Lotus Sutra says that unless this Great Law is revealed and spread, humankind will remain shrouded in darkness. Therefore, the Daishonin made a firm resolution. Only those who do "not hesitate even if it costs them their lives" are votaries of Lotus Sutra.

This in itself, however, cannot account for the extreme difficulty of the six difficult acts. In fact, the Lotus Sutra is not the only sutra to discuss difficulties. In this connection, we are better served if we focus on the problem of the fundamental darkness inherent in human life, to which we referred a little earlier.

The Lotus Sutra, remember, is the teaching for transforming life. It articulates the Great Law for conquering fundamental darkness or ignorance. Fundamental darkness is the underlying illusion inherent in life. While there are various points of view, Nichiren Daishonin says that "fundamental darkness manifests itself as the devil king of the sixth heaven" (WND-1, 1113). In "Letter to the Brothers" he wrote: "In each case, the devil king of the sixth heaven possessed these men of wisdom in order to deceive good people . . . The great demon of fundamental darkness can even enter the bodies of bodhisattvas who have reached near-perfect enlightenment and prevent them from attaining the Lotus Sutra's blessing of perfect enlightenment. How easily can he then obstruct those in any lower stage of practice!" (WND-1, 496).

Saito: A bodhisattva at the highest stage of practice has attained a level of enlightenment equal to that of the Buddha. The Daishonin is saying that even bodhisattvas at this stage have not yet conquered their fundamental darkness. Put another way, whether someone has conquered fundamental darkness determines whether that person has truly attained Buddhahood.

Endo: Both passages explain that fundamental darkness manifests as the devil king of the sixth heaven and functions to obstruct the practitioner of the Lotus Sutra. The devil king of the sixth heaven, the king who makes free use of the fruits of others' efforts for his own pleasure, is so called because it dwells in the highest of the six heavens of the world of desire. We could think of it as the embodiment of the devilish nature of power.

Ikeda: The devil king of the sixth heaven can be thought of as the fundamental tendency to seek to use everyone and everything as a means. In a sense, this is a natural inclination that all beings possess. By contrast, to actively seek to support other people and improve our environment is extremely difficult. Compassion, love of humanity, the spirit to serve others— these are wonderful qualities; but manifesting them in our actions is extremely difficult.

The universe and one's own life are in essence one. Even though people may understand this intellectually, usually they fail to grasp it in the depths of their lives. This could be termed fundamental darkness. Because of this ignorance about the true nature of life, people try to make everything and everyone in the universe serve them, to turn them into a means. This is the function of the devil king of the sixth heaven, of the devilish nature of power.

The Lotus Sutra explains that the self is one with the universe. The practice of the Lotus Sutra is the practice of compassion to respect and revere everyone as a treasure tower, and to become happy conjointly with others in accord with the principle of the oneness of self and others, while overcoming the various difficulties we face.

In the course of carrying out this practice, we will definitely have to battle our own fundamental darkness. Because by our efforts we are stimulating and activating the fundamental darkness in other people's lives, we are sure to encounter difficulties.

Those in positions of power are not the only ones influenced by the devilish nature of power. As indicated by the line, "the devil king of the sixth heaven possessed these men of wisdom in order to deceive good people," spiritual leaders who are revered in society may also brandish the devilish nature of power.

Saito: Such people represent the third of the three powerful enemies.[14]

Ikeda: Great persecutions usually result from the collusion of evil authorities and corrupt spiritual leaders. This holds true in the past and present, as it will in the future.

Endo: That's perfectly consistent with how, in making the *saha* world a land of tranquil light through the three transformations, Shakyamuni ultimately has to battle ignorance and delusion about the true nature of existence.

Saito: T'ien-t'ai's doctrine of the "three obstacles and four devils" originally referred to obstructions and negative functions that emerge from the depths of life in the process of developing "inner sight." To embody the principle of three thousand realms in a single moment of life, that is, to attain the awareness that our mind or life-moment is one with the universe, we have to overcome the seven inner obstacles and negative functions (i.e., three obstacles and four devils). In Nichiren Buddhism, this inner struggle is often played out in dynamic terms as a battle to defeat devils and obstacles that arise from without in the course of one's Buddhist practice.

Suda: Embracing the Lotus Sutra is the key to winning in the struggle against fundamental darkness and the devilish nature of power. Therefore, in the broadest sense, it is truly difficult.

Ikeda: In terms of difficulty, both the physical and the doctrinal tasks of the nine easy acts pale by comparison.

Endo: The physical tasks sound impossible, but when you examine them carefully, you see that they are all superficial. It may even be that the advancement of scientific technology has already brought some of them into the realm of possibility.

Ikeda: The point is that changing the inner world is far more difficult than changing the outer world. That's what the doctrine of the six difficult and nine easy acts teaches.

Suda: Regarding the doctrinal tasks, teaching and spreading sutras other than the Lotus Sutra is "easy" because these teachings do not enable one to conquer fundamental darkness.

Ikeda: We should be careful not to overly restrict the concepts of fundamental darkness and the devil king of the sixth heaven. The Lotus Sutra explains that fundamental darkness and the nature of enlightenment are in essence one.

The Daishonin says that even the devil king has both "body" and "function." The "body" is the devil king inherent in life in terms of the oneness of darkness and enlightenment. The "function" is the devil king of the sixth heaven as the function of life that derives from this essence (see GZ, 843). But why don't we take this up in detail another time?

Since darkness and enlightenment are essentially one, ultimately even the devil king functions to protect Buddhism. The Lotus Sutra says, "Although the devil and the devil's people will be there, they will all protect the Buddhist Law" (LSOC, 145). This time in our study of the Lotus Sutra we are focusing on the devil king function.

The Unifying Power of Compassion

Saito: And so we come to the devilish nature of power — this is a theme that we have to discuss time and again.

Ikeda: That's right. Just what is the evil of power? This fundamental issue has an important bearing on the twenty-first century. During the twentieth century, the evil of power assumed enormous proportions. Fascism and Stalinism are obvious examples.

Endo: While representing diametrically opposite ideological positions, rightist fascism and leftist Stalinism are similar in that they both produced fearfully oppressive totalitarian societies.

Ikeda: In a totalitarian system, everyone and everything is simply a means to be used by the powerful. Human beings are nothing more than tools, commodities, numbers. They are simply nonentities.

This is all too clear when we look at the Holocaust perpetrated by the Nazis and their atrocious behavior toward those whom they defined as "inferior." These are instances of such cruelty that it's hard even to discuss them. Under such systems, human beings are selected as "useful" or "useless" according to standards arbitrarily determined by those in power and then exploited or slaughtered at will.

Suda: In Japan's invasion of Asia, as well, there was a commodification of people that can only be described as insane.

Endo: While the devilish nature of power is present in any age, in the twentieth century it took on huge dimensions and became highly organized.

Ikeda: Not infrequently people have tried to justify such inhumanity on the basis of ideology.

Another factor in this century has been the advancement of science and technology, which has greatly expanded the scope of tragedy. The atom bomb and the gas chambers are symbolic of this trend. Such technology has put in people's hands the power to brutalize and kill human beings on a massive scale.

Science in essence tends to quantify everything; and soulless technology spurs on the commodification of human beings. Nuclear weapons symbolize the devilish nature of power. They are like the incarnation of the devil king. "Devil" means robber of life; the exact opposite of "Buddha," one who restores and invigorates life.

Saito: President Josei Toda's 1957 Declaration for the Abolition of Nuclear Weapons was based on such profound insight into the nature of life. He said, "Anyone who uses an atomic weapon is a devil and a Satan who threatens people's very right to existence."

Ikeda: President Toda fought with his entire being against the negative functions pervading the universe. His struggle was intense.

Probably no one can fully appreciate the anguish he went through and the strain he felt. The fierce pressures on his life would have caused another person to become violently ill or die or commit suicide or develop a severe psychological disorder.

I have described atomic weapons as the embodiment of darkness. But they could also be described as the incarnation of mistrust in, and hatred toward, human beings. The philosopher Max Picard argued that the atomic bomb is a symbol of a "disintegrating" world. Picard wrote:

> The very force which holds the atoms together as they form a world is now being used to explode that world. It is by no means accidental that the atom bomb was invented in the day and age which lives and which dies by disintegrating everything.[15]

The devilish nature of power functions to disintegrate and divide. It cuts people off from the universe, alienates them from other people, divides one country from another, and severs people's bonds with nature. On the other hand, compassion unifies. In the universe itself there is a unifying compassion.

The universe itself is originally compassion. In that sense, the universe is the perfect stage for the struggle between the Buddha and the devil, between compassion and the devilish nature of power, for the struggle between the desire to turn life into a means, and the compassion to make life the objective; for the battle between the power that attempts to turn people into grains of sands, to reduce them to nonentities, and the power that seeks to enable people to become treasure towers.

Saito: This reminds me of Immanuel Kant's famous definition of human worth known as his "categorical imperative." Kant held that people have absolute worth. He said, "Act so that you treat humanity, whether in your own person or in that of another, always as an end and never as a means only."[16]

Endo: Kant also said, "Two things fill the mind with ever new and increasing admiration and awe, the oftener and more steadily they are reflected on: the starry heavens above me and the moral law within me."[17]

The universe and the inner law—Buddhism teaches that these are not two but one. This has something in common with Goethe's comment that "Nothing's outside that's not within." Moreover, these both reflect the law of compassion, the power that unifies everything.

Ikeda: Norman Cousins wrote, "I see no separation between the universal order and the moral order"; and "I may not embrace or command this universal order, but I can be at one with it, for I am of it."[18]

The moment I met Dr. Cousins, I intuitively felt, "This person is a bodhisattva." He was a great man.

Suda: Dr. Cousins is famous for having worked very hard to get medical treatment for the Hiroshima Maidens, young girls who were victims of the atomic bombing of Hiroshima. He also worked to get psychological and medical treatment for a group of Polish women on whom the Nazis had conducted gruesome experiments.

Ikeda: The devilish nature of power is hideously cruel. Its antithesis is to love each person as an irreplaceable being, to exert oneself and suffer on others' behalf, and to regard doing so as a joy.

In a speech, the famous psychologist V. E. Frankl (author of *Man's Search for Meaning, an Introduction to Logotherapy*), a survivor of the Nazi concentration camps, showed the following passage from a letter by a mother:

> While in the uterus, my child's skull formed prematurely. As a result, when she was born on June 6, 1929, she was already fatally ill. I was eighteen years old at the time. I

worshipped my baby like a god and loved her bound-
lessly. My mother and I did everything we could to help
the poor baby. But it was no good. The child could neither walk nor speak. Still, I was young, and I did not
abandon hope. I worked day and night, just so that I
could buy nutritious food and medicine for my dear
daughter. I would wrap my daughter's frail arm around
my neck and ask her, "Do you love Mommy, dear?" And
she would hug me tight and smile, and awkwardly pat
my face. At those moments I was really happy. No matter how difficult things were, I felt boundless joy.[19]

This is the exact opposite of the devilish nature of power that
turns people into a means.

Saito: I feel as though I have come to understand a little of the profound meaning of the "Treasure Tower" chapter.

Ikeda: To put the devilish nature of power into more familiar terms,
one example of it would be a leader who foists hard work on others, making them do things that are unpleasant or difficult, while
taking it easy himself. Such people make others take responsibility and then claim all the credit.

Don Marquis, author of *The Lives and Times of Archy and Mehitabel*, writes:

> there is bound to be a certain amount of
> trouble running any country
> if you are president the trouble happens to you
> but if you are a tyrant you can arrange things so
> that most of the trouble happens to other people.[20]

The difference between a leader and a tyrant is that a leader
works hard for everyone else, while a tyrant makes others work
hard for him.

Nichiren Daishonin says that fundamental darkness manifests as the devil king of the sixth heaven, while the fundamental nature of enlightenment manifests as Brahma, Shakra and the other Buddhist gods (see WND-1, 1113). The devil king is a tyrant. Brahma and Shakra are leaders. The outward difference between the two is decisive; it is like the difference between heaven and earth. At the same time, in terms of a person's inner state of life, it is most subtle.

Saito: One has to exercise constant vigilance over one's spirit and intentions. In this light, it seems that the sense of powerlessness we talked about at the beginning is a major reason why people in modern society tend to be viewed only in terms of their function, or as the "means" to some end.

Endo: Similarly, for children it is no doubt a source of great anxiety to be evaluated and ranked simply on the basis of their grades in school. Even in the home, which ought to be a place where children are accepted as precious and irreplaceable, there is a tendency for parents to evaluate their children on the basis of grades —a very partial and fragmentary indicator. Under such circumstances, it's probably only natural that children fail to develop true self-confidence, that they do not acquire a sense of inner strength —the feeling, "No matter what happens, I will deal with things to the best of my ability."

Ikeda: Yes. There is no hierarchy or pecking order when it comes to life. All life has infinite worth. We have to educate children and adults alike so that no one is made to feel powerless. We have to provide nourishment for the heart. And we have to create true human solidarity. This will be the key to the present age. In that sense, the "Treasure Tower" chapter, which calls out to all: "You are a tower of treasure. Your life contains limitless strength and potential," offers a wealth of inspiration for this age.

Embracing the Lotus Sutra means continually fighting against all manifestations of the devilish nature of power. When we carry out this difficult task, motivated by love of humanity, our lives truly shine as treasure towers; we live each day in the presence of the Ceremony in the Air, in rhythm with eternity; and each moment brilliantly glows with the sheer joy of living.

NOTES

1. Norman Cousins, *Present Tense: An American Editor's Odyssey* (New York: McGraw-Hill Book Company, 1967), p. 373.

2. Ibid., p. 374.

3. Three thousand realms in a single moment of life: Actual, in contrast to theoretical, indicates the practical application of this principle to life.

4. "The Unanimous Declaration by the Buddhas of the Three Existences regarding the Classification of the Teachings and Which Are to Be Abandoned and Which Upheld" (WND-2, 835–61), written in October 1279 when the Daishonin was fifty-eight.

5. Goethe, *Poems and Epigrams*, trans. Michael Hamburger (London: Anvil Press Poetry, 1983), p. 90.

6. Ibid., p. 71.

7. See Shigeo Miki, *Seimei Keitai no Shizenshi* (Life Forms Natural Journal) (Tokyo: Ubusuna Shoin, 1989), pp. 5–9.

8. *Nayuta*: An Indian numerical unit corresponding to 100 billion.

9. *Saha* world: A land where people have to endure many hardships and trials.

10. Eight directions: North, south, east, west, northwest, northeast, southeast and southwest.

11. Six paths: The first six of the Ten Worlds—hell, hunger, animality, anger, humanity (or tranquillity) and heaven (or rapture). The six paths indicate states of delusion or suffering. One who is in these states is

governed by his reactions to external stimuli and is therefore never really free but constantly at the mercy of changing circumstances.

12. T'ien-t'ai, *The Words and Phrases of the Lotus Sutra*, vol. 8.

13. *Eppur si muove.* Attr. to Galileo after his recantation in 1632. The earliest appearance of the phrase is perhaps in Baretti, Italian Library (1757), p. 52.

14. Three powerful enemies: Three groups of people that the "Encouraging Devotion" (thirteenth) chapter of the Lotus Sutra predicts will persecute those who propagate the sutra in the future.

15. Max Picard, *Hitler in Our Selves*, trans. Heinrich Hauser (Hinsdale, IL: Henry Regnery Company, 1947), p. 266.

16. Immanuel Kant, *Foundations of the Metaphysics of Morals,* trans. Lewis White Beck (New York: The Bobbs-Merrill Company, Inc., 1969), p. 54.

17. Immanuel Kant, *Critique of Practical Reason and Other Writings in Moral Philosophy*, trans. Lewis White Beck (Chicago: The University of Chicago Press, 1949), p. 258.

18. Norman Cousins, *Present Tense*, p. 196.

19. Translated from Japanese: V. E. Frankl, *Soredemo jinsei ni iesu to iu* (I Still Say "Yes" to Life) trans. Kunio Yamada and Mika Matsuda (Tokyo: Shunjusha: 1993), p. 104.

20. Don Marquis, *The Lives and Times of Archy and Mehitabel* (New York: Doubleday, Doran and Company, Inc., 1942), "Archy Does His Part," p. 18.

PART II:

"Devadatta" Chapter

3 The Enlightenment of Evil People—
The Triumph of Good

"In future ages if there are good men or good women who, on hearing the Devadatta chapter of the Lotus Sutra of the Wonderful Law, believe and revere it with pure hearts and harbor no doubts or perplexities, they will never fall into the realm of hell, of hungry spirits, or of beasts, but will be born in the presence of the Buddhas of the ten directions, and in the place where they are born they will constantly hear this sutra. If they are born among human or heavenly beings, they will enjoy exceedingly wonderful delights, and if they are born in the presence of the Buddhas, they will be born by transformation from lotus flowers." (LSOC, 224)

Endo: The Lotus Sutra, which elucidates respect for all differences of social system, organization, culture and the like, connects people by urging them to conduct dialogue as human beings who are all on an equal footing.

Suda: Your trip abroad also speaks to the principle of the true aspect of all phenomena, a tenet central to the Lotus Sutra, which teaches us to realize that all phenomena in their magnificent diversity equally possess the true aspect. This is easy to say but very difficult to put into practice—all the more so on a global scale.

Ikeda: This is work that I want young people to carry on.

José Figueres Ferrer, the father of President José María Figueres Olsen of Costa Rica, is well-known for having abolished Costa Rica's military. Reportedly Mr. Figueres Ferrer's motto is *lucha sin fin* (endless struggle). He has used this motto since the days of his youth, even naming his farm Lucha Sin Fin.

Such a spirit is quite relevant for us as Buddhists. Buddhism is a teaching of endless struggle. The true aspect of life and society can be found in the eternal struggle between good and evil, between the nature of enlightenment and the nature of darkness, happiness and misery, peace and war, creation and destruction, harmony and turmoil. This is the true aspect of the universe.

Therefore, the only path is that of struggle. The only alternative is to win. Consequently, another name for the Buddha is Victorious One.

Saito: Shakyamuni spent his entire life engaged in unceasing and arduous struggle. But it seems that many people—perhaps because of the impression they were left with from seeing certain images of the Buddha and other relics—envision Buddhism as a teaching of tranquillity and repose. In reality, Shakyamuni's life was full of intense turmoil. It was a succession of fierce struggles.

Ikeda: That's right. It was because of his great struggles that the Buddha cultivated a state of life as tranquil as a calm sea. No matter how much commotion there was around him, no one could upset the inner world he had constructed. His serene, dignified state of life, as the Buddha enlightened since the remote past, shone brilliantly in his heart at all times.

Suda: Of Shakyamuni's many great struggles, the most famous concerns his betrayal by Devadatta. Unlike persecutions coming from without, this incident arose from within the Buddhist community. It was all the more serious because the traitor had conspired with the ruler of the land, King Ajatashatru,[1] to do away with Shakyamuni.

Endo: Devadatta truly represents the villain. He is known as "traitorous Devadatta," and it would be difficult to find a person of comparable villainy.

"Devadatta," the twelfth chapter of the Lotus Sutra, explains that even this great scoundrel will attain Buddhahood. On the face of it, this seems a most peculiar doctrine.

Saito: In addition to the "enlightenment of evil people," the "Devadatta" chapter explains the principle of the "enlightenment of women" because it chronicles the attainment of Buddhahood by the dragon king's daughter. In the pre-Lotus Sutra teachings, evildoers and women were described as incapable of becoming Buddhas.

In other words, it was a teaching that overturned the prevailing social ethos. This chapter gives dramatic expression to the Lotus Sutra's revelation that all people can attain Buddhahood.

Suda: It seems that the presence of the "Devadatta" chapter is one reason why, since ancient times, the Japanese have been especially fond of the Lotus Sutra. There is evidence that during the Heian period (781–1184), for example, ceremonial cycles of lectures on the Lotus Sutra were held for court nobles.[2] Since the "Devadatta" chapter was especially prized, lectures on the fifth volume,[3] which contains that chapter, are said to have been particularly well attended.

Ikeda: Regarding the fifth volume of the Lotus Sutra, Nichiren Daishonin says, "the fifth volume presents what is the heart and core of the entire sutra, the doctrine of attaining Buddhahood in one's present form" (WND-1, 930). There are, of course, many other important chapters, but the Daishonin says that the "Devadatta" chapter represents the very "heart and core of the entire sutra," suggesting that this chapter is the key to the principle of attaining Buddhahood in one's present form.

The spirit of the Lotus Sutra is to enable all people to become

Buddhas. For ordinary people, the simple fact that one can attain Buddhahood is a matter of far keener importance than any doctrine. The "Devadatta" chapter certainly offers a straightforward reply to that question.

The supremely evil Devadatta attempted to murder Shakyamuni and created a schism within the Buddhist order. Because she was a female, the dragon girl was discriminated against in society; in addition, her form was that of an animal. In terms of the cultural and social ethos of the time, both Devadatta and the dragon girl were probably seen as having not the dimmest prospect of ever attaining Buddhahood. The teaching that even Devadatta and the dragon girl can attain Buddhahood, therefore, clearly indicates that absolutely every being in the world can attain Buddhahood.

Through the concrete example of Devadatta and the dragon girl becoming Buddhas, people could accept this teaching not merely as theory but as an actuality. This is perhaps why people have felt a particular fondness for the "Devadatta" chapter.

Even Murasaki Shikibu, the eleventh-century Japanese court writer and author of *The Tale of Genji*, composed poems to describe how moved she was when she listened to a lecture on the "Devadatta" chapter and heard the doctrine of the enlightenment of women.

Saito: Nichiren Daishonin refers to the attainment of Buddhahood by Devadatta and the dragon girl as "two enlightening admonitions" (WND-1, 268). By explaining their attainment of Buddhahood, thereby revealing the Lotus Sutra's greatness, Shakyamuni is both encouraging and admonishing the bodhisattvas to propagate the Lotus Sutra after his passing.

In short, evil people and women represent all common mortals. That they can attain Buddhahood reveals the power of the Lotus Sutra to enable all people to do so. In that sense, relating their enlightenment amounts to encouraging and admonishing all people to spread the Lotus Sutra.

Endo: The doctrine that all beings can attain enlightenment has already been explained theoretically in "Expedient Means," the second chapter of the sutra. So, from a purely doctrinal standpoint, Nichiren Daishonin characterizes the "Devadatta" chapter as a "branch and leaf of the 'Expedient Means' chapter" (WND-I, 71).

Ikeda: Yes. But the reason Shakyamuni explains Devadatta's and the dragon girl's attainment of Buddhahood is probably because of the explanation's tremendous power to inspire. Devadatta had thoroughly turned against Shakyamuni Buddha. Since to turn against good is evil, Devadatta is a paragon of evil. The reason for the chapter's powerful impact is that it explains his attainment of Buddhahood.

Again, the dragon girl's becoming a Buddha is important because it indicates not only the enlightenment of women but the principle of attaining Buddhahood in one's present form. In other words, it teaches that ordinary people can become Buddhas without changing their form. This makes a powerful impression.

In this chapter, let's discuss the first of these cases, the enlightenment of evil people.

DEVADATTA WAS DESTROYED BY JEALOUSY

Saito: Why don't we begin by talking about just what kind of person Devadatta was? In the "Buddha" chapter of *The New Human Revolution*, President Ikeda, you offer a detailed description.

Suda: A great deal of lore has been handed down concerning Devadatta. Regarding his birth, some sources indicate he was a half-brother of Shakyamuni by a different mother, while others say he was Shakyamuni's cousin. The latter explanation seems to be the more common. In any event, Devadatta is thought to have been younger than Shakyamuni and to have renounced secular life about fifteen years after Shakyamuni attained enlightenment.

At first, Devadatta earnestly exerted himself in his Buddhist practice as a disciple of Shakyamuni. Because of his talent and ability, he gradually gained distinction in the Buddhist order. Later, however, it is said that he approached the prince Ajatashatru in order to gain backing and began trying to replace Shakyamuni as the head of the order.

Endo: It would appear that Devadatta was intelligent. The Daishonin says that he had "committed to memory . . . eighty thousand jeweled teachings" (WND-1, 342). That may be why he grew arrogant.

Ikeda: Intelligence makes a good person that much better and an evil person that much worse. Probably Devadatta's inner mind was not that of a person of faith but of a person of ambition. A person of faith seeks self-mastery; a person of ambition or power seeks to control others. A person of faith takes action, works hard and struggles to overcome his or her inner weakness; a person driven by a desire for power forces others to work for his own selfish purpose, never reflecting upon himself. Devadatta, perhaps on account of arrogance, was such a person, and so in the end he departed from the path of a person of faith.

Suda: When Shakyamuni was advanced in years, Devadatta approached him with the request that the Buddha invest him with control of the Buddhist order. The reason he gave was Shakyamuni's age. It is said that even though Shakyamuni refused immediately, Devadatta repeated his demand three times. Since many different writings are in agreement on this point, it is generally accepted as historically accurate.

Ikeda: No matter how seemingly sound his words might have been, religion for Devadatta was ultimately nothing more than a means for realizing personal ambition. Devadatta's words and actions in this incident make plain his ignoble intentions.

Saito: Shakyamuni rebuked him to his face, calling him a person who "licks the spit of others" ([WND-I, 245] referring to the fact that he had put himself under the protection of Ajatashatru). Devadatta solidified his traitorous resolve and left the order. Remarkably, Shakyamuni immediately instructed his disciples to spread word that Devadatta had evil intentions.

Ikeda: Shakyamuni did so because he did not want even one person to be led astray by Devadatta; such was his sense of responsibility. An evil person has to be clearly identified as evil. If measures to deal with such a person are halfhearted, everyone will be confused. Also, in a struggle of this kind, speed is essential. If one vacillates and fails to act resolutely and decisively, people will be consumed by devils.

Also, the reason Shakyamuni scolded Devadatta in front of others, I believe, was so they would thoroughly understand what was at stake. Devadatta's reaction is said to have been one of profound humiliation at having been put to shame in front of others. This shows that he no longer possessed the humble spirit of a disciple. His petty pride outstripped his seeking spirit.

It may be that in private Shakyamuni had previously warned Devadatta, and that he only took the step of a public reprimand because Devadatta had not heeded the Buddha's earlier warnings.

Suda: Thereafter, Devadatta, having resolved to turn against Shakyamuni, incited Ajatashatru to kill his father, King Bimbisara, and assume the throne. Another account has it that King Bimbisara willingly passed on the throne to his son.

Then, availing himself of King Ajatashatru's power, Devadatta hatched all manner of schemes to kill Shakyamuni. He dispatched assassins, set loose wild elephants, and, finally, rolled a huge stone down on him, but all of these attempts failed.

Ikeda: The Buddha's state of life is such that no power or scheme can harm him. Devadatta's failed attempts to do away with

Shakyamuni eloquently attest to this. We see the same in the case of Nichiren Daishonin. Even with the immense power of the ruling Kamakura shogunate at their disposal, the Daishonin's enemies could not make good on their schemes.

Saito: Devadatta also plotted to destroy the *sangha,* or community of Shakyamuni's followers. He tried to kill his mentor and to undermine Shakyamuni's bond with his disciples. In terms of precepts, Devadatta advocated monastic rules even stricter than those upheld in Shakyamuni's order and in this way tried to make himself appear superior to the Buddha. There are some discrepancies among different sources, but the precepts Devadatta put forth are more or less as follows:

(1) Practitioners should dwell in the woods away from villages or towns; those who enter villages or towns are committing an offense. (2) Practitioners should live on alms alone; those who accept invitations to banquets are committing an offense. (3) Practitioners should dress in rags; those who accept donated robes are committing an offense. (4) Practitioners should dwell under trees and not under a roof; those who go near a roofed abode are committing an offense. (5) Practitioners should not eat the flesh of animals or fish; those who break this precept are committing an offense.

Endo: In India at the time, practitioners who strove to curb desires were greatly respected. Devadatta probably thought he could win a following by advocating such severe precepts.

In fact, it is said that five hundred of the Buddha's disciples were deceived by Devadatta's words and became his followers. But these people later returned to Shakyamuni after Shariputra and Maudgalyayana, two of Shakyamuni's senior disciples, reasoned with them.

Those who remained with Devadatta created an order centering on the renegade disciple. This order, which revered Devadatta as an enlightened being, is thought to have survived in Indian society for as long as a thousand years.

Suda: These strict precepts must have sounded good. Indeed, they are so austere that Shakyamuni must have seemed decadent by comparison.

Ikeda: That was probably Devadatta's intention. An evil person, rather than present a face that says, "I am evil," will use evil wisdom and cunning to make himself appear otherwise. At a time when many people were carrying out extreme practices, it probably would have been easy to criticize Shakyamuni's practice of the Middle Way as decadent. As a matter of fact, before attaining enlightenment, Shakyamuni had rigorously pursued the limits of painful asceticism. When he rejected this path, he was severely criticized as decadent by five of his erstwhile fellow ascetics.

Naturally, Shakyamuni's order, while having a certain open-mindedness when it came to daily practice and the following of precepts—a quality intrinsic to the teaching of the Middle Way—no doubt maintained a spirit of the greatest austerity when it came to seeking the Way. Without a certain measure of flexibility and openness, it would not have been possible to include many different people. The purpose of Buddhist practice and of precepts is to enable many people to enter the path of good and guide them to happiness. To impose precepts with the express purpose of causing people to suffer is perverse. Religions that bind and restrict people with external rules prohibiting one thing after another cannot capture people's hearts. Moreover, anyone hypocritical enough to affect poverty and austerity out of personal vanity and scheming is abusing the spirit of religion.

In short, Devadatta desperately wanted to be respected more highly than Shakyamuni. He was motivated by jealousy, and it was probably for this reason that he thought up his five precepts.

Endo: At its root, the idea can only have arisen from sheer madness.

Saito: I think Devadatta was destroyed by his own jealousy.

Ikeda: President Toda often said that Devadatta represented male jealousy. He would often point out that while jealousy is usually associated with women, it is not uncommon in men, in whom it may take a particularly virulent form.

Jealousy, instead of leading to appreciation of the greatness or outstanding qualities of others, impels us to try to find fault with, injure or somehow drag the other person down. That is its fearful power. But the net effect of jealousy is to injure and drag oneself down. The Greek philosopher Antisthenes said, "As iron is eaten away by rust, so are the envious consumed by their own passion."[4]

Saito: It seems to me that the state of Japan today is no different than when Nichiren Daishonin wrote: "The men of Japan are like Devadatta" (WND-1, 963–64). In a country ruled by jealousy, people cannot respect greatness and they regard tripping others up through underhanded means as natural behavior. It's truly a sad situation.

Ikeda: Devadatta saw only that Shakyamuni was widely respected; he did not attempt to understand Shakyamuni's heart. Shakyamuni, unbeknownst to others, must have agonized day and night over the question of how to lead people to happiness and make them aware of the treasure of their own lives. How he must have struggled to gain self-mastery! What continuous and painstaking efforts he must have made! But Devadatta did not try to understand Shakyamuni's difficult ordeal.

Why couldn't he see this? Most likely it's because he had given up his own internal struggle. If we perceive our inner evil but neglect efforts to conquer it, then our lives are instantaneously stained with evil. In that sense, a good person is someone who struggles against evil. It is by fighting the evil around us that we eradicate evil within our lives and so purify them. That is the path of human revolution.

Saito: Perceiving inner evil—this brings us to the doctrine of three thousand realms in a single moment of life. The extreme evil that Devadatta represents, dwelling in the world of hell, exists even in the life of the Buddha, a being of the utmost goodness. That's because of the mutual possession of the Ten Worlds and three thousand realms in a single moment of life.

Ikeda: Exactly. In that sense, the Lotus Sutra's doctrine of three thousand realms in a single moment of life is the ultimate philosophy of self-reflection. It is a philosophy of equality that does not permit anyone the arrogance to claim special nobility or status. It is a philosophy of the sanctity of all life.

According to three thousand realms in a single moment of life, even a supremely benevolent being such as the Buddha possesses the nature of evil, and even a great villain like Devadatta possesses the Buddha nature. On this premise, the paths of good and evil diverge greatly, going in completely opposite directions; the path we take depends on whether we continue struggling against evil. This is in fact the key to understanding the "Devadatta" chapter. In conclusion, a spirit of resolute struggle against evil runs throughout the chapter.

The Buddha Turned Even Devadatta Into a "Good Friend"

Endo: I'd like to turn to the outline of the "Devadatta" chapter. Shakyamuni begins by explaining his karmic relationship from the past with Devadatta. Shakyamuni relates that he had once been the king of a great country, and that he had carried out a bodhisattva practice and devoted himself to the well-being of the people, expending his life and using his wealth without hesitation on their behalf.

Saito: He must have been a great ruler. The basic spirit of governing is compassion. In fact, it is essentially bodhisattva practice.

Endo: But the king was still not satisfied and continued searching for the Law of the great vehicle that could lead all people to happiness. He sought a philosophy that would make it possible to bring people true peace and tranquillity. An outstanding leader seeks a great philosophy for the people.

Suda: The sutra says that he abandoned his throne in search of such a philosophy. This is the exact opposite of the befuddled leaders we often see who try to control the minds of the people and use religion to maintain their power and protect their interests.

Endo: In response to the king's seeking spirit, a seer named Asita came forth. The seer told the king that if he practiced as instructed, then he, the seer, would expound the Sutra of the Lotus of the Wonderful Law for him. The king rejoiced and earnestly went to work serving the seer, drawing water for him, collecting firewood and performing other chores. Although he continued this practice for a thousand years, he did not become fatigued in either body or mind because in his heart he sought the Mystic Law. As a result, the king eventually attained Buddhahood.

The curious thing about this story is that although it emphasizes that the king undertook extraordinarily difficult practice in service of the seer, termed "millennial service," it does not make it entirely clear whether or at what point he was taught the Lotus Sutra.

Ikeda: On this point, Nichiren Daishonin explains in *The Record of the Orally Transmitted Teachings* that the king carried out no actions apart from these in order to receive the transmission of the Law (see OTT, 102). In other words, the Lotus Sutra is transmitted through everyday practice, through strenuous action. The Mystic Law manifests in a heart that thoroughly seeks the Mystic Law. Our practice of chanting daimoku for the happiness of ourselves and others is itself the practice of receiving, upholding and transmitting the Mystic Law.

In the present age, carrying out millennial service means exerting oneself body and mind for kosen-rufu.

Endo: After relating this episode from his past, Shakyamuni reveals that the seer who had served as his mentor was in fact Devadatta. Further, Shakyamuni attributes the fact of his own enlightenment along with his ability to broadly lead people to happiness to the role Devadatta played in his life as a "good friend." He also predicts that, because of these past causes and conditions, after immeasurable kalpas have passed, Devadatta will become a Buddha called Heavenly King Thus Come One.

Saito: For Shakyamuni at the time, Devadatta was an "evil friend." He tried to kill Shakyamuni; disrupted the unity of Shakyamuni's followers, creating a schism in the Buddhist order, and had a follower of Shakyamuni (the nun Utpalavarna) beaten to death. Shakyamuni reveals that in a past life this man of great evil had been a good friend. Good and evil are thus completely reversed.

More to the point, Shakyamuni explains that, incredible as it might seem, in the past Devadatta had also been his teacher. In terms of common sense, the notion that a villain like Devadatta could have been the teacher of the Buddha is unthinkable.

Suda: The line in the "Devadatta" chapter where Shakyamuni explains his attaining Buddhahood, "The fact that I have attained impartial and correct enlightenment and can save living beings on a broad scale is all due to Devadatta, who was a good friend" (LSOC, 223), seems to offer a clue. In other words, had it not been for Devadatta, even Shakyamuni could not have become a Buddha.

The Great Teacher T'ien-t'ai of China says in the fifth volume of the *Profound Meaning of the Lotus Sutra*: "Good exists in response to evil. There is no good in isolation from evil"; and, "Evil supports good. Without evil there would also be no good."

Ikeda: That's it exactly. Good and evil are not absolutes, they are relative. Therefore, we cannot say conclusively that a particular person is intrinsically good or intrinsically evil.

Tsunesaburo Makiguchi, the first Soka Gakkai president, said: "Even a good person, if he opposes great good, immediately becomes a person of great evil. Even an evil person, if he opposes great evil, immediately becomes a person of great good."[5] He used the following illustration to clarify his meaning: "Had Yen Hui opposed Confucius, then this sage, who was second in order of esteem, would have immediately become a person of great evil. Had Confucius opposed Shakyamuni, he would have immediately created effects of supreme evil."[6]

Endo: Yen Hui was one of Confucius's major disciples; he was a sage second in order of esteem, that is, second in wisdom only to Confucius. For Yen Hui to turn his back on Confucius would be for a person of medium good to oppose a person of great good; he would at once have turned into a person of great evil. Similarly, had Confucius opposed the Buddha, a person of supreme good, he would have become a person of supreme evil. This is the relation of good and evil.

Ikeda: But President Makiguchi also said that if Confucius, Jesus Christ or Mohammed were to meet Shakyamuni, it is doubtful that they would have opposed him. He explained: "That's because they all alike disregarded the self and had no concerns apart from their desire to lead people to happiness. They were not egoists."[7]

It seems that President Makiguchi regarded leading people to happiness as the ultimate good. By contrast, the egoism that allows one to think only about personal interests is the root of evil.

Mr. Makiguchi said:

> Generally speaking, people who pride themselves on being good or extraordinarily good should be well prepared to recognize someone superior to them or to recognize a method other than their own. In actuality,

however, the higher a person's position, the more likely that he or she will make causes of great evil or extraordinary great evil.

Had Nichiren Daishonin not appeared, then Ryokan,[8] Doryu[9] and others [who were venerated by society in the Daishonin's day] would likely have ended their lives revered as living Buddhas. Unfortunately for them, unable to accept the supremacy of the Daishonin's teaching and consumed by concern for their personal interests, they became priests of the greatest evil.[10]

It seems they became people of evil on account of jealousy.

Saito: President Makiguchi defined "good" as something contributing toward or providing public benefit. The Lotus Sutra is the teaching that enables all people to attain Buddhahood. In that sense, we can say that the Lotus Sutra aims for the greatest public benefit, the greatest good.

Ikeda: That is also the Buddha's spirit. The Buddha, therefore, is a person of supreme good. But this is not to say that there is no evil in the life of the Buddha. It exists, of course, as a potential. Because the Buddha aims for the ultimate good and relentlessly struggles against evil, good is what manifests from his life.

Nichiren Daishonin says: "The opposite of good we call bad, the opposite of bad we call good. Hence we know that outside of the mind there is no good and there is no bad" (WND-2, 843). Good and bad in themselves have no substance. In other words, they are not in themselves absolute but reflect relative distinctions. It is important, therefore, to ceaselessly direct our hearts, and take action, toward good.

The Oneness of Good and Evil

Suda: It's a bit complicated, but the Daishonin's work "The Entity of the Mystic Law" says the following with regard to this point:

The mystic principle of the true aspect of reality is like this. The mystic principle of the true aspect of reality is one, but if it encounters evil influences, it will manifest delusion, while if it encounters good influences, it will manifest enlightenment. Enlightenment means enlightenment to the essential nature of phenomena, and delusion, ignorance of it.

It is like the case of a person who in a dream sees himself performing various good and evil actions. After he wakes up and considers the matter, he realizes that it was all a dream produced by his own mind. This mind of his corresponds to the single principle of the essential nature of phenomena, the true aspect of reality, while the good and evil that appeared in the dream correspond to enlightenment and delusion. When one becomes aware of this, it is clear that one should discard the ignorance associated with evil and delusion, and take as one's basis the awakening that is characterized by goodness and enlightenment. (WND-I, 417–18)

The true aspect of life embodies the oneness of good and evil. Both good and evil exist in life. For precisely this reason, in terms of practice we have to base ourselves on the nature of enlightenment and strive for good.

Ikeda: That's right. Buddhism is a contest, an endless struggle. Because Shakyamuni defeated Devadatta, Devadatta's evil helped prove Shakyamuni's good. On the other hand, had Shakyamuni been defeated by evil, then it certainly would not have been possible for him to call Devadatta a good friend.

President Toda clarified this matter as follows:

Devadatta was the slanderer in Shakyamuni's lifetime; he cut all the roots of goodness in the world. The pre-Lotus Sutra teachings say: "Without the existence of evil, wise actions of good cannot be manifested. For this reason, Devadatta had for immeasurable kalpas always been together with Shakyamuni, and when Shakyamuni practiced the Buddha way, Devadatta practiced injustice. In this way, they mutually inspired each other." Once good is completely revealed, however, evil in its entirety becomes good. Therefore, the Lotus Sutra teaches the oneness of good and evil, the oneness of the erroneous and the true, and the oneness of a reverse relationship and a positive relationship. This is the inner doctrine that had not been revealed in the pre-Lotus Sutra teachings.[11]

If evil functions to reveal good, then evil in its entirety becomes good. This is truly the oneness of good and evil. But if evil is simply allowed to run its course, then it does not become good. Only when evil is thoroughly challenged and conquered does it become an entity of the oneness of good and evil.

In that sense, the enlightenment of evil people presented in the "Devadatta" chapter is great proof of the victory won by Shakyamuni. It is his victory declaration. Only when he stands in this lofty state of life as a winner can he say that Devadatta had in a past life been a good friend and mentor and had in this life aided his efforts to instruct people.

Saito: Isn't the point of this explanation to reveal the principle of life rather than to provide specific facts about their past relationship?

Ikeda: We could say that it explains the reality of life. Devadatta, too, in terms of the true aspect of his life also embodies the oneness of good and evil. Darkness and enlightenment are two facets of the one entity of the Mystic Law. Devadatta, who had been Shakyamuni's teacher in a past life, was in fact the entity of the Mystic Law. Therefore, Nichiren Daishonin says: "Devadatta is another name for

Myoho-renge-kyo. In a past existence he was the seer Asita. The seer Asita is another name for *myoho*, the Wonderful Law" (OTT, 101).

Shakyamuni attained Buddhahood with the fundamental Mystic Law as his teacher. This is what is expressed by the formulation in the "Devadatta" chapter of his having practiced and attained Buddhahood under Asita in a past life.

Endo: The oneness of good and evil certainly does not mean that good and evil are the same.

Suda: Such a way of thinking amounts to an affirmation of evil; it is comparable to the erroneous concept of "original enlightenment"—the notion that all people are Buddhas just as they are, without having to carry out any practice—to which the Japanese Tendai school succumbed. By contrast, the Lotus Sutra's doctrine of the oneness of good and evil is about constantly striving to create good and changing even evil into good.

Ikeda: That's right. The power of the Mystic Law enables us to change even bad friends into good friends. The strength of our mind of faith changes suffering into joy, into a tailwind to propel our further advance. This is what the "Devadatta" chapter teaches.

Nichiren Daishonin says: "Devadatta was the foremost good friend to the Thus Come One Shakyamuni. In this age as well, it is not one's allies but one's powerful enemies who assist one's progress" (WND-1, 770). To attain Buddhahood, we have to thoroughly conquer our own inner evil. The concrete means for doing so is struggling against and defeating external evil. Struggling to defeat evil enables us to polish and purify our lives and attain Buddhahood. Because we strive against the ultimate evil, we attain the ultimate good.

Even ultimate evil, when viewed in terms of its essential function of enabling us to polish our lives and attain Buddhahood, can be thought of as a teacher. The point, therefore, is Shakyamuni's victorious state of life in explaining that even the supremely evil

Devadatta had been his teacher in the past. Because Shakyamuni won, he could say this; because he won, he became a Buddha.

Nichiren Daishonin, likewise, having realized great victory, could say, "For me, Nichiren, my best allies in attaining Buddhahood are Kagenobu, the priests Ryokan, Doryu, and Doamidabutsu, and Hei no Saemon and the lord of Sagami. I am grateful when I think that without them I could not have proved myself to be the votary of the Lotus Sutra" (WND-1, 770). In other words, these evil people who had persecuted the original Buddha were changed into good people by his victory.

Because of the model of such struggle set by Shakyamuni and the Daishonin, we of later generations know where the correct path lies. In that sense, Devadatta, Hei no Saemon and the others functioned in part as teachers who revealed the path of good for later generations.

The Soka Gakkai has struggled against and triumphed over all manner of persecution, repression and scheming. As a result of these struggles, we could all deepen and strengthen our faith. If it were possible to accomplish kosen-rufu easily and without obstacles, then we would not have the opportunity to polish ourselves or to carry out our practice for attaining Buddhahood.

Difficulties equal progress. Earthly desires are enlightenment. The key is to use all sufferings as fuel to become happy; to use all evil as firewood to cause the light of good to burn brighter still.

Endo: Those who heard the "Devadatta" chapter the first time it was expounded must have been rather startled.

Suda: Even if he had made sincere penance for his evil deeds, the idea of the supremely evil Devadatta receiving a prophecy of enlightenment would have been utterly unthinkable in the pre-Lotus Sutra teachings.

Saito: Shakyamuni expounded the principle of the true aspect of all phenomena in the "Expedient Means" chapter; so, theoretically, people must have had a sense of the doctrine of the mutual possession of the Ten Worlds. Still, it may be that even Shariputra, known as the foremost in wisdom, did not realize that this doctrine meant that evil people and women could attain enlightenment.

Ikeda: That's right. Later in the "Devadatta" chapter it is revealed that Shariputra has a streak of obstinacy that prevents him from believing that women can attain Buddhahood. It's often the case that even if we understand something theoretically, our lives are still dominated by darkness. Therefore, it is important to have a practice for polishing our lives.

Endo: Fundamentally, all people can equally attain Buddhahood. Since that is the spirit of the entire Lotus Sutra, it would be a contradiction if Devadatta were excluded. Rather, in terms of the spirit of the Lotus Sutra, it can be said that the prediction of enlightenment for Devadatta is necessary. Nichiren Daishonin explains that the prophecy of enlightenment for Devadatta "indicates that the world of hell also contains Buddhahood" (WND-1, 357).

Saito: It occurs to me that since everyone has in his or her life an evil nature as heinous as Devadatta's, if it were the case that those with evil in their lives could not attain Buddhahood, it would mean that no one could. In other words, whether evil people can attain Buddhahood is not only an issue of concern for evil people; it in fact concerns all people. This is analogous to the principle we earlier discussed in connection with the enlightenment of the people of the two vehicles, i.e., voice-hearers and cause-awakened ones.

Ikeda: The doctrine of the mutual possession of the Ten Worlds indicates that evil exists even within the life of the Buddha, and that the Buddha nature exists even within the lives of evil people. This is indicated directly by Devadatta's attainment of Buddhahood. It could be said, therefore, that if Devadatta's attainment of enlightenment had not been expounded, the Lotus Sutra would not be complete.

Endo: It's easy to understand the narrow view that the Buddha should be the polar opposite of evil, someone who has completely eradicated evil from his life. But real people have an evil nature, and it cannot be completely eradicated. Therefore, if a Buddha were entirely free of evil, then the Buddha would simply be an abstract being, a myth, making it impossible for any ordinary person to actually become a Buddha.

The Daishonin indicates this when he says, "If we inquire into the truth of the matter, we will find that the sutras prior to the Lotus show us only a provisional type of Buddha and do not reveal any way in which ordinary people can attain Buddhahood" (WND-2, 62).

Ikeda: Because the doctrine of three thousand realms in a single moment of life had not yet been revealed, the pre-Lotus Sutra teachings, even where they talk about people attaining Buddhahood, are empty words; they are all talk and no substance. The Lotus Sutra, however, is not an abstract doctrine. It has the power to actually remove the blade of suffering from people's lives and lead them to happiness. The entity of the Law of the Lotus Sutra, which is the fundamental power to help people attain Buddhahood, is Nam-myoho-renge-kyo.

Saito: There are various ways of looking at the relationship between good and evil. One is as fixed forces that are in opposition to each other. This is the perspective we find in the pre-Lotus Sutra teachings. Another view holds that good and evil are different sides or aspects of the same thing, like the front and back sides of a coin.

Ikeda: We might surmise that the oneness of good and evil corresponds to the latter view, but it does not. If that were the case, good and evil would be merely differences in perspective, and life itself would become static and unchanging. From that standpoint, it would be impossible to capture the dynamism and ceaseless change that are the true aspects of life.

We must recognize that, while one in essence, life at times produces positive value and at other times produces negative value.

Suda: That gives us three ways of looking at good and evil. These correspond to the three interpretations of the concept of "oneness" given by the Chinese Tendai priest Chih-li. They are "dualism of separate entities," "dualism of the same entity" and "an integrated whole."

The view that good and evil exist separately, such that good appears when evil is extinguished, corresponds to the first interpretation. The view of good and evil as like the front and back sides of a coin corresponds to the second interpretation. The third interpretation is the view that while good and evil always manifest in opposition, they arise from the true aspect of all phenomena, which itself embodies the oneness of good and evil.

Ikeda: That classification is rather complex. The Daishonin says, "Anger can be either a good and a bad thing" (WND-2, 931). Anger directed toward bad is good. Anger that derives from egotism is bad. Anger itself cannot be called either good or bad. Good and bad exist in the context of relationships. It is important, therefore, that we actively seek to create "good" relations.

President Makiguchi continued to conduct dialogue even in prison. He would ask, loudly enough for people in other cells to hear, "Isn't not doing good the same as doing evil?"[12] In that way, he encouraged them to think about what was going on around them.

Ordinarily, most people probably suppose that doing evil is worse than simply not doing good. Not doing evil, but not doing any good either—this is how most people in the modern age live. President Makiguchi, however, argued that not to do good is the same as doing evil.

To illustrate, let us say that someone places a rock on a railroad track. That is evil. Let us say that someone else sees the rock on the tracks but fails to alert anyone to the situation and just lets the rock be. It may well be true that this person has not committed evil, but neither has he done any good. If as a result of his inaction the train gets derailed, then it is the same as if he had committed evil.[13]

Not to fight against evil is itself evil. It was with this conviction that Mr. Makiguchi taught the importance of leading a life of actively creating good, a conviction he put into practice.

He also argued that the accumulation of minor good is ultimately to no avail. "It has been said that the accumulation of particles of dust will form a mountain, but at most all you can create from specks of dust is a mound of dust."[14] President Makiguchi had an interesting way of putting things, and his words were really on the mark. He concluded: "Mountains are formed by upheavals in earth's crust. Unless we change human beings and society from the very foundation, it will be too late for humankind. Creating such change is great good; it is spreading the Lotus Sutra."

Saito: In other words, not fighting against evil is the same as committing evil. It seems to me that this is a shrill warning to the people of the present age, who are inclined to live their lives oblivious to what is going on around them.

Ikeda: That was certainly the attitude of Dr. Martin Luther King Jr. Dr. King believed those who stood by quietly in the face of evil were aiding and abetting evil, and that not to oppose evil was to comply with it.

Suda: Throughout the world, I believe, there is a great deal of vagueness and ambiguity surrounding the question of just what good and evil are. I think that under such circumstances the Buddhist ideal of actively creating good is like a beacon in the fog.

Ikeda: Exactly. We must be careful lest this age, which is largely devoid of philosophy and ideology, give way to a dangerous era in which egoism is allowed to run amok. We must not allow nihilism to prevail. We have to show people a sure path to follow and bring about the ascendance of a sun of hope.

Many philosophical arguments have been made about good and evil in both past and present, East and West. Without going into these various perspectives, the point that life is the objective and the end and must not be turned into a means is key; this is the major premise. To enrich this supremely noble life and make it shine is good; to turn life into a means and cause it to contract is evil.

Also, unity is good while fragmentation is evil. The highest good, therefore, is to help people open up the world of Buddhahood in their lives and to forge a global solidarity of good will. The movement for peace, culture and education based on Buddhism, that is to say, our movement of kosen-rufu, accords entirely with this objective. Carrying out these activities means putting the principle of the oneness of good and evil, in which evil is embraced and transformed by good, into dynamic practice.

The point is to advance while intently reflecting on and grappling to master the self; to defeat one's inner weaknesses and advance. When we do so, we are truly reading the "Devadatta" chapter. Ultimately, the bitter struggle between Shakyamuni and Devadatta exists within each of our lives. When we understand the sutra in this light we are reading it from the standpoint of Nichiren Buddhism.

The Indian poet Rabindranath Tagore compares the function of evil to the banks of a river. The river banks are obstructions, but they are necessary for keeping the river on track and flowing steadily forward. Without banks, the river would overflow, causing destruction instead of creating value.[15]

Like the river, let us use every obstruction to our benefit as we continue our endless struggle against evil. Let us strive to further increase the volume of water in our "river of good" and extend its flow worldwide.

NOTES

1. Ajatashatru: King of Magadha in Shakyamuni's time. Under his reign, Magadha became the most powerful kingdom in India at that time. Later, he converted to Buddhism.

2. These consisted of lectures on each of the eight volumes of the Lotus Sutra held morning and evening over four successive days.

3. The fifth volume of the Lotus Sutra includes the "Devadatta" (twelfth), "Encouraging Devotion" (thirteenth), "Peaceful Practices" (fourteenth), and "Emerging from the Earth" (fifteenth) chapters.

4. *The Macmillan Book of Proverbs, Maxims, and Famous Phrases*, ed. Burton Stevenson (New York: Macmillan Publishing Company, 1948), p. 701.

5. *Makiguchi Tsunesaburo zenshu* (Collected Writings of Tsunesaburo Makiguchi) (Tokyo: Daisan Bummeisha, 1987), vol. 10, p. 31.

6. Ibid., p. 33.

7. *Makiguchi Tsunesaburo shingenshu* (Collection of Tsunesaburo Makiguchi's Sayings), ed. Takehisa Tsuji (Tokyo: Daisan Bummeisha, 1979), p. 169.

8. Ryokan (1217–1303): A priest of the Shingon-Ritsu school during the Kamakura period.

9. Doryu (1213–1278): A priest of the Rinzai school of Zen, also called Rankei. In 1246, he came to Japan from China. He opposed the Daishonin and, with Ryokan and others, plotted against him.

10. *Makiguchi Tsunesaburo shingenshu*, p. 169.

11. *Toda Josei zenshu*, vol. 6, pp. 360–61.

12. *Makiguchi Tsunesaburo zenshu*, vol. 10, p. 30.

13. *Makiguchi Tsunesaburo shingenshu*, p. 184.

14. Ibid., p. 23.

15. See Rabindranath Tagore, *Sadhana: The Realisation of Life* (New York: The Macmillan Company, 1929), p. 47.

4   The Dragon Girl's Enlightenment
Is a Grand Declaration of Equality

Endo: In this chapter, let's take up the enlightenment of the young lady known as the dragon girl,[1] which is described in the latter half of the "Devadatta" chapter.

Suda: The dragon girl is best known for providing women a model of attaining Buddhahood.

Ikeda: The enlightenment of women is a key theme of the Lotus Sutra. For us, a group of men, to discuss the enlightenment of women may prove a challenge.

President Hassan Gouled Aptidon of Djibouti, Africa, whom I met in 1995, told me that should there ever be a war between men and women, he would have no problem deciding which side to take—that of the women.

"You can count me in, too," I told him.

When I mentioned this to Alexander Yakovlev of Russia and his wife, Dr. Yakovlev remarked that before it came to war, he would raise a white flag and surrender. Against a phalanx of women, men wouldn't stand a chance, he said, humorously confiding that during fifty years of married life he had not once managed to sway his wife once she had made up her mind.

From one standpoint, the discussion of the dragon girl in the "Devadatta" chapter is a tale about how arrogant men are defeated by women. Even Shariputra, known as the foremost in wisdom, is no match in faith for the dragon girl. It is also a grand declaration of human rights that refutes, by means of actual proof, ideas and beliefs that discriminate against women.

It seems that misunderstanding still lingers about the enlightenment of women as taught in the Lotus Sutra. Let's try to get an accurate grasp of the concept.

THE DRAGON GIRL'S BUDDHAHOOD IS MET WITH DISBELIEF

> *At that time Shariputra said to the dragon girl, "You suppose that in this short time you have been able to attain the unsurpassed way. But this is difficult to believe. Why? Because a woman's body is soiled and defiled, not a vessel for the Law. How could you attain the unsurpassed enlihtenment?. . ."*
>
> *At that time the dragon girl had a precious jewel worth as much as the major world system, which she presented to the Buddha. The Buddha immediately accepted it . . .*
>
> *The girl said, "Employ your supernatural powers and watch me attain Buddhahood. It will be even quicker than that!"*
> (LSOC, 227)

Suda: First, let's consider the flow of the "Devadatta" chapter.

After Shakyamuni completes his prophecy that the great villain Devadatta would attain enlightenment, one of the followers of Many Treasures Buddha, known as Bodhisattva Wisdom Accumulated, suggests to Many Treasures that they return home to the land of Treasure Purity. If his name is any indication, he must have been not only perceptive but also highly intelligent. He must have thought that the teaching was finished, having just heard Shakyamuni preach the doctrine of the enlightenment of evil people and urge his followers to "make certain the Law will long endure" (LSOC, 217), i.e., spread the Lotus Sutra after his passing.

Endo: But he was premature in coming to this conclusion. Shakyamuni had not yet finished his instruction.

Ikeda: That's right. There was more to the story, something even Wisdom Accumulated did not comprehend; namely, the doctrine of attaining Buddhahood in one's present form.

Suda: Yes. Thereupon, Shakyamuni says to Wisdom Accumulated: "Good man, wait a little while. There is a bodhisattva named Manjushri[2] here whom you should see. Debate and discuss the wonderful Law with him, and then you may return to your homeland" (LSOC, 224). Manjushri, who had just arrived from the palace of the dragon king in the ocean where he had been spreading the Buddha's teachings, appears at the Ceremony in the Air accompanied by many bodhisattvas under his instruction. A discussion between Wisdom Accumulated and Manjushri ensues.

Wisdom Accumulated starts out by asking Manjushri, "When you went to the palace of the dragon king, how many living beings did you convert?" Manjushri explains that in the palace of the dragon king he had "constantly expounded the Lotus Sutra of the Wonderful Law alone" (LSOC, 225), converting countless beings, and that the eight-year-old daughter of the dragon king heard the Lotus Sutra and immediately attained *bodhi*, or enlightenment.

Wisdom Accumulated doesn't believe a word of this. Convinced that Buddhahood can only be attained by bodhisattvas after they have carried out difficult and painful practices for immeasurable kalpas, he cannot believe that the dragon girl could have attained Buddhahood in the brief time of Manjushri's stay at the dragon king's palace.

Saito: The Daishonin says in his writings that Manjushri's propagation at the palace of the dragon king took place during the short interval while Shakyamuni was expounding "The Emergence of the Treasure Tower," the eleventh chapter. That Manjushri could convert many beings, he explains, and that the dragon girl could attain enlightenment during that brief interlude indicates the power of the Lotus Sutra.

[Nichiren Daishonin writes: "And yet, contrary to all expectations, through the instruction of Manjushri, in the short space of time between the 'Teacher of the Law' and 'Devadatta' chapters when the Buddha was preaching the 'Treasure Tower' chapter, she attained Buddhahood in the midst of the ocean. This was a most wonderful happening! If it had not been for the power of the Lotus Sutra, the foremost among all the teachings of the Buddha's lifetime, how could such a thing have come about?" (WND-1, 341)]

Ikeda: Wisdom Accumulated obviously did not understand the power of the Lotus Sutra. That's why he couldn't believe it when he heard Manjushri relate that the dragon girl had attained Buddhahood in her present form.

Nichiren Daishonin says that such disbelief in the Mystic Law is a manifestation of fundamental darkness. In this context, fundamental darkness means we have a mistaken notion about the true nature of our existence and, ultimately, the potential of our lives. Also, the Daishonin characterizes the disbelief of Wisdom Accumulated as according with the "viewpoint ... of the specific teaching"[3] (see OTT, 105). In other words, Wisdom Accumulated represents the rather limited point of view that one can attain Buddhahood only by first passing through many stages of practice, for example, the fifty-two stages of bodhisattva practice.

By contrast, the dragon girl represents the perfect teaching of the Lotus Sutra. The dragon girl reveals with her life "new" thinking that flies in the face of the patriarchal old way of thinking. The "Devadatta" chapter can be likened to a philosophical drama. It presents profound ideas in the form of a dramatic narrative with deep meaning. I think that is why one never tires of hearing it.

Endo: That's true. Before Wisdom Accumulated has even finished stating his disbelief, the dragon girl herself suddenly appears.

Suda: And what a dramatic entry it is!

Endo: She greets the Buddha, vowing:

> The Buddha alone can bear witness to this [the fact
>   I attained Buddhahood].
> I unfold the doctrines of the great vehicle [of the
>   Lotus Sutra]
> to rescue living beings from suffering. (LSOC, 227)

Ikeda: "I unfold the doctrines of the great vehicle to rescue living beings from suffering" — these are notable words. It's a wonderful passage.

She says, in other words: "Everyone might ridicule me, but that does not concern me in the least. The Buddha knows the truth. I will simply devote myself to helping people become happy through the power of the Mystic Law that has saved me." Attaining Buddhahood in our present form means developing in ourselves the Buddha's strong spirit to unhesitatingly lead all suffering people to happiness. It is to take action cheerfully and with composure to help those who are suffering, even though one might be subject to ridicule or discrimination. Those who carry out such a practice shine as Buddhas just as they are.

Suda: Still the men, hopelessly stubborn and missing the point, continue to express disbelief.

This time it is Shariputra who voices doubts after hearing the dragon girl's determination. There are two reasons for Shariputra's disbelief. In the first place, Shariputra, like Wisdom Accumulated, has the fixed notion that the Buddha's enlightenment can only be attained by carrying out painful practices over an extremely long period of time. The second reason relates to the "five obstacles"; the view that a woman cannot become a (Brahma) heavenly king, a King Shakra,[4] a devil king, a wheel-turning sage king[5] or a Buddha. Therefore, he criticizes the dragon girl, declaring it impossible that in her form as a woman she could have quickly become a Buddha.

Saito: The Great Teacher T'ien-t'ai of China says, "Shariputra argues employing the provisional teachings of the Tripitaka."[6] The Tripitaka, or Hinayana, are provisional teachings in which the five obstacles are discussed.

Endo: In this "scene," Shariputra, as a proponent of the Theravada teachings, plays the role of "bad guy."

Ikeda: That the dragon girl has attained Buddhahood in her present form wonderfully overturns both the commonly held view that attaining Buddhahood requires practice over an extremely long period and the doctrine of the five obstacles.

Suda: Yes. Next the dragon girl takes up a jewel that the sutra says is equal in value to the major world system, a metaphor for the entire universe, and offers it to Shakyamuni, who accepts it immediately. The dragon girl then declares to Shariputra, who has watched this, that her own attainment of Buddhahood will be accomplished in less time than it took for her to present the jewel to Shakyamuni and for Shakyamuni to accept it.

Ikeda: This gesture, while highly symbolic, does indeed amount to a fundamental refutation of the previous, prevailing understanding about the nature of enlightenment.

The "jewel worth as much as the major world system" represents the Mystic Law, which is the wellspring of the universe and of all life. We can also say that it symbolizes one's own life, which is an entity of the Mystic Law. Offering the jewel to the Buddha means offering one's own life, which is infinitely precious and irreplaceable. In other words, it is to devote one's life, in the sense of the term *namu*[7]; it is to have faith.

The Buddha's acceptance of the jewel indicates that the lives of the dragon girl and the Buddha have become one. In other words, by this action Shakyamuni provides actual proof of the dragon girl's attainment of Buddhahood.

We could also say that the jewel is the jewel of three thousand realms in a single moment of life. By making this offering to the Buddha, the dragon girl indicates she has awakened to this mystic principle.

Endo: The Record of the Orally Transmitted Teachings says: "At the time when the precious jewel was still in the hands of the dragon girl, it represented the attainments that were inherent in her nature. But when the Buddha accepted the precious jewel, it became representative of the attainments acquired through religious practice" (OTT, 108).

THE DRAGON GIRL'S ENLIGHTENMENT MEANS THAT MEN CAN BECOME BUDDHAS, TOO

Ikeda: Everyone, men and women alike, possesses the "attainments that were inherent in her nature." It is a jewel that exists in the lives of all living beings. This is the meaning of the mutual possession of the Ten Worlds and three thousand realms in a single moment of life; this is the Lotus Sutra's fundamental revelation.

The Ten Worlds include the realm of animals. The dragon girl has the form of an animal, and naturally the world of Buddhahood is also inherent in the realm of animals. Her Buddhahood is invisible, however, to an eye that is tainted by prejudice.

The Lotus Sutra teaches that all living beings possess the world of Buddhahood. There is not even a hint of discrimination toward women. If it were true that women could not become Buddhas, then the doctrine of three thousand realms in a single moment of life would fall apart. To deny three thousand realms in a single moment of life is to deny the possibility of anyone's attainment of Buddhahood. Therefore, the dragon girl's enlightenment signifies not only the enlightenment of all women but the enlightenment of all men as well.

If there are men who deny the enlightenment of women, they

are denying the possibility of their own enlightenment. This is a point that not everyone understands.

Saito: Earlier when we discussed the enlightenment of voice-hearers and cause-awakened ones, we noted that the bodhisattvas had thought that while they were capable of attaining Buddhahood, the people of the two vehicles[8] were not. But once they grasped the doctrine of three thousand realms in a single moment of life, it dawned on them that if the people of the two vehicles were incapable of attaining Buddhahood, then they, too, could not attain Buddhahood. For it would mean that the worlds of voice-hearers (learning) and cause-awakened ones (realization) in their own lives did not contain, and so could not manifest, the condition of Buddhahood. This parallels the case of the enlightenment of women.

Suda: As the Daishonin says, "If others could not attain Buddhahood, then they themselves could not do so, that if others could attain Buddhahood, then they themselves could do so." (WND-2, 59). The bodhisattvas had failed to understand this.

Ikeda: They thought that whether other people could become Buddhas had nothing to do with their own attainment of Buddhahood. But to discriminate against others—in any way—is to discriminate against your own life.

Therefore, the dragon girl exhorts Shariputra and Wisdom Accumulated to "employ your supernatural powers and watch me attain Buddhahood" (LSOC, 227). The Daishonin comments on this as follows: "Shariputra thinks she is referring only to her own attainment of Buddhahood, but this is an error. She is rebuking him by saying, 'Watch how one attains Buddhahood.'" (OTT, 109).

Endo: Shariputra and Bodhisattva Wisdom Accumulated take quite a drubbing.

A bodhisattva, in the original sense of the term, is someone who has vowed to attain Buddhahood only after enabling all other beings to do so. Since half the people in the world are women, if women were incapable of attaining Buddhahood, then it would naturally follow that no bodhisattva could attain Buddhahood.

Suda: But the roots of discrimination run deep. It is very difficult to let go of one's attachments to such views merely through logic and reasoning. In that sense, I think the purpose of the metaphors and analogies found in the "Devadatta" chapter is to drive home with actual proof the principle of women attaining Buddhahood.

The Dragon Girl's Transformation Into a Man Is an Expedient Means

Ikeda: That may be so. The dragon girl next transforms into a man, thereby concretely revealing her attainment of Buddhahood.

Suda: Yes. She tells them, "watch me attain Buddhahood" and then turns into a man before everyone's eyes. She immediately carries out all the practices of a bodhisattva and then proceeds southward to a land called Spotless World. To cause everyone to understand the actual proof of her enlightenment, she manifests the Buddha's thirty-two features and eighty characteristics[9] and preaches the Mystic Law to all people in that land. The beings of the *saha* world, seeing her from afar, greatly rejoice and bow with deep reverence. And they, too, attain the stage of "no regression" and receive prophecies of future enlightenment.

Confronted with such actual proof, Bodhisattva Wisdom Accumulated and Shariputra "silently believed and accepted these things" (lsoc, 228). This brings us to the close of the "Devadatta" chapter.

Saito: Regarding the description of how the dragon girl "in the space of an instant change[d] into a man" (lsoc, 227), some have suggested that if she has to take on the form of a man in order to attain Buddhahood, then the Lotus Sutra still presents a discriminatory view of women.

Ikeda: That's an incorrect reading of what happened. The dragon girl's enlightenment indicates the principle of attaining Buddhahood in one's present form. The crucial point is that she had already become a Buddha in her female form.

The dragon girl's changing into a man is nothing more than an expedient means that she employs to drive home the fact of her Buddhahood to Shariputra and the others, who were convinced only men could attain Buddhahood. It does not mean that a woman can only attain Buddhahood by first turning into a man. This has been clear from the first with Bodhisattva Manjushri's introduction of the dragon girl.

Endo: It's a bit lengthy, but since it's an important passage I'll read Manjushri's remarks in their entirety:

> There is the daughter of the dragon king Sagara, who has just turned eight. Her wisdom has keen roots and she is good at understanding the activities and deeds of the sense organs of living beings. She has mastered the dharanis, has been able to accept and embrace all the storehouse of profound secrets preached by the Buddhas, has entered deep into meditation, thoroughly grasped the doctrines, and in the space of an instant conceived the desire for enlightenment and reached the level of no regression. Her eloquence knows no hindrance, and she thinks of living beings with compassion as though they were her own children. She is fully endowed with blessings, and when it comes to conceiving in mind and expounding by mouth, she is subtle, wonderful, comprehensive and great. Kind, compassionate, benevolent, yielding, she is gentle and refined in will, capable of attaining enlightenment. (LSOC, 226)

Ikeda: This truly describes a Buddha. I think we could say it also presents an ideal not only for women but for all human beings.

Saito: Since she has "thoroughly grasped the doctrines," "reached the level of no regression," possesses the compassion, wisdom and power to lead people to happiness, and is "capable of attaining enlightenment," she has already in fact attained Buddhahood. The dragon girl herself says, "I have attained enlightenment" (LSOC, 227).

Endo: In terms of the ordinary view of attaining Buddhahood that we find in sutras expounded before the Lotus Sutra, the circumstances of the dragon girl would suggest that, among all the Buddha's followers, she has the dimmest prospects of attaining Buddhahood. Namely, she (1) has the form of an animal; (2) is a woman; and (3) is very young in years, being only eight years old.

Even if it were said that this dragon girl had become a Buddha, her outward appearance alone would have definitely prevented people from understanding and believing this. And so, for the benefit of Shariputra and the others, she manifests a form that will be convincing to those who are obstinate and a bit slow to understand. That is the reason she changed into a man.

Ikeda: Indeed. Speaking of women changing into men, we find similar accounts in many Mahayana sutras other than the Lotus Sutra. In light of the truth of nonsubstantiality, which is one of the basic principles of Mahayana Buddhism, for one to fixate on superficial differences between men and women is pointless and unnecessary.

However, Shakyamuni must have foreseen that there would be great resistance to the idea that women could become Buddhas.

Endo: Indian society at the time was highly discriminatory toward women. And in Buddhism, too, in the Hinayana teachings, discrimination toward women is very much evident. Therefore, it may be that by explaining that women would first become men and then attain Buddhahood, Mahayana Buddhism sought to cushion the blow, as it were, and make it easier for people to accept the idea of women attaining Buddhahood.

Suda: The doctrine of women transforming into men could therefore perhaps be characterized as a product of compromise.

Ikeda: That's certainly one way to look at it.

Fundamentally, Buddhism views all living beings as individual manifestations of a single great golden life. This is the truth to which Shakyamuni had become enlightened. This is what is illustrated by the principles of dependent origination and nonsubstantiality. This, in essence, is the Mystic Law. From this enlightened standpoint, it would be ludicrous to assert that one sex is superior to the other.

To cause that Law to spread and take root in society, however, the Buddha had to consider how to explain it in terms people would accept. Under certain circumstances, Shakyamuni, while fundamentally determined to teach the Law "according with the Buddha's own mind," had to employ wisdom and adapt his teaching to the capacities of his listeners simply to get a hearing; he had to draw others gradually toward his own enlightened state of life.

The explanation we find in Mahayana sutras of women turning into men could, therefore, be seen as a revolutionary doctrine refuting the Theravada notion that women could never become Buddhas.

Saito: Had Shakyamuni simply told people the entire truth from the outset, the resistance would have been too great. When he expounds the Lotus Sutra, he declares for the first time the teaching "according with the Buddha's own mind" that women can attain enlightenment without changing form.

Ikeda: When explanations are tailored to the biases of society in this fashion, however, there is a danger that even people of sincere faith will become attached to those biases, leading to a distorted interpretation of the teaching. The effect often is that when a distorted teaching gets handed down it does nothing but exacerbate and harden the discriminatory attitudes of society. If we were to trace the historical view of women in Buddhism, we would probably find many such instances.

Endo: I think so. The five obstacles that Shariputra mentions are a good example. This doctrine is thought to have appeared after Shakyamuni's death during the period when Hinayana Buddhism prospered. Monks and the Buddhist order became highly authoritarian; and, in a reflection of the bigotry of Indian society at the time, there was open discrimination against women and lay people. Many of the Buddhist monks were from Brahman families, and it may be that their inability to completely discard the discriminatory and elitist assumptions of their class was a factor in the discriminatory character of Hinayana Buddhism.

SHAKYAMUNI FOUGHT DISCRIMINATION IN SOCIETY

Suda: Discrimination against women goes directly against the spirit of Shakyamuni. Indian society in Shakyamuni's day was disparaging toward women in the extreme. The Brahman scriptures, too, teem with abuse and vilification of women.

Despite the times, Shakyamuni did not discriminate against women in the least. After deliberating the matter, he allowed women to become nuns and carry out monastic practice. Both Mahaprajapati, the aunt who had raised him, and Yashodhara, his wife from before renouncing the world, became nuns. This is said to have been a landmark development for the time.

Endo: That's because in Brahmanism only men could take up the monastic life.

Suda: In Buddhism, however, during Shakyamuni's lifetime and the period shortly after his death, many women left secular life and were active in the *sangha.* We get a glimpse of the situation at the time from a Pali text titled the *Therigatha* (Confessions of Nuns).

In an afterword to the work, the translator, the renowned Japanese Buddhologist Hajime Nakamura, writes: "The appearance [in Buddhism] of an order of nuns was an astonishing development in world religious history. No such female religious order existed in Europe, North Africa, West Asia or East Asia at the time. Buddhism was the first tradition to produce one."[10]

The women who became nuns had a variety of backgrounds. Dr. Nakamura explains:

> Formerly, when they lived in the secular world, the nuns had been ordinary women. Living in a polluted age, they had fully experienced the pain and hardship of life in this world. Some had lost husbands, some had lost children, some had been ostracized, and some had been so destitute that they had only just managed to survive. Some had experienced bad luck with men, and been married a number of times, only to have the relationship always end in disaster. Some women were simply poor and ill-fated ... There were also women who had at one time determined to take their own lives on account of the overwhelming hardships they faced.[11]

Of course, the order also included women who had been wealthy and who had been endowed with intelligence and beauty. But even such women could not avoid the suffering of aging and the problem of death. Shakyamuni taught many such women the path to happiness.

Ikeda: People's worries are still the same.

Since Shakyamuni did not discriminate between clerics and lay people, he also taught laywomen the path to happiness. Shakyamuni's laywomen followers included Vaidehi, the wife of King Bimbisara of Magadha and mother of Ajatashatru; and Shrimala, the queen of Ayodhya, an ancient city in central India. But Shakyamuni treated these prominent women the same way he treated women from ordinary backgrounds.

There is a famous saying, "Not by birth does one become an outcaste, not by birth does one become a Brahman. By action one becomes an outcaste, by action one becomes a Brahman."[12] In a fiercely discriminatory society, Shakyamuni staunchly refused to allow his actions to be colored by distinctions of class, gender, birth or religious role. As a result, the conservative elements in society who had a stake in the status quo saw him as a dangerous person.

Endo: At the outset, the *sangha* pulsed vibrantly with Shakyamuni's spirit of equality. A nun gives an account of calmly rebutting someone who had been whispering that women could not attain enlightenment. Pointing out that women are able to quiet their minds, manifest wisdom and attain awakening, she asks, "How is it possible, then, that being a woman could be an obstacle to attaining enlightenment?"[13]

Teachings of Shakyamuni that seem to back up the words of this nun have also been handed down. One text cites him as saying: "There are differences between men and women, but there is no basis for discriminating among people in terms of the essential nature of life. Just as a man can practice the Way and attain enlightenment, if a woman practices and passes through the necessary courses of the heart, she will without a doubt arrive at enlightenment."[14]

Ikeda: Whether male or female, one's nobility or vulgarity depends entirely on what one has done. Our actions and sincerity are what count. That is Shakyamuni's spirit.

Saito: Early Buddhist texts attribute various negative statements regarding women to Shakyamuni. But these are thought to have been intended, rather, as admonitions to help male practitioners avoid being distracted.

Endo: Certainly, some point to the fact that Shakyamuni's teachings to monks and nuns regarding women are completely different from those addressed to lay people. Nevertheless, I think it is a mistake to conclude that the Buddha was prejudiced against women. Shakyamuni's teachings to monks and nuns were obviously intended to help them maintain a strict practice.

Suda: Monks had 250 precepts, but nuns had many more — 348 or, according to some sources, 500. I think the fact that things were stricter for women could be related to the social conditions of the day.

Ikeda: At the least, we can say that there is some uncertainty as to how much the early Buddhist sutras represent what was truly in Shakyamuni's heart. In any event, it is a fact that Shakyamuni allowed women to take clerical vows and to carry out strict practice. Naturally, the major premise of carrying out Buddhist practice is that you can attain enlightenment by doing so. If that were not possible, he certainly would not have allowed women practitioners. From this alone, we get a sense of Shakyamuni's egalitarianism.

In the *Therigatha*, many nuns express their joy in attaining the state of inner calm and tranquility that Shakyamuni taught: One says, "My heart was liberated."[15] Another says, "I have fully understood and cast aside the roots that give rise to all sufferings."[16] And a third nun says, "I have in fact awakened to peace of mind and have glimpsed the mirror of the truth."[17]

Suda: During the age when Hinayana Buddhism flourished, this original spirit of Shakyamuni all but disappeared. Generally speaking, Theravada Buddhism deified Shakyamuni as a super-human being. It asserted not only that most people could not become Buddhas but that unless you were a monk, you could not even attain the state of *arhat*, the highest enlightenment of voice-hearers. And it blatantly discriminated against both lay people and women.

The doctrine of the five obstacles is thought to have appeared at that time.

Endo: The decline of monastic Buddhism was evident already during the reign of King Ashoka, just a hundred years after Shakyamuni's death.[18] Hinayana Buddhism had strong authoritarian and discriminatory leanings and had lost Shakyamuni's spirit. By contrast, a new current of Buddhism, known as Mahayana, gave rise to a renaissance aimed at returning to Shakyamuni's original spirit.

The Mahayana sutras explain women's attainment of Buddhahood in a variety of ways. For example, the Sukhavativyuha, which is variously translated as the "Sutra of the Buddha of Infinite Life" and "Great Sutra of Amida Buddha," gives "causing women to be reborn in the pure land" as one of Amida's vows. The idea, however, was that women would be reborn in the pure land not as women but as men.

Also, the Shrimala Sutra and Vimalakirti Sutra, which emphasize the doctrine of nonsubstantiality, assert that to distinguish between men and women is itself a meaningless illusion, and they criticize the Hinayana teachings' discrimination against women.

Saito: Many other Mahayana texts similarly explain that women can attain Buddhahood after first transforming into men. These include the Hoshaku Sutra, the Sutra of Great Assembly, and the Wisdom sutras. On the surface, the explanation that the dragon girl turned into a man in the "Devadatta" chapter can be seen as an extension of these other Mahayana sutras.

But the Lotus Sutra teaches the principle of attaining Buddhahood in one's present form. In other words, it does not present changing into a man as a condition for women to attain Buddhahood. The Lotus Sutra, therefore, fundamentally differs from these other texts.

Ikeda: The Lotus Sutra teaches that men and women are equal both in enlightenment and in practice. For example, "The Teacher of the Law" chapter says, "These good men and good women should enter the Thus Come One's room, put on the Thus Come One's robe, sit in the Thus Come One's seat, and then for the sake of the four kinds of believers broadly expound this sutra" (LSOC, 205). This amounts to a declaration that men and women are equally qualified to expound the Law in the Buddha's stead.

In the "Encouraging Devotion" chapter, Shakyamuni bestows prophecies of future enlightenment upon a multitude of women. And the people to whom Bodhisattva Never Disparaging bows in reverence (acknowledging their inherent Buddha nature), saying, "I have profound reverence for you, I would never dare treat you with disparagement or arrogance" (LSOC, 308), include both laymen and laywomen, priests and nuns. The premise here naturally is that women equally can attain Buddhahood.

Nichiren Daishonin says, "With the exception of this Lotus Sutra, the attainment of Buddhahood is not regarded as a possibility" (WND-2, 308), in reference to the Lotus Sutra. And:

> When she [the dragon girl] attained Buddhahood, this does not mean simply that one person did so. It reveals the fact that all women will attain Buddhahood. In the various Hinayana sutras that were preached before the Lotus Sutra, it is denied that women can ever attain Buddhahood. In the Mahayana sutras other than the Lotus Sutra, it would appear that women can attain Buddhahood or be reborn in the pure land. But they may do so only after they have changed into some other

form. It is not the kind of immediate attainment of Buddhahood that is based on the doctrine of three thousand realms in a single moment of life. Thus it is an attainment of Buddhahood or rebirth in the pure land in name only and not in reality. (WND-1, 269)

Endo: The idea was that women could only become Buddhas after first changing their form, i.e., transforming into men. This notion reveals a lack of understanding of the doctrines of the mutual possession of the Ten Worlds and of three thousand realms in a single moment of life. Without a correct understanding of the true aspect of all phenomena, or three thousand realms in a single moment of life, any claims of attaining Buddhahood or gaining rebirth in the pure land are just words without any substance — empty promises. That's why the Daishonin says that this is attainment "in name only and not in reality."

Suda: In Nichiren Buddhism, there is equality of the sexes through and through. In one famous passage the Daishonin says, "There should be no discrimination among those who propagate the five characters of Myoho-renge-kyo in the Latter Day of the Law, be they men or women" (WND-1, 385). He also says, "a woman who embraces this sutra not only excels all other women, but also surpasses all men" (WND-1, 464).

Saito: Nichiren gave some women the honorific title of "sage," such as Sage Nichimyo. This is still further evidence of the Daishonin's liberality.

Ikeda: The Daishonin's actions in this regard stand out as very much the exception in Japanese society and the Buddhist world of his day. Probably no other Buddhist figure of the time praised and respected women as highly as did the Daishonin.

Suda: At the time, women were prohibited from entering the

Buddhist learning centers at Mount Hiei and Mount Koya,[19] as well as Todai-ji and Daigo-ji, all state-supported temples of the old Buddhist schools. Unlike these traditional schools, the Pure Land and Zen schools and other so-called new Buddhist schools of the Kamakura period (1185–1333) addressed the issue of the salvation of women, but they taught that to attain Buddhahood or gain rebirth in the pure land women had to first be reborn as men.

Ikeda: By contrast, the Daishonin declared, "Are not all practitioners of the Lotus Sutra, both men and women, World-Honored Ones?" (GZ, 813). In this we see his greatness.

THE FIRST PERSON IN JAPAN TO LEAVE SECULAR LIFE WAS A WOMAN

Saito: Women weren't always excluded from Buddhism in Japan. In fact, the first person in Japan to renounce secular life and take Buddhist vows was a woman.

Ikeda: That was the nun Zenshin-ni.[20]

Saito: Yes. She is thought to have been the daughter of Shiba Tatsuto, who came to Japan from China (in 522). Zenshin-ni became a nun in 584. Two others took their vows at the same time, and it seems that they, too, were women. I think this could be taken as evidence that there was little if any discrimination against women in early Japanese Buddhism.

Endo: It seems that women on the whole enjoyed high status in Japanese society around that time (between the sixth and eighth centuries), because there was also a succession of emperesses.

Saito: During the Nara period (710–94), temples for nuns were built in provinces throughout the realm. The famous Hokke-ji in Nara was one such temple. The nuns at these temples, known as

"Temples of the Lotus Sutra for the Expiation of Sin," were supposed to pray for women's peace and security through the benefit of the Lotus Sutra. This institution declined after the ninth century, however, and the nunneries were abandoned, turned into monasteries, or became branches of major temples.

Suda: In attempting to account for this, I think we have to consider Buddhism's development into a kind of national ideology, as well as its relation to the indigenous Shinto tradition. In any event, as in India, we see that in Japan, too, the original egalitarian spirit of Buddhism proved extremely difficult to maintain.

Ikeda: We have to make continuous and unceasing efforts to return to the spirit of the founder. Religion ultimately comes down to people. The character of a religion is determined by the character of its adherents.

Also, from another angle, change is continuous. The present patriarchal society will not—must not—continue indefinitely.

Saito: Looking at the broad sweep of history before the start of the common era, we find evidence of an extremely long period, several millennia, during which human society was predominantly matriarchal. Thereafter, society became patriarchal. By comparison, the period of patriarchal society has thus far been of much shorter duration.

Ikeda: In the future, rather than a situation where one sex dominates society, it will be necessary to develop a completely new civilization in which there is balance and harmony between the sexes.

Nichiren's teaching is thoroughly egalitarian. For instance, the Daishonin says that "all living beings are the dragon king's daughter as an essential or intrinsic quality" (OTT, 230). In that sense, the dragon girl represents all people. That's why the dragon girl proclaims that her attainment of Buddhahood is also Shariputra's attainment of Buddhahood.

First Strive To Shine as a Human Being

Endo: How, then, does Buddhism see the difference between men and women? I understand the concept of equality of the sexes—the fact that men and women alike are entities of three thousand realms in a single moment of life. And yet, differences between men and women do exist.

Suda: In terms of gender differences, it has often been said that women, for example, are far more perceptive than men; which might explain why women are so much quicker than men to see through lies and deceit.

Endo: Whatever else may be said, the ability to bear children, obviously, is an exclusive characteristic of female sexuality. Because women are directly involved with giving birth to life, some view women as being in some sense more closely connected to the real essence of life.

Saito: Researchers in the field of depth psychology have investigated the characteristics of men and women fairly extensively. For example, the Jungian psychologist Hayao Kawai says that the maternal principle manifests in the faculty to embrace all things equally, whereas the paternal principle is evident in the faculty to divide and analyze things in terms of dualisms like subjective and objective, or good and evil.[21]

Ikeda: There are many different points of view. The key issue, however, is whether these differences are inherited or learned. That is, are they universally held in common by people in all ages and all societies? Or are they acquired in life due to the culture and traditions to which people are exposed? When it comes to any particular trait, determining to which category it should be attributed is very difficult. I hope future studies will shed light on the matter.

In the meantime, an American researcher points out that, while men are generally raised from childhood to risk danger, women are encouraged to seek safety. She writes: "If a girl seeks out danger, people think that she wants to be like a boy. Even [the Austrian psychiatrist] Alfred Adler says that a girl who climbs trees wants to imitate boys. It doesn't occur to him that girls might also find it interesting to climb trees. Nor does he realize that by seeking out danger as boys do, girls can develop independence."[22]

It is a fact that cultural traditions developed over long periods of time have deeply influenced images of masculinity and femininity in our consciousness. The influence of these traditions thoroughly pervades every aspect of the social ethos, including language, religion, systems of organization, education and scholarship. Therefore, it seems to me that the important thing is not that society come up with a particular model of how men and women ought to behave, but that people first and foremost make tenacious effort to live as decent human beings and allow others to do the same.

In Buddhism, too, there are various explanations about the roles of men and women. But these naturally are colored by the views of men and women prevalent when and where these teachings were expounded. They cannot be taken as having universal application. The important thing is that both women and men become happy as human beings. Becoming happy is the objective; everything else is a means.

Anytime someone decides the way people ought to be, no matter how correct the idea might seem, what good is it if in the implementation people become miserable? Nor is it possible that only one sex could become happy at the expense of the other.

Endo: It's enough that men and women, through cultivating their humanity, come to exhibit the hues of masculinity and femininity that naturally permeate their lives.

Suda: One book that sparked the postwar movement for gender equality in the United States was Betty Friedan's *The Feminine Mystique*, originally published in 1963.

In the first chapter, titled "The Problem That Has No Name," Friedan paints a picture of the suffering of many women in a climate where a woman was expected to be "concerned only about her husband, her children, her home."[23] She writes:

> Sometimes a woman would say "I feel empty somehow . . . incomplete." Or she would say, "I feel as if I don't exist." Sometimes she blotted out the feeling with a tranquilizer.". . . [She described her symptoms:] "A tired feeling. . . I get so angry with the children it scares me . . . . I feel like crying without any reason.". . . Sometimes a woman would tell me that the feeling gets so strong she runs out of the house and walks through the streets. Or she stays inside her house and cries.[24]

Endo: Middle-class American women in the 1950s were associated with a lifestyle of brightness and abundance featuring such amenities as large lawns, gardens and labor-saving electronic appliances. It seems to me that this was the stereotype conveyed even in Japan. But behind this facade, many suffered in a spiritual void.

Suda: I think that reaction to the tendency to try to make women fit a particular stereotype played a major role in inspiring the movement for gender equality. The purpose must always be the genuine happiness of individuals.

Saito: Because there is also much diversity among women, there is sure to be a certain amount of difference of opinion. A Christian school of thought known as "feminist theology" is the focus of considerable attention. Proponents criticize the tendency of mainstream theology to accord superior status to men and argue that church teachings have been used by men as a tool to control women.

Endo: Identifying the concept of "God the Father" as the wellspring of discrimination against women, some assert that the deity should instead be referred to as "God our Mother and Father."

Saito: Such revisionist movements certainly have their critics, but it seems to me that the sincerity of their proponents is commendable.

WOMEN AND MEN: FROM OPPOSITION TO HARMONY

Ikeda: From the standpoint of life's eternity, distinctions of male and female are not set in stone. Rather, we may be born as a man in one life and as a woman in another. Moreover, all people have both male and female aspects.

Suda: Physiologically, all people are born with both male and female hormones.

Ikeda: That's indeed a clear illustration.

The point is that we must learn to balance these two sides. That's an important part of becoming a mature and self-actualized individual. In other words, if a man only possesses so-called masculine traits, he will be a boor. To be well-rounded, we need to give play to our feminine qualities as well; for example, we need to cultivate the sensitivity and openness to understand another person's heart. By the same token, it's not enough for a woman to possess only so-called feminine traits. Otherwise she cannot bring her life to fruition.

In any society, certain qualities will be sought in men and in women according to the standards of that society. The more closely people try to match those stereotypes, the more other traits within them will tend to be repressed.

That people will try to match such cultural norms is to some extent inevitable. But wouldn't it be better if men and women, recognizing this sort of gender-typing, instead tried to learn from one another and round out their own character? I think that part of the significance of marriage lies in such self-completion. This is not to say, of course, that to develop character one has to be married.

Endo: A psychologist has said: "For both men and women, opposing factors of day and night, above and below, patriarchal and matriarchal consciousness fuse together; they complement each other, each gender manifesting its own productivity, and bring it to fruition together. Only then is wholeness attained."[25]

POETS WHO SOUGHT THE FEMININE

Ikeda: Since my youth, Dante's *Divine Comedy* and Goethe's *Faust* have continued to hold a strong attraction for me. Both of these works, of which I have spoken numerous times, portray a certain longing and admiration for the feminine.

Needless to say, in the *Divine Comedy*, Beatrice (Dante's first love) is presented as a "star" to guide the character Dante to the world of heaven; and Mary, the mother of Christ, also figures prominently. Incidentally, it has been argued that belief in Mary answers a need among Christians for the sanctification of the feminine.

Endo: Christianity on the whole is a religion in which the masculine side is more pronounced. It has been suggested that the cult of Mary may have arisen to supplement this dominant aspect.

Ikeda: Perhaps Dante, for the sake of his own completion as a human being, required an ideal image of the feminine and found this in Beatrice.

The following famous lines conclude Goethe's *Faust*:

> *Woman, eternally,*
> *shows us the way.*[26]

It may be that Goethe, as a man, kept seeking the "eternal feminine" in a spiritual struggle to become a complete human being.

The Buddha, who embodies the principle of three thousand realms in a single moment of life, is the epitome of the complete human being. In that sense, it seems significant that the "Devadatta" chapter explains both the enlightenment of evil people and the enlightenment of women.

Each Person Has the Nature of Both Devadatta and the Dragon Girl

Saito: Some have argued that there is no logical connection between the chapter's first and second halves. But it seems to me that only when we put these two sides together do we get an image of the total human being. When we say that each person has both a masculine and a feminine side, doesn't this mean that both the Devadatta side and the dragon girl side within each person have to attain Buddhahood?

Ikeda: That's right. Nichiren Daishonin says, "Devadatta represents the spiritual aspect of enlightenment, and the dragon king's daughter, the physical aspect" (WND-1, 963). And, "Devadatta also represents the principle that our earthly desires are none other than enlightenment. The dragon girl represents the principle that the sufferings of birth and death are none other than nirvana" (OTT, 107). Since we have these two sides, when we attain enlightenment we do so in both body and mind.

Endo: In the case of the dragon girl, the main point is that she attains Buddhahood in her present animal form. That's why her Buddhahood symbolizes the physical aspect of enlightenment.

In the case of the enlightenment of evil people, the issue of good and evil pertains to the heart; that is, being good or evil does not make one physically different from anyone else. I think this is why, if we contrast it with the case of the dragon girl, the enlightenment of Devadatta symbolizes the spiritual aspect.

Suda: "Earthly desires are enlightenment" indicates attaining Buddhahood on a spiritual level, whereas "the sufferings of birth and death are nirvana" points to enlightenment on the level of the totality of our being, including our physical form. Putting these together, we get the enlightenment of life as an entity of the oneness of body and mind. Therefore, the "Devadatta" chapter in its entirety expresses the Buddhahood of both the physical and spiritual aspects, of both masculine and feminine dimensions.

Ikeda: That's right. But this is definitely not just a matter of theory. Attaining enlightenment comes down to the question of how deeply we can close in upon the essence of the self. While he was in exile on Sado Island, facing the greatest difficulties of his lifetime, Nichiren Daishonin turned inward to reflect upon himself as a human being. In "Letter from Sado," he writes: "Nichiren, . . . in this life was born poor and lowly to a chandala[27] family. In my heart I cherish some faith in the Lotus Sutra, but my body, while outwardly human, is fundamentally that of an animal . . . Since my heart believes in the Lotus Sutra, I do not fear even Brahma or Shakra . . ." (WND-1, 303).

The Daishonin was an exile; he had no status, wealth or power. His situation was exactly the opposite of powerful figures of the day who were persecuting him. He lacked adequate food, clothing and shelter. All he possessed was his life. In truth, he had been stripped down to his bare humanity.

Under such circumstances, the Daishonin declares that his body is "that of an animal." Certainly, when we get right down to it, in our physical form we belong to the animal kingdom. In that sense, therefore, the dragon girl's enlightenment in animal form represents our own enlightenment; it does not pertain only to women. At the same time, the Daishonin says that he "do[es] not fear even Brahma or Shakra." With his powerful spirit, and that alone, the Daishonin pitted himself against the immense power of the Kamakura shogunate.

In conclusion, after further self-reflection, the Daishonin proclaims that, because he has thoroughly and sincerely dedicated himself body and mind to the Lotus Sutra, he will attain enlightenment in both body and mind and is certain to become a Buddha.

Saito: He says, "Since Nichiren is making the same cause as Never Disparaging, how could it be that he would not become a Buddha equal to Shakyamuni?" (WND-1, 305).

Ikeda: The Daishonin here teaches that encountering and fighting to overcome great persecution is the key to actualizing the principle of attaining Buddhahood in one's present form. This is the point we have to bear in mind when we read the "Devadatta" chapter; otherwise it becomes merely abstract theory.

WOMEN ACTING IN SOLIDARITY CAN CHANGE THE TENOR OF THE AGE

Ikeda: The so-called masculine side has both positive and negative aspects. For example, the free exercise of power is key to construction and growth; but under certain circumstances it can manifest as thirst for power or be expressed as violence and destructiveness. The latter certainly represents the actions of an evil person, a Devadatta. On the other hand, the capacity to embrace all things, which some have suggested is a characteristically feminine trait, may sometimes manifest as avarice or profligate consumption.

Endo: The Mother of Demon Children[28] typifies this.

Ikeda: Attaining Buddhahood, that is to say, showing actual proof of the principles that earthly desires are enlightenment and that the sufferings of birth and death are nirvana, causes the positive aspects of the lives of Devadatta and the dragon girl to shine most brightly.

Further, because the dragon girl is a woman, she can more easily understand the sufferings of women and lead them to happiness. All of her sufferings as a woman fuel her ability to help others also attain enlightenment. Such is the power of the Mystic Law. Herein lies the significance of the dragon girl's attainment of Buddhahood.

The dragon girl was perceived as having virtually no chance of ever attaining Buddhahood because she was a woman, was very young, and had the body of an animal. She was, however, the first to attain Buddhahood in her present form. This is very significant. The dragon girl's enlightenment in an oppressively discriminatory society amounts to a ringing declaration of human rights.

The human rights declaration of the French Revolution is well known. Yet it defines "people" as meaning only men. A woman named Olympe de Gouges criticized this document and in 1791 announced a "Declaration of the Rights of Women and Female Citizens." But she was branded an anti-revolutionary and sent to the guillotine. She was one of countless people who lost their lives in the effort to secure rights for women.

The fundamental point of the declaration of women's rights arising from the Lotus Sutra is that each person has the innate potential and the right to realize a state of life of the greatest happiness. Our realizing such happiness will ensure that this noble history of sacrifice and struggle has not been in vain. The goal is for each person, like the dragon girl, to set out on a voyage to attain absolute happiness, while helping those adrift on the sea of suffering do the same—without anyone being victimized.

"All women have the right to become happy. They have to become happy without fail." That is the spirit of the Lotus Sutra.

In combining the words *dragon*, which stands for her father, the dragon king, and *girl*, which stands for herself, the daughter, the term *dragon girl* expresses the oneness of parent and child. The child, through attaining enlightenment, leads the parent to happiness.

The land where the dragon girl attains Buddhahood and leads others to happiness is called Spotless World. This suggests that when one woman attains enlightenment, it causes her surroundings to turn into a world of purity and beauty. A solidarity of women awakened to the nobility of their own lives will doubtless change the tenor of the age and the very character of civilization. The SGI women's and young women's division members are the pioneers and nucleus for the development of such solidarity. They are infinitely respectworthy. They are truly irreplaceable individuals who can answer the expectations of people around the world.

The Indian poet Rabindranath Tagore characterized modern civilization as a "civilization of power" dominated by men and yearned for the development, through the efforts of women, of a "civilization of the spirit" based on compassion.[29]

Saito: Certainly, whether we're talking about the destruction of nature or the tendency of science to reduce human beings to machines, it can be argued that a masculine tendency toward control is the root cause of many of modern society's ills.

Ikeda: In that sense, the "Devadatta" chapter contains important suggestions for transforming the very make-up of modern civilization. Simply put, it is a shift from a material civilization to a civilization of life; and from a society of control to a society of cooperation and compassion.

I think that Bodhisattva Manjushri's words in praise of the dragon girl offer an important key to this transformation: "She thinks of living beings with compassion as though they were her own children" (LSOC, 226). To compassionately embrace all living beings as one's own children — this is a state of life that all people, women and men alike, should strive to attain. Herein lies the true significance, for civilization and for the age, of the dragon girl's enlightenment.

1. Dragon girl: The daughter of Sagara, one of the eight dragon kings said to dwell in a palace at the bottom of the sea.

2. Manjushri: A bodhisattva who plays an important role in the Lotus Sutra and other sutras. He is symbolic of the perfection of wisdom and is revered as chief of the bodhisattvas.

3. Specific teaching: One of the eight teachings in T'ien-t'ai's comparative classification of the Buddhist teachings. The eight teachings consist of four teachings of doctrine and four teachings of method. The four teachings of doctrine is a classification according to content and consists of the Tripitaka teaching, the connecting teaching, the specific teaching and the perfect teaching. These correspond to the Hinayana, the introductory Mahayana, the Mahayana teaching specifically for bodhisattvas, and the perfect teaching, which encompasses and unifies the other three.

4. Shakra: Originally the god of thunder in Indian mythology, he was later incorporated into Buddhism as a protective deity.

5. Wheel-turning sage king: An ideal ruler in Indian mythology. In Buddhism, the wheel-turning kings rule by justice rather than force.

6. *The Words and Phrases of the Lotus Sutra*, vol. 8.

7. *Namu*: Or *nam*, the first syllable of Nam-myoho-renge-kyo. It is a transliteration of the Sanskrit term *namas*, which means "devotion."

8. People of the two vehicles: People of the worlds of voice-hearers (learning) and cause-awakened ones (realization, or *pratyekabuddhas*).

9. The Buddha's thirty-two features and eighty characteristics: Extraordinary attributes described in the provisional teachings to represent the Buddha's wisdom, ability, compassion and so on.

10. From the Japanese translation of the *Therigatha: Niso no kokuhaku* (Confessions of Nuns), trans. Hajime Nakamura (Tokyo: Iwanami Bunko, 1982), p. 120.

11. Ibid., p. 119.

12. *The Group of Discourses* (Sutta-nipata), vol. 2, trans. K.R. Norman (Oxford: The Pali Text Society, 1995), p. 16.

13. *Therigatha*, p.21.

14. Translated from Japanese: *Taishu Tagami, Bukkyo to Seisabetsu* (Buddhism and Gender Discrimination) (Tokyo: Tokyo Shoseki, 1992), p. 195.

15. *Therigatha*, p. 11.

16. Ibid., pp. 34–35.

17. Ibid., p. 50.

18. Two hundred years, according to some sources.

19. Mount Hiei and Mount Koya were the centers of the Tendai and Shingon schools, respectively.

20. Zenshin-ni: The first Japanese Buddhist nun, also known by her lay name Shimajo.

21. Hayao Kawai, *Bosei shakai Nihon no byori* (The Pathology of Japan's Maternal Society) (Tokyo: Chuokoronsha, 1976), pp. 9–10.

22. Translated from Japanese: Grace Halsell, *Watashi ga motometa sozojin-sei — Yume to jiyu to boken to* (Dreams, Freedom and Adventures: My Odyssey in Pursuit of a Creative Life), trans. Taoko Hori (Tokyo: The Simul Press, Inc., 1994), p. 73.

23. Betty Friedan, *The Feminine Mystique* (New York: W. W. Norton & Company, Inc., 1963), p. 18.

24. Ibid., pp. 20–21.

25. Translated from Japanese: Erich Neumann, *Josei no shinso* (The Psychology of the Feminine), trans. Yoichi Matsushiro and Teruo Kamata (Tokyo: Kinokuniya Shoten, 1980), p. 131.

26. Johan von Goethe, *Goethe's Collected Works*, vol. 2, *Faust I & II*, ed. and trans. Stuart Atkins (Cambridge, MA: Suhrkamp/Insel Publishers Boston, Inc., 1983), p. 305.

27. Chandala (candala): A Sanskrit term designating the lowest social class, comprised of those whose profession required them to kill living creatures. The Daishonin was born to a family of fishermen.

28. Mother of Demon Children (also, Kishimojin): A demon whose children are known as the ten demon daughters. Said to have fed her children the babies of others, she symbolizes the selfish nature of a

mother who protects her own offspring but cares nothing for other children. In the "Dharani" chapter of the Lotus Sutra, she and her daughters pledge to protect the votaries of the Lotus Sutra.

29. See Rabindranath Tagore, *Personality* (London: Macmillan and Co., Limited, 1921), pp. 172, 182–83.

PART III

"Encouraging Devotion" Chapter

5　A Disciple Battles the Three Powerful Enemies

Ikeda: How to live the very best life; how to be truly human —these thoughts are constantly on my mind. In this connection, let's talk a bit about the great renaissance artist Michelangelo.

Michelangelo's works from his later years include the huge fresco *The Last Judgment* (which measures forty-eight feet high by forty-three feet wide). The painting includes a self-portrait. The manner in which he depicts himself is quite horrid; the flayed skin of Saint Bartholomew, which hangs limply in another's grasp, carries the tragic mask of Michelangelo. As the vehicle for his self-portrait, he chose the raw flesh of a saint who in his martyrdom had been skinned alive.

Why does he depict himself—and only himself—in this fashion? There are many possible interpretations, but it seems to me that this is the image of someone who has truly lived his life for all it was worth. All the other figures in the fresco are drawn to perfection, their lifelike appearances given to them by Michelangelo. He gave and gave, giving everything of himself to others, until at death he was reduced to a shapeless mass of discarded flesh.

This is the way of life of a bodhisattva. Seeing this painting, I sensed the ardent spirit of someone who, to paraphrase the Lotus Sutra, does not begrudge his own life (see LSOC, 233–34).

Endo: As a matter of fact, biographical accounts describe Michelangelo as very muscular, and as having a powerful and large frame.

In contrast, in this painting he reduces himself to nothing more than a mass of skin.

Ikeda: Michelangelo was truly human, and he achieved excellence as an ordinary human being. Therein lay his greatness.

On another level, the essence of Buddhism is to live one's life as a great ordinary person. To completely dedicate one's life to others; to thoroughly exert oneself for the Law and for society; and to die having fully expended oneself—that is the way of life of a bodhisattva and a Buddha. It's a matter of laying down one's life; of fearlessly speaking out on behalf of justice; of exhausting one's energy to bring people true happiness. Where this spirit is lacking, Buddhism does not exist.

The Lotus Sutra describes this selfless dedication with the words, "We care nothing for our bodies or lives / but are anxious only for the unsurpassed way" (LSOC, 233). This is the spirit of the "Encouraging Devotion" chapter, which we are discussing in this chapter. This is also the essence of the spirit of the Soka movement. Fundamentally, the Soka movement exists only where people dedicate their lives to spreading the Law.

Saito: The purpose of Buddhist study, too, lies in thoroughly internalizing this essential spirit. In "The Emergence of the Treasure Tower," which we discussed before, Shakyamuni indicates just how difficult it will be to expound the Lotus Sutra after his death, admonishing his listeners (in the "three pronouncements") to determine firmly to spread the sutra. In the subsequent "Devadatta" chapter, the great power of the Lotus Sutra is revealed through the enlightenment of evil people and women (i.e., the "two admonitions").

The bodhisattvas, having heard these teachings, vow to expound the Lotus Sutra steadfastly, no matter how they are persecuted and attacked. It is here, in the "Encouraging Devotion" chapter, that they make this vow.

Suda: We could say that the vows of disciples constitute the theme of this chapter.

Saito: Their vows clarify the specific pattern that persecution follows.

Suda: Namely, they describe the "three powerful enemies," a theme we have often discussed.

Ikeda: Because the concept of the three powerful enemies is such a familiar motif, let's try to get to the heart of what they represent. Why don't we make the three powerful enemies our focus in discussing the "Encouraging Devotion" chapter?

STRUGGLE FOR THE LAW WHERE YOU ARE NOW

> *In a muddied kalpa, in an evil age*
> *there will be many things to fear.*
> *Evil demons will take possession of others*
> *and through them curse, revile, and heap shame on us.*
> *But we, reverently trusting in the Buddha,*
> *will put on the armor of perseverance.*
> *In order to preach this sutra*
> *we will bear these difficult things.*
> *We care nothing for our bodies or lives*
> *but are anxious only for the unsurpassed way.*
> (LSOC, 233)

Endo: I'd like to begin by looking at the outline of the "Encouraging Devotion" chapter.

Two chapters earlier, in "Treasure Tower," Shakyamuni turns to his disciples and asks who among them will expound the Lotus Sutra in the strife-ridden *saha* world after his death. He tells them, in other words, that he is not long for this world and that he wishes to pass the baton by entrusting someone with the Lotus Sutra. He explains that after he has entered extinction it will be very difficult for people to uphold this sutra, but those who do will "win the admiration of the Buddhas" and "quickly attain the unsurpassed Buddha way." If anyone can uphold this sutra after the Buddha's death, he says,

> Now in the presence of the Buddha
> let him come forward and speak his vow!
> (LSOC, 220)

In response to the Buddha's entreaty, Bodhisattva Medicine King, Bodhisattva Great Joy of Preaching and others make this vow:

> We beg the World-Honored One to have no further worry. After the Buddha has entered extinction we will honor, embrace, read, recite, and preach this sutra. Living beings in the evil age to come will have fewer and fewer good roots. Many will be overbearingly arrogant and greedy for offerings and other forms of gain, increasing the roots that are not good and moving farther away than ever from emancipation. But although it will be difficult to teach and convert them, we will summon up the power of great patience and will read and recite this sutra, embrace, preach, and copy it, offering it many kinds of alms and never begrudging our bodies or lives. (LSOC, 229)

Ikeda: "Never begrudging our bodies or lives," they say, vowing to propagate the Lotus Sutra in the *saha* world despite the many difficulties this will entail.

Endo: Next, vows are recited by a succession of other disciples who had earlier received assurances that in the future they would become Buddhas.

Ikeda: Their vows, however, are decidedly different from the vows of Bodhisattva Medicine King and the disciples in the first group.

Endo: Yes. The first group of bodhisattvas determines to spread the sutra in this world. But the next group of disciples says that, "Because in this saha world the people are given to corruption and evil," they will broadly preach the sutra "in lands other than this one." The reason they give is that the people of the *saha* world are ridden with faults; they are described as "beset by over-bearing arrogance, shallow in blessings, irascible . . . and their hearts are not sincere" (LSOC, 229–30).

Ikeda: That's quite a laundry list! Sadly, however, this is indeed the true state of people's lives.

Endo: This second group of disciples, the voice-hearers,[1] had received prophecies of future enlightenment from Shakyamuni. By this point they had already entered the path of the bodhisattva. But since they are still "novice bodhisattvas," they think they cannot endure the difficulty of spreading the teaching in the *saha* world, so replete with corruption and evil. This is the interpretation of the Great Teacher T'ien-t'ai of China.[2]

Ikeda: Their saying that they will go to "lands other than this one" might express a universal tendency among people to want to shy away from difficult circumstances and go instead somewhere peaceful. But the spirit of the Lotus Sutra is to live with blazing vigor and joy right where we are, basking in the brilliance of the world of Buddhahood inherently possessed and eternally existing in our lives. As Nichiren Daishonin says, "It is not that he [a practitioner of the Lotus Sutra] leaves his present place and goes to some other place" (OTT, 192).

Saito: In his preaching, Shakyamuni had urged them to spread the Lotus Sutra in the *saha* world. While all the disciples were overjoyed to know that they would attain enlightenment, only those in the first group replied to the Buddha's true intent.

Suda: No doubt Shakyamuni was disappointed with those who didn't.

Ikeda: Nichiren Daishonin says: "How exasperated the Buddha must have been! That is why the Buddha turned aside and looked earnestly at the eight hundred thousand million nayutas of bodhisattvas" (WND-1, 1105–06). He is referring to the scene where women who had received prophecies of enlightenment vow that they, too, will spread this sutra in "lands in other directions" (LSOC, 231).

Suda: Shakyamuni had just given prophecies of enlightenment to the nuns Mahaprajapati, his aunt, and Yashodhara, his wife before leaving secular life, and their followers.

Saito: It appears that, even after the dragon girl attained enlightenment, these women still worried about whether they, too, could become Buddhas. Immediately sensing their anxiety, Shakyamuni announces to them that if they practice the bodhisattva way they can definitely attain enlightenment.

Ikeda: Nichiren Daishonin says: "When [the dragon girl] attained Buddhahood, this does not mean simply that one person did so. It reveals the fact that all women will attain Buddhahood" (WND-1, 269). In other words, the dragon girl's enlightenment in "Devadatta" indicates the enlightenment of all women — not just the dragon girl. The dragon girl symbolizes all women.

But while some, upon hearing such a general pronouncement, will immediately understand that the same applies to them, others will not make this connection. That's why it is important to offer specific encouragement to each person.

If only large meetings were held, it would be difficult for all members to gain heartfelt understanding and make a deep determination in faith. The importance of giving detailed consideration to the situation of each person through one-to-one dialogue cannot be emphasized too strongly; encouraging individuals should be our primary concern. The SGI has developed to the extent it has because we have steadfastly adhered to this principle.

Saito: Mahaprajapati and Yashodhara were related to Shakyamuni. It seems to me significant that the Buddha makes prophecies of enlightenment for the members of his family only after he has already predicted Buddhahood for many others. Similarly, among his ten major disciples,[3] Shakyamuni's son, Rahula,[4] and Shakyamuni's cousin, Ananda,[5] are the last to receive predictions of enlightenment (in the "Prophecies Conferred on Learners and Adepts" chapter).

Ikeda: Perhaps this is a sign of just how difficult it is to teach the members of one's own family about Buddhism. From Shakyamuni's perspective, of course, all people were equal. He would never give people special or deferential treatment because they were his relatives. Consequently, the existence of this bond, rather than facilitating their receptivity to Shakyamuni's teaching, may have actually made it that much more difficult for them to accept it. All the same, in the end, they each successfully entered the path of Buddhahood.

We can interpret the fact that they were the last to receive prophecies as indicative of this principle. There is no need to be impatient, therefore, if your spouse or your parents are reluctant to begin practicing, or if your children hesitate to embrace faith. Nichiren Daishonin says, "Be firmly convinced that the benefits from this will extend to your parents, your grandparents, nay, even to countless living beings . . ." (WND-1, 533).

The important thing is that we ourselves are strong in faith, for we thereby open a path for everyone around us. Therefore, you can put your worries to rest. Once the sun rises in our lives, we can illuminate everything. That is why we should strive to become the sun of our homes and our families.

Saito: After this prophecy of enlightenment for women, countless other bodhisattvas approach Shakyamuni and, pressing their palms together, think, "If the World-Honored One should order us to embrace and preach this sutra, we would do as the Buddha instructed and broadly propagate this Law" (LSOC, 231). But the Buddha says nothing. "The Buddha now is silent and gives us no such order," they think. "What shall we do?" (LSOC, 231).

Suda: At this point the bodhisattvas harden their resolve, intent upon replying to the Buddha's spirit and devoting their lives to their own original vow! And then they make a vow: "After the Thus Come One has entered extinction we will travel here and there, back and forth through the worlds in the ten directions [to spread this sutra]" (LSOC, 231–32).

Ikeda: In this passage, propagating the Lotus Sutra is termed "travel[ing] here and there, back and forth through the worlds in the ten directions" (LSOC, 232). The bodhisattvas are filled with the determination to travel anywhere to spread the Law.

Global kosen-rufu can only advance in reality if people take action traveling around the world time and again. It is with just this kind of determination that I have resolutely worked to open a path of worldwide kosen-rufu where none existed before. What remains is the question of how those who follow will further expand and develop that path.

Suda: I have had the opportunity to travel abroad a number of times. Whenever I see how the SGI is developing in different parts of the world, I deeply sense the rising tide of world kosen-rufu. And I am overwhelmed by the thought of how difficult it must have been to develop things to this point.

Endo: The earnestness and vigor of the disciples' vow are expressed by the famous line "to roar the lion's roar" (LSOC, 231–32). Nichiren Daishonin explains the original meaning of the two Chinese characters for "lion": "The first *shi* of the word *shishi*, or 'lion' [which means 'teacher'], is the Wonderful Law that is passed on by the teacher. The second *shi* [which means 'child'] is the Wonderful Law as it is received by the disciples. The 'roar' is the sound of the teacher and the disciples chanting in unison" (OTT, 111).

Ikeda: This is the united action of mentor and disciple.

Endo: The Daishonin says, " 'To roar the lion's roar' means to invoke Nam-myoho-renge-kyo in the Latter Day of the Law" (see OTT, 111).

Ikeda: Here, "invoke" also carries the meaning of "to take the initiative," to take positive action. This is entirely different from doing something because someone has told you to; such a passive practice has nothing to do with the lion's roar. That's why Shakyamuni quietly watched to see what his disciples would do. The mentor roars; but then it is up to the disciples to roar in response. Shakyamuni patiently waited and observed them.

Saito: In the Sanskrit text of the sutra, the "Encouraging Devotion" chapter is titled "Inexhaustible Effort," expressing the vow of the disciples.

Suda: The entire chapter truly is a recitation of vows.

THE THREE POWERFUL ENEMIES

Suda: Next, I'd like to look closely at the so-called twenty-line verse that describes the three powerful enemies. This extended verse passage also expresses in its entirety the vow spoken by the bodhisattvas.

Saito: It could be said that the twenty-line verse explains the concrete form that the six difficult acts, of the "six difficult and nine easy acts" expounded in the earlier "Treasure Tower" chapter, will take.

Suda: Though known as the twenty-line verse, the section in fact consists of twenty four-line passages.

Endo: Toward the beginning of this section, we come upon the following description of the first of the three powerful enemies:

> There will be many ignorant people
> who will curse and speak ill of us
> and will attack us with swords and staves,
> but we will endure all these things. (LSOC, 232)

As the Great Teacher Miao-lo of China indicates, this passage reveals the powerful enemy identified as ignorant lay people.

Suda: It explains that laymen and laywomen who are ignorant of Buddhism will verbally harass and commit physical violence against the votaries of the Lotus Sutra.

Ikeda: One or two instances of verbal harassment or of people cursing and speaking ill of you is easy to endure. But to be ceaselessly cursed and vilified by many people is a hardship defying description.

The French philosopher Alain[6] says: "Without a doubt there is not even one person who could stand fast against a universal and constant barrage of curses and insults. The person being cursed races toward his ruin."[7]

I think he's entirely correct. Unless you have directly experienced such abuse, you cannot understand it. But a true bodhisattva is someone who, despite this mistreatment, continues calmly advancing and shielding others.

Endo: Ignorant lay people are those who do not understand the important distinctions between superior and inferior and profound and shallow when it comes to Buddhist teachings. That they nonetheless persist in persecuting the Lotus Sutra's votaries indicates that they are in part spurred to action by the second and third powerful enemies—arrogant and cunning priests who slander the votaries, and priests revered by the general public who, fearful of losing fame or profit, induce the authorities to persecute the votaries.

Saito: Probably the most distinguishing characteristic of ignorant lay people is that by relying on authorities, they turn hostile to the true teaching. Such people never bother to try to discover the truth for themselves.

Ikeda: They blindly follow authority because they lack the ability to judge true and false on their own; they place their trust in authorities and do their bidding. This underlines how important it is that the people become wise.

Endo: The next lines (the third passage) concern arrogant and cunning priests, the second powerful enemy:

> In that evil age there will be monks
> with perverse wisdom and hearts that are fawning
>   and crooked
> who will suppose they have attained what they have
>   not attained,
> being proud and boastful in heart. (LSOC, 232)

Suda: These are people who have renounced secular life. They are characterized by "perverse wisdom" and "hearts that are fawning and crooked."

Saito: Although these people have studied Buddhism, the wisdom they have succeeded in acquiring can only be called "perverse."

That their hearts are "fawning and crooked" means that they grovel before and seek to ingratiate themselves with the powerful. Their tendency, on the other hand, is to behave arrogantly toward those whom they perceive as weak.

Suda: They have a minuscule understanding of Buddhism. But their scant knowledge, rather than inspiring them to improve themselves, only makes them ill-natured and vicious. Not only do they conceal the truth from others, but they think nothing of twisting and distorting the teachings of the Buddha to suit themselves and their circumstances.

Ikeda: Consequently, if they are told there is a teaching superior to the one to which they ascribe—a discovery which, by rights, ought to be a cause for joy—they react with anger. They cannot honestly respect any teaching as superior or any person as having achieved insight and wisdom superior to their own. They are, in a word, conceited.

False Sages Who "Despise and Look Down on All Humankind"

Saito: Next, we come (in the fourth passage) to the lines describing false sages, the third powerful enemy:

> Or there will be forest-dwelling monks
> wearing clothing of patched rags and living
>   in retirement,
> who will claim they are practicing the true way,
> despising and looking down on all humankind.
> (LSOC, 232)

Ikeda: It says that they despise and look down on all humankind. This is the main characteristic of false sages—their condescending attitude toward others. Such an attitude goes directly against the spirit of the Lotus Sutra, which teaches that all living beings are infinitely respectworthy. Therefore, such people will inevitably become enemies of the practitioners of the Lotus Sutra.

Suda: The traitorous Devadatta was one such person. This is how a modern novel describes him: "Devadatta despised and detested people. Because his life was steeped in everything that is ugly and hateful in human nature, even people appeared to him to be foul and contemptible."[8]

Saito: The description of such people as despising and looking down on all humankind is right on the mark.

Endo: The next passage (the fifth) further exposes that side of false sages:

> Greedy for profit and support,
> they will preach the Law to white-robed laymen
> and will be respected and revered by the world
> as though they were arhats who possess the six
>   transcendental powers.
> (LSOC, 232)

Ikeda: False sages use Buddhism to realize personal profit. Even so, they are revered by the world as sages. They haven't the spirit to help suffering people or to dedicate their lives to kosen-rufu. They are hypocrites who use religion.

Nichiren Daishonin calls people who preach Buddhism in order to gain fame and wealth "Law-devouring hungry spirits" (WND-1, 191). Spiritually depraved, they devise cunning schemes to gain popularity and win adulation and applause in the world of Buddhism.

Suda: "Law-devouring hungry spirits" is certainly a fitting description of Nichiren Shoshu and those of their ilk who, using Nichiren

Buddhism as a means, wallow in decadence and prey upon lay practitioners.

Saito: The sixth passage reads:

> These men [false sages] with evil in their hearts,
> constantly thinking of worldly affairs,
> will borrow the name of forest-dwelling monks
> and take delight in proclaiming our faults,...
> (LSOC, 232–33)

In other words, when a votary of the Lotus Sutra opposes them, they fabricate charges of wrongdoing and denounce the person.

Ikeda: What hypocrites most fear is that the truth about them will be revealed. Therefore, a votary of the Lotus Sutra who proclaims the truth represents a definite threat.

Endo: That's why they use lies to try to do away with such people.

Suda: Lies are the tools of their trade.

USING FABRICATIONS TO PERSECUTE THE LOTUS SUTRA'S VOTARIES

Ikeda: The Lotus Sutra clarifies their modus operandi in detail.

Saito: Yes. The seventh and eighth passages explain that false sages criticize the votaries of the Lotus Sutra saying:

> "These monks are greedy
> for profit and support
> and therefore they preach non-Buddhist doctrines
> and fabricate their own scriptures
> to delude the people of the world.

Because they hope to gain fame and renown thereby they make distinctions when preaching this sutra." (LSOC, 233)

Endo: I am reminded of how the priesthood labeled us as non-Buddhist, among other things.

Saito: They certainly are quick to resort to malicious lies and fabrication.

Suda: Moreover, the contents of their charges are nothing more than a description of themselves. The members of the priesthood have indeed shown themselves to be "greedy for profit and support" and to "preach non-Buddhist doctrines."

Ikeda: That's right. Using sleight of hand, false sages accuse the votaries of the Lotus Sutra of the very things of which they themselves are guilty. It's as though they're vilifying and denouncing the ugliness of their own reflection.

Endo: I think that in characterizing the third powerful enemy as false sages, Miao-lo really put his finger on their true nature. These are people who pass themselves off as sages. While others regard them as sages, they are not the genuine article. Their true nature is just the opposite.

Somewhere in their hearts they realize that, when all is said and done, they are not sages; they are merely living out a charade. But because of the depth of their arrogance, they cannot directly face and recognize the ugliness that is the reality of their lives. So they constantly suppress their true nature.

When a votary of the Lotus Sutra, a genuine Buddhist, appears before them, however, they are compelled to gaze upon their own mean and petty nature; it is as though their lives are suddenly illuminated in the bright light of the sun. For a person of towering arrogance, this is unbearable. So they make up their minds that everything will be all right if they can just get rid of the votary.

Saito: It's a matter of jealousy.

Suda: They behave like people who are so miserable that they have contorted their faces into the most horrible expressions, but rather than accepting their ugliness, they get angry at the clear mirror that reflects them.

CONNIVING WITH POWERFUL PEOPLE BEHIND THE SCENES

Endo: In the ninth and tenth passages, we get a clarification of the ties that develop between false sages and secular authorities:

> Because in the midst of the great assemblies
> they constantly try to defame us [the votaries
>   of the Lotus Sutra],
> they will address the rulers, high ministers,
> Brahmans, and householders,
> as well as the other monks,
> slandering and speaking evil of us,
> saying, "These are men of perverted views
> who preach non-Buddhist doctrines!" (LSOC, 233)

Ikeda: They don't confront the votaries of the Lotus Sutra directly; rather they always try to manipulate things behind the scenes. This is the tendency of false sages — so deeply ingrained in their lives is the habit of living behind a facade. They are in fact cowards.

🌢 And so they turn instead to society. Addressing themselves to people in positions of power and authority, they repeatedly slander and impugn the integrity of the votaries of the Lotus Sutra.

Suda: They use lay people who are ignorant of Buddhism as their minions. From this alone it is clear just how unscrupulous and base they are.

Saito: Similarly, it appears that during the Inquisition that plagued Europe, members of the clergy did not become directly involved in the executions. Using information provided by secret informants and gained through torture, they arbitrarily condemned people to death. But instead of carrying out the sentences themselves, they merely handed their hapless victims over to the secular authorities.

Endo: They didn't want to dirty their hands. Hypocrites are hypocrites through and through.

Ikeda: Moreover, when they handed a victim over to the authorities, it is said that they would give the person a written pronouncement, stating something to the effect that: "We mercifully hope that your life may be saved. Nevertheless, we have no choice but to hand you over to the secular courts." Yet they turned people over on the precondition that they be executed. This is the height of hypocrisy.

It is the nature of evil people to collude with one another, to form a united front. They unite to get their share of the spoils. In the meantime, good people, because they are unconcerned with profit, tend to become isolated. This tragic state of affairs has to be changed. Those on the side of good have to stand together.

Suda: Next, the eleventh passage says that the three powerful enemies will ridicule the votaries of the Lotus Sutra:

> Though they treat us with contempt, saying,
> "You are all no doubt Buddhas!"
> (LSOC, 233)

"They think they're all Buddhas," they sneer. These are words that arise from contempt.

Ikeda: To tell people, as did Bodhisattva Never Disparaging, "You are all no doubt Buddhas!" (LSOC, 233) is an expression of the highest respect. The three powerful enemies employ even these words to express derision and contempt. This vividly expresses the depravity of those who only look down on others.

Endo: The twelfth and thirteenth passages say:

> In a muddied kalpa, in an evil age,
> there will be many things to fear.
> Evil demons will take possession of others
> and through them curse, revile, and heap shame on us.
> (LSOC, 233)

It further explains that the votaries put on the "armor of perseverance" (LSOC, 233, thirteenth passage) and teach people the Lotus Sutra. Their spirit in doing so is described by the lines (in passage fourteen):

> We care nothing for our bodies or lives
> but are anxious only for the unsurpassed way.
> (LSOC, 233)

Ikeda: Nichiren Daishonin says: "The 'unsurpassed way' is Nam-myoho-renge-kyo. Now Nichiren and his followers are even more anxious with regard to Nam-myoho-renge-kyo than they are with regard to their own lives" (OTT, 114). The ultimate meaning of faith is to treasure Nam-myoho-renge-kyo even more highly than our own lives. It is to devote ourselves entirely to achieving the widespread propagation of the Mystic Law.

Concretely speaking, this means advancing together with the SGI, thoroughly protecting the SGI, and practicing together with the SGI, in both times of hardship and times of joy. Apart from the SGI, there is no kosen-rufu of the Mystic Law. This is the meaning of the statement by Josei Toda, the second Soka Gakkai president, "The Soka Gakkai organization is more precious than my life."

Saito: The sixteenth and seventeenth passages explain:

> The evil monks of that muddied age,
> failing to understand the Buddha's expedient means,
> how he preaches the Law in accordance with what is
>   appropriate,
> will confront us with foul language and angry frowns;
> again and again we will be banished
> to a place far removed from towers and temples.
>   (LSOC, 234)

Ikeda: "Again and again we will be banished." Regarding this passage, Nichiren Daishonin declares: "But if Nichiren had not been banished time and again for the sake of the Lotus Sutra, what would these words 'again and again' have meant? Even T'ien-t'ai and Dengyo were not able to fulfill this prediction represented by the words 'again and again,' much less was anyone else" (WND-1, 242).

Only Nichiren Daishonin read this passage with his life. The twenty-line verse is, therefore, documentary proof that Nichiren Daishonin is the true votary of the Lotus Sutra.

Saito: In recent times, no one has been as severely persecuted by the three powerful enemies as have the members of the SGI. This is actual proof that we are truly carrying out the practice of the Lotus Sutra.

THE STRUGGLE WITH THE THREE POWERFUL ENEMIES IS A GENUINE STRUGGLE FOR HUMAN RIGHTS

Ikeda: When we look at things in this light, we find a clear contrast between the votaries of the Lotus Sutra and the three powerful enemies, particularly false sages. On one hand, there is an attitude of respect for human beings; on the other, an attitude of outright contempt. This translates into the difference between a religion that exists for the people and one that exists to perpetuate its own authority; between a religion that struggles against corrupt power and one that acts in league with corrupt figures of power and authority. It is also the difference between a true person of religion who is persecuted and attacked and a religious charlatan who persecutes others.

The Lotus Sutra, which explains that all people can attain Buddhahood and that all people are Buddhas, embodies a spirit of supreme respect for human beings. By contrast, those teachings and ideas that seek to turn people into objects to be exploited embody ultimate disrespect for human beings. Such disrespect is an expression of fundamental darkness.

On the level of the individual, practicing the Lotus Sutra means confronting the fundamental darkness in one's own life. In terms of society, it means confronting corrupt power and authority. Practicing the Lotus Sutra, therefore, necessarily entails challenging great difficulties. Someone who does not confront great hardship is not a true votary of the Lotus Sutra.

Saito: Your mention of the human tendency to despise others reminds me of an episode from the life of the German philosopher Immanuel Kant. Kant says that reading Jean-Jacques Rousseau's *Emile* caused him to reflect on his own condescending attitude toward people.

Suda: That's a well-known episode. Kant, who was in the habit of taking a walk at precisely the same time each day, became so absorbed in *Emile* that one day he even forgot to take his walk.

Saito: That's right. Kant says: "I had disparaged those who were not learned. Rousseau has straightened me out. Eliminating this blinding sense of special privilege from my heart, I will learn to respect humanity."[9]

Endo: In a speech, President Ikeda, you once talked about Rousseau's *Emile* and cited these words from the text: "Man is the same in all stations. If that is so, the stations having the most members merit the most respect."[10] You argued that the people must become the sovereigns of society.

Ikeda: "I will learn to respect humanity"—these are really wonderful words, aren't they? The extent to which we can respect others determines the true value of our own lives. Respect for other people is the point of departure for human rights. We must not look down on anyone; this is Buddhist humanism.

Saito: The establishment of human rights is the most important issue. In that connection I cannot forget the words of Austregésilo de Athayde, president of the Brazilian Academy of Letters. Mr. Athayde, a true crusader for human rights, said to you, "Unless we see that the divine exists in all people, the idea of respect for human beings will remain empty and rootless." In that sense, I am confident that the Lotus Sutra offers the most fundamental philosophy of human rights.

Endo: The struggle against the three powerful enemies is a struggle for human rights that is pervaded with respect for the dignity of all.

Ikeda: The problem is that false sages always try to pass themselves off as allies of human rights and champions of the people. As a result, it is no easy matter to discern their true nature.

Endo: The Great Teacher Miao-lo says: "Of these three, the first [ignorant lay people] can be endured. The second [arrogant and cunning priest] exceeds the first, and the third [false sages] is the most formidable of all. This is because the second and third ones are increasingly harder to recognize for what they really are" (WND-1, 270).

Suda: A great many people in society today pose as fighters for human rights and peace. For precisely this reason, we need a discerning eye toward people's true natures so as not to be deceived by their words or the images they project.

Saito: In "The Opening of the Eyes," Nichiren Daishonin says, "Those without eyes, those with only one eye, and those with distorted vision cannot see these three types of enemies of the Lotus Sutra who have appeared at the beginning of the Latter Day of the Law," whereas the votaries of the Lotus Sutra "have attained a portion of the Buddha eye" to discern the three powerful enemies (WND-1, 277).

Ikeda: Only people of action, people who struggle, can recognize evil for what it is. A youth once asked President Makiguchi how one could develop the ability to judge good and evil. President Makiguchi replied: "If you have the tenacity and courage to practice the world's foremost religion, you will come to understand."

Suda: Even though false sages know better, they nonetheless claim that they "are practicing the true way" (LSOC, 232). In that way, they flatter themselves that they are better than everyone else and look down on others. That is their nature. What psychology do you suppose is fundamentally at work here?

Saito: Generally speaking, a highly conceited person is someone who has extremely strong narcissistic tendencies.

Suda: Such people are intoxicated with themselves. If they could just be content with gazing raptly at themselves in the mirror, they wouldn't cause anyone any trouble. But when they are in fact revered by society as though they were the greatest of beings, they conduct themselves in the belief that this is indeed the case.

Endo: The psychoanalyst Erich Fromm offers an analysis of the narcissism of powerful people who are, as he puts it, "on the borderline between sanity and insanity." He says that such people think that their power is unlimited, and that they can have whoever and whatever they want. In other words, he says, they try to become gods.

Fromm writes: "The more he tries to be god, the more he isolates himself from the human race; this isolation makes him more frightened, everybody becomes his enemy, and in order to stand the resulting fright he has to increase his power, his ruthlessness and his narcissism."[11]

Saito: To believe that one is a god—what an extreme form of self-love.

Suda: Such people are constantly smitten with anxiety at the thought that everyone else doubts and rejects their authority, and as a result they are reduced to a writhing mass of hostility and suspicion. And this only aggravates their "insanity." It's exhausting just to talk with this type of individual.

Ikeda: That's one perspective on the psychology of evil. As the French philosopher Blaise Pascal put it, "Man is neither angel nor beast, and it is a misfortune that whoever tries to play the angel ends by playing the beast."[12] Human beings, finally, cannot be anything more than human beings. The correct path, therefore, is to live out one's life as a human being—not as a "big shot" but as an ordinary person.

Saito: To make themselves appear superior, false sages require a degree of distance to insulate themselves from others. The statement that they "dwell in forests" (see LSOC, 232) is very interesting in that regard.

For precisely that reason, they cannot stand the egalitarian ideas of the Lotus Sutra, which teaches that all people are Buddhas. For their purposes, Buddhahood cannot be easily attained. The more the Buddha is seen as somehow beyond the reach of human beings, the more their own authority as intermediaries between the people and the Buddha increases. It could be said that false sages try to establish a monopoly on the Buddha.

Suda: Nichiren Shoshu is a case in point. It has tried to increase the distance between people and the Daishonin by telling them that they cannot attain enlightenment unless they have a special "secret transmission."

Endo: They are like an unscrupulous salesman who arbitrarily raises prices to maximize profits. Fundamentally, Nichiren Buddhism teaches direct fusion between the self and the Gohonzon according to the principle that embracing the Gohonzon is observing one's own mind (and perceiving the Ten Worlds within it) and that of quickly attaining true perception (i.e., attaining Buddhahood in one's present form). But the priesthood has twisted this and tried to interpose itself between people and the Gohonzon.

Ikeda: The important thing is to have faith and a connection with someone who teaches the correct way of practice. In the world of Nichiren Buddhism, there is no need—not now and not ever—for priests who neither have faith nor carry out Buddhist practice but who merely brandish authority.

Hypocrites use all kinds of means to try to make themselves appear superior and dignified. This was certainly the case with Devadatta. To make himself appear more noble-minded than Shakyamuni, he advocated extreme monastic rules.

Endo: Devadatta at one point pressed Shakyamuni to establish five severe precepts: (1) for as long as they live, monks should not take salt with their meals; (2) for as long as they live, monks should not drink curdled milk; (3) for as long as they live, monks should not eat the flesh of animals or fish; (4) for as long as they live, monks should carry out the practice of begging for alms and should not accept invitations to dine in people's homes; and (5) monks should dwell outside during the eight months of spring and summer, and may dwell in thatched huts only during the four winter months; and they should not accept offerings of lodging.

He schemed to elevate his standing in the *sangha* by criticizing the teaching of his mentor as too mild. In this way, he aimed to make himself appear more spiritually accomplished than he actually was. Devadatta tried to establish himself as a new Buddha to replace his teacher Shakyamuni.

Ikeda: It is enough that we are simply true to ourselves—that we remain ordinary people, unadorned and unaffected. It is enough that we attain enlightenment by revealing our intrinsic nature, just as we are, as common mortals of time without beginning. Our enlightenment, in other words, is not something that could ever have been "improved upon, but that exists [in our lives] just as it always has" (OTT, 141). A true Buddha dons no embellishment or ornamentation. He or she does not manifest the thirty-two features and eighty characteristics.[13]

To put on airs out of vanity is the action of a false sage. The Buddha revealed in the depths of the Lotus Sutra is a common mortal. While his true identity is that of the Buddha, in appearance and action, he is a bodhisattva. He is a "bodhisattva-Buddha." The Buddha is not arrogant. He lives among the people and shares their sufferings and joys.

Suda: This is certainly the opposite of narcissistic false sages.

Endo: Fromm says: "It is the goal of man to overcome one's narcissism. Perhaps this principle is nowhere expressed more radically than in Buddhism . . . The 'awakened' person of whom Buddhist teaching speaks is the person who has overcome his narcissism and who is therefore capable of being fully awake."[14]

Ikeda: That's an astute point. It could be said that the human revolution is a great struggle with the self. Specifically, it is the struggle to achieve the state of "car[ing] nothing for our bodies or lives." By undergoing difficulties and struggling to overcome them, we can eradicate the fundamental darkness in our lives. Apart from this, there is no true attainment of Buddhahood.

A PRIEST WHO LINED HIS POCKETS

Suda: In Nichiren Daishonin's day, the priest Ryokan of Goku-raku-ji temple was a typical example of such a false sage. He carried out a great many public projects, such as building bridges, and charitable works, such as helping victims of leprosy. He was widely venerated as a living Buddha and a bodhisattva.

Saito: But Nichiren Daishonin deftly perceived the true nature behind Ryokan's facade. He writes:

> If we examine the behavior of the priests of today who supposedly observe the precepts, we find that they hoard silks, wealth, and jewels, and concern themselves with lending money at interest . . .
>
> And as for this matter of building roads and constructing bridges, it only causes people trouble. The charitable activities at the port of Iijima and the collecting of rice at the Mutsura Barrier have brought unhappiness to a great many people, and the setting up of barriers along the seven highways of the various provinces has imposed a hardship upon travelers. These

are things that are happening right in front of your eyes. Can't you see what is going on? (WND-1, 102)

Ryokan is credited with building 189 bridges, building or repairing 71 roads, and digging 33 wells in various parts of the country. His temple, Gokuraku-ji, was strategically located where the Tokaido Road (a major transportation route linking Kyoto's ancient capital and cultural center with Kamakura, the seat of the military government) enters Kamakura. At a barrier along this important thoroughfare, Ryokan levied a transit tax on each person passing through.

Endo: He also collected a rice tax at points strategically located along the sea route, such as the ports of Iijima and Mutsura. It seems that he held enormous concessions.

Saito: Historical accounts back up the Daishonin's point. Ryokan and others who carried out such charitable works were also avid consumers of luxury items. They accumulated a great deal of wealth and ran money-lending operations. Collecting transit tax and carrying out public works no doubt enabled them to realize handsome profits. As the Daishonin sternly points out, however, these taxes must have been a great hardship for ordinary people.

Endo: In fact, current research corroborates the point that the barrier stations did in fact greatly burden people's lives. Later, during the fifteenth century, there were even popular uprisings against such oppressive taxation.

Ikeda: In any event, the true activities of people such as Ryokan were a far cry from the carefully cultivated behavior of priests who made upholding the precepts a top priority. There is a diary titled *Towazugatari* (Confession of Lady Nijo),[15] in which the author, Lady Nijo, describes her journey through various provinces.

Among her recollections are her impressions of Kamakura shortly after the Daishonin's passing. Ryokan was seventy-three and at the height of his power and influence in society.

Having traveled from Kyoto, the author finds the narrow and constrained condition of people's lives in Kamakura most pitiful. But when she goes to Gokuraku-ji, she records sensing in the conduct of the priests the charm of Kyoto and confesses to feeling homesick.

Saito: One can well imagine that the priests of Gokuraku-ji enjoyed a degree of elegance far removed from the impoverished conditions of the ordinary people of the day.

Ikeda: Yes. Nichiren Daishonin says of Ryokan, "On his body he wears his three robes like a hide that he can never take off" (WND-2, 692). Ryokan made a show of simplicity, but this was nothing more than a pose. In actuality, he was in league with those in power and held concessions that gave him the right to collect tolls and taxes, causing the people a great deal of suffering. Truly, he was the very image of a monk "greedy for profit." This is the true nature of a false sage.

Also, a priest's robes were originally supposed to be work clothes for helping and serving others. To become robes of authority is a complete reversal.

Suda: I feel we sometimes see the same sort of inversion in the way the physicians' white smock and the lapel badges sported by lawyers and politicians in Japan have become symbols of authority.

Endo: In 1271, Ryokan was defeated by the Daishonin in a contest to pray for rain. His ensuing desperate actions exposed his true nature.

Saito: Ryokan had promised that, if defeated, he would become the Daishonin's follower. But when he lost, rather than honor his agreement, he began working behind the scenes to have the Daishonin persecuted.

Endo: First, he schemed to get the priest Gyobin[17] of Jokomyo-ji temple to challenge the Daishonin in debate. When the Daishonin asserted in reply that rather than holding a private debate they should confront each other in a proper public forum, Ryokan and others submitted a letter of complaint to the Board of Inquiry at Kamakura in Gyobin's name, slandering the Daishonin.

The Daishonin discerned that Ryokan was behind this. In his writing "Response to the Petition from Gyobin," he pointed out that Ryokan had been slandering him to the constables and stewards of various provinces throughout the land, alleging that he and his followers had "set fire to and cast into the water images of Amida Buddha" and urging [constables and stewards] "to cut off our heads, or banish us from our lands" (WND-2, 388). Ryokan, in other words, caused the Daishonin and his followers to be persecuted by spreading lies about them. That is how such people operate.

Saito: According to the Daishonin's writing, "The Letter of Petition from Yorimoto," Ryokan and his cohorts urged in their letter of complaint to the authorities that the Daishonin be executed. It seems the Daishonin had solid proof of this (see WND-1, 807).

Ikeda: Ryokan preached against killing any living being and was revered as a priest who staunchly upheld the precepts. This person thought to be above killing even an insect instigated an appeal to have the Daishonin put to death. This was the truth about this so-called living Buddha.

Saito: At the time, very few people could see through the deceptiveness and perceive the true nature of this false sage. Even now, Ryokan is on the whole respected by the Japanese. The people of Kamakura probably thought, "It's intolerable for that Nichiren to be maliciously vilifying such a wonderful priest as Ryokan."

Endo: They were simply swayed by appearances and made no attempt to find out who was correct. Much of the media today, because it is devoid of guiding principles, treats information simply as a commodity. The attitude seems to be that anything that attracts people's attention and boosts sales is printworthy.

Saito: Ultimately, the only way out of this kind of situation is for people to become wise; to create a world in which false sages are not at liberty to do as they please.

Ikeda: Every age has certain icons that are considered sacred and inviolable; any challenge to those is regarded as taboo. This sacredness and inviolability carry the weight of authority. False sages conceal their true nature behind this type of facade. This type of authoritarianism is not limited to religion, however. In different times and different places, different people and groups will don this mask.

But while the manner in which false sages appear changes, the principle is always the same. They will use the institutions and whatever else a society regards as sacred to persecute the votaries of the Lotus Sutra.

Endo: Regarding the false sages of the present age, President Toda said: "When scholars, writers and other opinion leaders who are trusted by the people, as well as major newspapers and other kinds of media that influence society, ally themselves with the authorities to persecute, out of personal interest and emotionalism, this Buddhism of sowing and our activities for kosen-rufu . . . we can pronounce that the three powerful enemies have appeared."[18]

Suda: That is indeed the situation today.

Saito: In the present age, what people regard as sacred is certainly not limited to religion. In his discussions with you, President Ikeda, the British historian Arnold J. Toynbee remarked that the void created in the West by the recession of Christianity in the seventeenth century had been filled by the rise of three new "religions": nationalism, communism and the belief in the inevitability of progress through the systematic application of science to technology.[19]

Ikeda: That's right. Dr. Toynbee's conclusion was that these three beliefs were showing signs of having outlived their usefulness. Our joint conclusion was that a new religion, a religion for the future of humankind, was necessary.

Endo: I recall that at the beginning of this series we talked about how the present dearth of philosophy and spiritual void are prompting many people to seek new principles of synthesis and integration. This may partially account for the spread of nationalism and other kinds of religions and ideologies.

Suda: What is considered sacred is often what holds the fabric of human society together; without it, society cannot sustain itself.

Ikeda: To summarize Dr. Toynbee's comments, it's not that people in Western Europe have ceased to embrace religion but that they have placed their faith in different things. The sacred never ceases to exist; it merely changes form.

Suda: A French social psychologist writes: "(Thus in theory) societies have all they need at any time to give themselves the gods they require. And it seems certain that the time must never come when science will be able to let them do without them, or create afresh a substitute for religion."[20]

Saito: In the early decades of the twentieth century, Japan was a kind of religious state. It might be that in the postwar period the economy has assumed the mantle of the sacred.

Ikeda: But the idea of economics for the people's happiness was at some point supplanted by economic development for its own sake. Instead of economic development for human beings, we tend to see human beings as existing for the sake of the economy.

The same reversal can and has in fact occurred in all areas of human endeavor such as medicine, scholarship, politics, science and education. The Lotus Sutra can reorient all enterprises and institutions to function for the happiness and well-being of human beings and society.

Endo: We have to make human beings genuinely the prime concern. We have to establish true respect for human dignity. Otherwise, while people continue to place their belief in those ideas and institutions that their age defines as sacred, sooner or later society will become dominated by "false sages donning the mask of the sacred."

Fascism would be an extreme example. In such cases, when people finally realize what is happening, it is already too late.

Suda: A Japanese philosopher has commented that if the Japanese had from the outset experienced the tragic circumstances that militarism finally brought upon them, then it is likely that many people would have stood up in opposition. But by the time they realized what was happening, it was too late.

Ikeda: It is important to expose the true nature of false sages to the people. Bringing about change in society will take more than just a few people with their eyes open. Therefore, we have to take bold action and smoke out the false sages.

Ultimately, people will either abandon the votaries of the Lotus Sutra or they will abandon the false sages. A society that abandons the votaries of the Lotus Sutra will be manipulated by false sages and follow a path to certain ruin. We are struggling to prevent this from happening. The struggle against the three powerful enemies is a struggle to actualize the principle of peace and prosperity based on the philosophy and principles of Nichiren Buddhism.

Selfless Dedication
Is the Life of Religion

Ikeda: The Austrian writer Stefan Zweig, who struggled against the totalitarianism of the Nazi regime, once wrote that for any school of thought to have a lasting impact on the world, it would have to produce people of conviction, whom he called "witnesses" willing to give their lives for what they believed.[21]

Individuals of selfless dedication are the pride and honor of a religion. They are the foundation of any religious body. The death of religion begins when such a spirit is lost.

Endo: This spirit, it seems to me, is the vital essence of the "Encouraging Devotion" chapter.

Ikeda: The three powerful enemies seek to persecute and kill people because of religion. By contrast, the votaries of the Lotus Sutra devote their lives to their beliefs.

Nichiren Daishonin was such a person. So were Tsunesaburo Makiguchi and Josei Toda. President Toda often said: "I shall rejoice when they [the three powerful enemies] appear. I would like you all to feel the same. When that time comes, let us fight with all our might."

In the twenty-line verse section of the "Encouraging Devotion" chapter, the bodhisattvas vow, "We care nothing for our bodies or lives / but are anxious only for the unsurpassed way" (LSOC, 233). Those who practice with this spirit of caring nothing for their lives will attain enlightenment. Those who stand up and selflessly spread the Mystic Law will become Buddhas.

Saito: Gandhi said, "Even if I am all alone . . ."

In an address at the East-West Center in Hawaii, President Ikeda, you cited Gandhi: "You have to stand against the whole world although you may have to stand alone. You have to stare the world in the face although the world may look at you with blood-shot eyes. Do not fear. Trust that little thing that resides in your heart."[22]

When he heard President Ikeda's speech, Dr. Robert Thurman, chairman of Columbia University's Religion Department remarked:

> For there to be world peace, more people have to be willing to die not to do violence than are already willing to die to do violence. And that's actually the bottom line of what President Ikeda calls "human revolution," or maybe it should be translated as "personal revolution" — that there are more persons on this planet who are ready to die not to be violent than there are already persons who are ready to die in the process of being violent. And then there will be world peace.[23]

Now is the time when we, as disciples, should bravely roar the lion's roar for justice and truth.

Notes

1. Voice-hearers (Skt *shravaka*): The people of learning who listen to the teaching of Shakyamuni Buddha.

2. *The Words and Phrases of the Lotus Sutra*, vol. 8.

3. Ten major disciples: These disciples waged an all-out struggle to spread the Law, using as "weapons" the individual character and unparalleled gifts they had developed by practicing under their mentor.

4. Rahula: The foremost in inconspicuous practice. Inconspicuous practice means a form of practice in which good deeds are carried out secretly without others being aware of them.

5. Ananda: The foremost in hearing the Buddha's teachings. He continually accompanied the Buddha and heard more of his teachings than any other disciple.

6. Alain: The pen name of Emile-Auguste Chartier (1868–1951).

7. Alain, *Définitions* (Paris: Gallimard, 1953), pp. 140–41.

8. Kansuke Naka, *Daibadatta* (Devadatta) (Tokyo: Iwanami Bunko, 1985), p. 131.

9. Translated from Japanese: *Kanto zenshu* (Collected Works of Kant), trans. Tatsuo Owatari (Tokyo: Risosha, 1966), vol. 16, p. 295.

10. Jean-Jacques Rousseau (1712–78), *Emile or On Education*, trans. Allan Bloom (New York: Basic Books, Inc., Publishers, 1979), p. 225.

11. Erich Fromm, *The Heart of Man: Its Genius for Good and Evil* (New York, Evanston and London: Harper & Row, Publishers, 1964), p. 66.

12. Pascal's *Pensées*, trans. Martin Turnell (London: Harvill Press, 1962), p. 173.

13. The Buddha's thirty-two features and eighty characteristics: Attributes described in the provisional teachings. These unusual qualities represent the Buddha's wisdom, ability, compassion, etc.

14. Fromm, op. cit., p. 88.

15. *Towazugatari* (Confession of Lady Nijo): Autobiographical narrative covering thirty-six years (1271–1306) in the life of Lady Nijo, a high-ranking Kyoto aristocrat. *Towazugatari*, the culminating work in the long court tradition of autobiographical writing, describes life during a time of transition from an aristocratic culture to one dominated by the warrior class.

16. Three robes: The only personal belongings that the precepts allow a monk to possess. They symbolize the simplicity and nonattachment of monastic life.

17. Gyobin: A Nembutsu priest during the days of the Daishonin. Dates of birth and death are not known. In July 1271, he challenged the Daishonin to a debate.

18. *Toda Josei zenshu* (Collected Writings of Josei Toda) (Tokyo: Seikyo Shimbunsha, 1986), vol. 6, p. 400.

19. *The Toynbee–Ikeda Dialogue: Man Himself Must Choose* (Tokyo, New York and San Francisco: Kodansha International, Ltd., 1976), p. 292.

20. Serge Moscovici, *The Invention of Society, Psychological Explanations for Social Phenomena*, trans. W. D. Halls (Cambridge: Polity Press, 1993), p. 37.

21. Stefan Zweig, *Kenryoku to tatakau ryoshin* (The Conscience to Fight Against Power) (Tokyo: Misuzu Shobo, 1973), p. 23.

22. Mohandas K. Gandhi, *All Men Are Brothers*, ed. Krishna Kripalani (New York: Continuum, 1990), p. 49.

23. *Boston Research Center for the 21st Century Newsletter*, Spring 1995, no. 3, p. 10.

PART IV

"Peaceful Practices" Chapter

6   The Lotus Sutra Enables All People To Attain Absolute Peace and Happiness

Saito: In our investigation of the Lotus Sutra, we have at last come to the threshold of the essential teaching. Beginning here, we will discuss the "Peaceful Practices" chapter, which is the last of the fourteen chapters making up the theoretical teaching.

Suda: "Peaceful practices" has the ring of a relaxed and effortless practice.

Ikeda: It would be nice if such a Buddhist practice were possible. But, alas, it is not to be.

Nichiren Daishonin clearly says, "Concerning . . . the practice carried out by Nichiren and his followers now in the Latter Day of the Law, you should understand that . . . difficulties will arise, and these are to be looked on as 'peaceful' practices" (OTT, 115). In other words, struggling to overcome obstacles is the state of true peacefulness. The basic message of the "Peaceful Practices" chapter is that we can establish a state of life of such composure that we can even regard the obstacles we encounter as causes for a peaceful life.

The word *peaceful* (Jpn *anraku*) in the chapter's title is written with two Chinese characters. The Great Teacher T'ien-t'ai of China interprets the first character, *an,* as meaning "unmoving" and the second, *raku,* as meaning "free of worry."[1] Peaceful does not mean a state of life free of toil and suffering. Rather it means living without being swayed and without worries, no matter what happens. This is a state of true peace and happiness.

In other words, by practicing the supreme Law of Nam-myoho-renge-kyo, we can turn any and all circumstances into causes for peace and happiness. This is the principle that earthly desires are enlightenment, and it is the practice for attaining Buddhahood in one's present existence.

Compared to the Buddhist teachings that say you must practice for countless *kalpas* to attain Buddhahood, this is truly a peaceful practice. It is deceptively easy as well. We can say that embracing the Law of Nam-myoho-renge-kyo, or the Gohonzon, is itself the true peaceful practice.

ABILITY TO TAKE ACTION
IS GOOD FORTUNE

Endo: The history of the Soka Gakkai certainly proves that peacefulness can be found in encountering hardships. The Soka Gakkai was built through the all-out struggles of ordinary people. Every time I glimpse this history, I am filled with profound solemnity.

Saito: I heard the following experience from a couple who has practiced for more than forty years.

When they began practicing (in 1956), they were unimaginably poor. After taking faith they were advised that by propagating this Buddhism they could accumulate good fortune. They enthusiastically began telling people about Buddhism, beginning with their siblings and relatives.

They initially expected that when people heard what they had to say, they, too, would gladly begin practicing. But what actually happened was just the opposite: People completely broke off relations with them. When they went to people suffering from poverty or illness, as they themselves were, to talk about Buddhism, they had salt thrown at them [a gesture meaning "Go away!"] or bathwater dumped on them countless times.

The couple and their three children lived in a storeroom that they rented in someone's house. But when the owner found out that they were Soka Gakkai members, they were forced to move. On top of everything else, they suffered from night blindness, perhaps because they were practically starving themselves to keep their children fed.

Once, after visiting a friend to talk about Buddhism, the mother made her way home in a drizzling rain, carrying one child on her back and leading another by the hand. A kindly bus driver pulled up at the side of the road for them, even though they were not at a bus stop, but they couldn't accept his offer for a ride because they didn't have the fare. They had to walk in the rain more than an hour. While chanting daimoku, the mother thought, "Someday, I will come home down that road in a taxi."

Suda: She must have been mortified by her inability to respond to the bus driver's kindness.

Saito: The couple went on to introduce more than a hundred families to the Daishonin's teaching. A leader had told them that the greater people's worries, the greater the benefit they receive through faith in the Mystic Law.

No matter how destitute they became, they always exerted themselves thoroughly in faith. As a result, they eventually became healthy. They opened a food shop with a small amount of capital they had managed to scrape together, and it began to prosper. This benefit filled them with appreciation, which enabled them to receive still greater benefit. In this way, their lives developed steadily.

Today, in addition to operating stores of their own, they have a large factory and distribute goods nationwide. They reportedly have a customer base of 3,600 households and receive new orders daily. They built a large home with the strong desire to open it up as a place for chapter meetings. It has a parking lot for up to sixty cars, and the tricolor flag of the Soka Gakkai flies from a pole in the front.

Endo: That's wonderful actual proof.

Saito: "Nothing is more joyful than Soka Gakkai activities," they say with complete earnestness. There was a period when they couldn't do many activities because they had been encouraged to make overcoming their economic difficulties their first priority. Of that time they say, "Nothing was more painful." "To work for kosen-rufu, that has been our greatest happiness."

When conniving Nichiren Shoshu priests, attracted by the couple's wealth, tried to entice them to leave the Soka Gakkai, the priests were firmly rebuffed.

Suda: The path of SGI activities truly is one in which encountering difficulties is peaceful.

Ikeda: I know that couple very well; I never forget those who exert themselves behind the scenes to support the Soka Gakkai. While battling difficulties in their own lives, they have silently supported the Soka Gakkai and wholeheartedly exerted themselves for kosen-rufu and their fellow members. Yet they neither stand out particularly, nor do they enjoy great status in society. From the viewpoint of Buddhism, none are more worthy of respect than these people.

I would like to scour the earth in search of such people, give them due recognition and repay their efforts. These are my true sentiments.

I want people to say, "I'm so glad I'm a member of the SGI," "I'm so glad I have struggled hard." That is the world of faith I want to create. Though we know the Buddhist principle that encountering difficulties is peaceful, unless leaders have the spirit to guide members to attain a state of peace and happiness without fail, it is nothing more than theory.

Since my youth, my constant prayer has been to open a path of boundless hope for the Soka Gakkai and for all fellow members.

Spread the Law With Wisdom
and the Spirit Not To Begrudge Your Life

Anyone who reads this sutra
will at all times be free of worry and anxiety;
likewise he will be without illness or pain,
his expression fresh and bright.

• • •

He will stroll about without fear
like the lion king.
The brilliance of his wisdom
will be like the shining of the sun . . . (LSOC, 248–49)

Endo: The "Peaceful Practices" chapter is mainly concerned with explaining the four peaceful ways of practice. They can also be thought of as the four "rules" of practice. They describe the action, speech, thought and vow proper for bodhisattvas. The Daishonin designates these practices as *shoju*,[2] which means the type of propagation in which one gradually leads another to the supreme teaching without refuting his or her attachment to inferior teachings.

Suda: Yes. The practice that T'ien-t'ai established during the Middle Day of the Law,[3] the Daishonin explains, was based on the "Peaceful Practices" and "Encouragements of the Bodhisattva Universal Worthy" chapters and falls into the category of *shoju*. In contrast, the practice of Nichiren Buddhism in the Latter Day of the Law is the practice of *shakubuku* and is based on the "Encouraging Devotion" and "The Bodhisattva Never Disparaging" chapters.

Endo: The Daishonin says that someone who carries out the four peaceful ways of practice during the Latter Day is like a rooster that crows at dusk rather than in the morning (see WND-1, 394). That's because the Latter Day of the Law is the time for *shakubuku*.

Saito: On that premise, the Daishonin teaches that one should decide which method to make primary in a given situation depending on the conditions of the land and the people. He says:

> When the country is full of evil people without wisdom, then shoju is the primary method to be applied, as described in the "Peaceful Practices" chapter. But at a time when there are many people of perverse views who slander the Law, then shakubuku should come first, as described in the "Never Disparaging" chapter. . . .
>
> In the Latter Day of the Law, however, both shoju and shakubuku are to be used. This is because there are two kinds of countries, the country that is passively evil,[4] and the kind that actively seeks to destroy the Law. (WND-1, 285)

It becomes a question of how we interpret *shoju* and *shakubuku*.

Ikeda: First, as the major premise, all efforts to teach people about Nam-myoho-renge-kyo in the Latter Day constitute *shakubuku*. Basing ourselves on the spirit of *shakubuku* to teach others about the Mystic Law without selfish concern, at times we might strictly refute a person's mistaken views, while at other times we might explain the truth with a broad-minded spirit of tolerance for the other person's beliefs.

Suda: The concepts represented by the words *shakubuku* and *shoju* are not exclusive to Buddhism. They reportedly were common in ancient Indian society. *Shakubuku* is the translation of the Pali term *niggaha*, meaning to reproach, and the Sanskrit term *abhibhava*, meaning to defeat through superior strength. And *shoju* is the translation of the Pali term *paggaha*, which means to extend help or shower blessings.

Endo: Both terms point to one's conduct and attitude.

Ikeda: It is important to have the wisdom to use each of them correctly. As we discussed in connection with "The Teacher of the Law" chapter, *shakubuku* in essence means to declare the truth. All our efforts to explain Buddhism with a sincere and earnest desire to help others become happy are *shakubuku*.

Saito: Being coercive is not *shakubuku*.

Ikeda: In a situation where the other person has been poisoned by erroneous views and vilifies the Mystic Law, efforts to refute the person's mistaken beliefs should naturally come to the fore. Someone who forgets the refutation aspect is no disciple of Nichiren Daishonin. The Soka Gakkai spirit does not exist in those who have lost the spirit to refute evil.

On the other hand, the manner of explanation will naturally be different in the case of someone free of such bias.

Endo: Asserting that "Nembutsu leads to the hell of incessant suffering!" will be completely incomprehensible to someone who knows nothing about Japanese Buddhism. We should, of course, explain the Mystic Law in a manner that is easy to understand based on the culture and way of life of the particular country we are in.

Saito: It seems to me that the "Peaceful Practices" chapter explains a number of cautionary points for bodhisattvas who are novices at propagating the Lotus Sutra to ensure that they do not denigrate the Law by getting enmeshed in senseless quarrels or become confused and deviate from the path of Buddhahood.

Ikeda: From our standpoint, this means that even when we are spreading the Law without concern for our lives, we absolutely must not do anything that would reflect badly on the Law. Because we have the highest concern for the Law, we need to fully exercise our wisdom in propagating it. This is the heart of "Peaceful

Practices." It explains the spirit to always ask: "How can I help all people receive the benefit of the Mystic Law?" The "Peaceful Practices" chapter, therefore, finds full expression in our efforts to pray earnestly for the happiness of friends and to use our wisdom to tell others about Buddhism.

While teaching his followers the *shakubuku* spirit of not begrudging one's life, Nichiren Daishonin also emphasized the importance of showing people genuine courtesy and respect and of conducting oneself with wisdom.

Endo: SGI members have been selflessly leading people to happiness just as the Daishonin taught. Such all-encompassing wisdom, I believe, is the product of serious, determined dedication to the Law.

Saito: This truly amounts to a revolution in propagation. High Priest Nichijun praised the Soka Gakkai highly for propagating the Daishonin's teaching in a manner according with the times. The Soka Gakkai's appearance, he said, marked the transition from an age of protection [of the Mystic Law] to an age of transmission and widespread propagation.[5]

Ikeda: The "Peaceful Practices" chapter says that those who practice the Mystic Law will "stroll about without fear like the lion king" and possess wisdom brilliant as the sun (see LSOC, 249).

Kosen-rufu is a religious movement to illuminate the world with great wisdom just as the sun illuminates the earth. The idea is for each person to become a light of wisdom; when there are many such lights, the entire world will be illuminated. Kosen-rufu could be described as the grand art of revolutionizing the inner state of one's life. In concrete terms, it comes down to the expansion of peace, culture and education.

"Peaceful" Means Embracing the Fundamental Law

Endo: The "Peaceful Practices" chapter begins with Bodhisattva Manjushri asking Shakyamuni how the Lotus Sutra should be taught in the evil age to come.

In response, Shakyamuni explains the concepts of peaceful action, peaceful speech, peaceful thought and peaceful vow, which together make up the four peaceful ways of practice.

Suda: Simply put, peaceful action means to quiet the body, avoid evil influences, and practice in a place of peace and tranquillity. Peaceful speech means to calmly expound the Lotus Sutra, without thoughtlessly disparaging or praising other persons or sutras. Peaceful thought means to uphold, read and expound the sutra without harboring jealousy, arrogance or a fawning attitude, and to avoid doctrinal disputes. And peaceful vow means to make a deeply compassionate vow for the salvation of all beings and to practice accordingly.

Endo: T'ien-t'ai says that these four peaceful ways of practice concern method.[6] In other words, they explain the method for spreading the Lotus Sutra without allowing oneself to be troubled physically and spiritually by the various negative influences that accompany an evil age.

Saito: T'ien-t'ai says that while no explanation is necessary for seasoned bodhisattvas (i.e., those who have attained profound practice), novice bodhisattvas (those whose practice is still shallow) would be incapable of completing their practice either for themselves or for others unless Shakyamuni instructed them in method. These peaceful practices, therefore, could be likened to a lifeboat for the practice of novices.

Ikeda: If "Peaceful Practices" is a discourse on method, then the immediately preceding "Encouraging Devotion" chapter is an explanation of spirit; namely, the spirit of not begrudging one's life. It is the spirit to prize the Law more highly even than one's life. Unless we interpret "Peaceful Practices" based on this spirit, we may be left with the impression that all we need to consider is the shallow question of "How can I carry out a peaceful practice?"

"Peaceful," in "four peaceful ways of practice," fundamentally means practicing the Mystic Law in thought, word and deed—the three categories of action—that is to say, with one's entire being. By carrying out such a practice, one's life becomes saturated with peace and happiness. Nam-myoho-renge-kyo is the Law of true peace and happiness.

Saito: For us, the important question is what specifically we must do to carry out these peaceful practices and experience such peace and happiness. *The Record of the Orally Transmitted Teachings* says, "The essence of these peaceful practices is this Nam-myoho-renge-kyo that was transmitted to the Bodhisattva Superior Practices" (OTT, 232). In other words, the primary component of peaceful practice is the teaching of Nam-myoho-renge-kyo of the Three Great Secret Laws transmitted to Bodhisattva Superior Practices in the Lotus Sutra, which he spreads in the Latter Day of the Law.

Ikeda: Here, the Daishonin is explaining this from the standpoint of the implicit teaching of the Lotus Sutra. In a lecture on the portion of *The Record of the Orally Transmitted Teachings* dealing with the "Peaceful Practices" chapter, President Toda said:

> There are four peaceful ways of practice, each of which is actually quite a bother . . . But the Daishonin went beyond this categorization, saying in effect that, since by chanting Nam-myoho-renge-kyo everyone can attain peace and happiness, that alone is sufficient.

The "Peaceful Practices" chapter of Shakyamuni's Buddhism sets various conditions: we are told to think certain thoughts, say certain words, take certain actions and make certain vows. But the Daishonin's "Peaceful Practices" chapter is far simpler. It says that if you are having troubles, then chant Nam-myoho-renge-kyo to the Gohonzon. When we do so, don't we experience peace and joy? Why should we need to do anything else?

The Record of the Orally Transmitted Teachings says, "Since they are 'the true aspect of all phenomena' (chapter two, Expedient Means), there are none that are not peaceful practices" (OTT, 232). President Toda also said:

> The true aspect of life permeates all existences and phenomena of the world. There's no need to do something particular to get close to it. We should do what we are inclined to do. The true aspect of life exists for a dog as a dog, and for a human being as a human being. Whether beings manifest their true aspect depends entirely on whether they chant Nam-myoho-renge-kyo . . . When we are living honestly and true to ourselves, we are living the "Peaceful Practices" chapter.

Faith means living true to ourselves, as we are, and realizing a state in which we can genuinely say, "Ah, this is true satisfaction," "My life is a great victory." This is peace and happiness.

Everyone without exception seeks happiness and peace. One person may pursue treasures of the storehouse, while another pursues treasures of the body such as status or health. But true happiness lies in accumulating treasures of the heart. And the substance of the treasures of the heart is a great state of life totally dedicated to faith.

Nichiren Daishonin says: "There is no true happiness for human beings other than chanting Nam-myoho-renge-kyo . . . There is no true happiness other than upholding faith in the Lotus Sutra." He exhorts us to "regard both suffering and joy as facts of life, and continue chanting Nam-myoho-renge-kyo" (WND-1, 681).

This happiness cannot be gained by satisfying cravings or desires. It's a matter of experiencing "the boundless joy of the Law," which wells forth from our lives. Each of us can definitely attain such a state of peace and happiness. Moreover, because this peace and happiness comes from our own lives, it is enduring.

In reference to such a state of peace and happiness, the Lotus Sutra speaks of "peace and security in [the] present existence" (LSOC, 136). Nichiren Daishonin says that the appearance of the three powerful enemies proves the passage "peace and security in the present existence" (GZ, 825).

Suda: This is all the exact opposite of the usual view of peace and security.

Ikeda: It's not a matter of leading a timid and weak existence, seeking to avoid obstacles and difficulties. Rather, we should have the spirit: "Come what may, I will survive! I will climb another mountain! And the more I climb, the more I can enjoy my life, and the more people I can help become happy."

Nichiren Buddhism is the teaching for leading the ultimate active life.

THE FOUR PEACEFUL WAYS OF PRACTICE

Ikeda: With all of this as the premise, why don't we look at the specific content of the four peaceful ways of practice?

Suda: Certainly. First, peaceful action addresses how bodhisattvas should behave, in other words, their actions and how they should conduct themselves with others, or their associations. In terms of their actions, it says that a bodhisattva "takes his stand on perseverance, is gentle and compliant, never violent, and never alarmed in mind," and that he "observes the true aspect of phenomena without ... making any distinction" (LSOC, 235). Each of these is important. In terms of associations, it explains that bodhisattvas should not go any place where they might be tempted to stray from Buddhism and lose their spirit of practice; and that they should not consort with powerful people or go to places of amusement. It also says that men, in explaining the teachings of Buddhism to women, should not harbor ulterior motives or base intentions.

Next the sutra explains the basic attitude underlying these practices, which is the understanding that, because all phenomena are nonsubstantial, they should be viewed neither as existing nor nonexisting and should not become objects of attachment (see LSOC, 237).

Saito: In rough terms, this teaches a certain code of conduct for people, a common sense or etiquette. It is cautioning practitioners to avoid evil influences, biases and erroneous views.

Suda: Next, peaceful speech cautions against certain types of speech. It says that practitioners, among other things, "should not delight in speaking of the faults of other people or scriptures ... should not display contempt for other teachers of the Law ... [and] should not refer to them by name and describe their faults, or name them and praise their good points" (LSOC, 240). This certainly sounds like *shoju.*

Endo: It emphasizes that one should "employ expedient means and thereby cause all listeners to aspire to enlightenment, and gradually enter the Buddha way"; "preach the Law with a compassionate mind"; "day and night one should constantly expound the teachings of the unsurpassed way, employing causes and conditions, similes and parables to instruct living beings and cause them all to be joyful"; "reply to questions not in terms of the teachings of the lesser vehicle, but ... solely in terms of the great vehicle so that people can acquire all-embracing wisdom"; and "desire to enable all people to complete the Buddha way" (LSOC, 240–42). It seems to me that these are all relevant to the conduct of Buddhist leaders today.

Ikeda: A leader has to consider what to impart to others. Even just a few words may be enough: "You seem tired. Have you been very busy?" "How is your husband doing? Please dress warmly to avoid catching cold." "Thank you for allowing us to use this wonderful room for our meeting." You might bring a snack like a rice cracker or piece of fruit for members to enjoy on their way home.

What you choose to do is up to you, but a leader should always ponder: "What can I do to raise everyone's spirits?" "How can I give people hope and peace of mind?"

Suda: Next is the practice of peaceful thought. Here, Shakyamuni teaches that in preaching the Lotus Sutra one "must set aside jealousy, hatred, arrogance, / a mind that is fawning, deceitful and false." Also, he indicates that one must not treat those desiring to learn about Buddhism with contempt or arouse in them worries or doubts, and should revere and respect those who spread the Law (see LSOC, 242–45).

Saito: This, too, is an important attitude for leaders.

Ikeda: I find particularly noteworthy the statement: "To all living beings preach the Law in an equitable manner. Because a person is heedful of the Law, that does not mean one should vary the amount of preaching. Even to those who show a profound love for the Law one should not on that account preach at greater length" (LSOC, 243).

Many people are so busy with their work or raising children and looking after their families that they have a hard time attending activities. Also, some people continue practicing faith but for some reason find it difficult to connect with the organization. Broadly interpreting the above passage in modern terms, I think it means that leaders should warmly embrace such individuals, become close to them, listen to what they have to say and try to encourage them.

Suda: The last rule of practice is peaceful vow. Here Shakyamuni says that those who embrace the Lotus Sutra should arouse a mind of great compassion toward others and think to themselves: "Though the Thus Come One as an expedient means preached the Law in accordance with what is appropriate, they do not listen, do not know, do not realize, do not inquire, do not believe, do not understand . . . But when I have attained supreme perfect enlightenment, wherever I may happen to be, I will . . . cause them to abide in this Law" (see LSOC, 244–45).

Saito: In other words, this is saying that no matter how obstinate people may be, we must absolutely never abandon them.

OUR VOW IS TO LEAD PEOPLE TO HAPPINESS

Ikeda: President Toda said: "This is extremely easygoing. It says that one should make the vow, 'If I attain Buddhahood, then I will help others.' That's a peaceful practice all right — it means that you don't have to do shakubuku any time soon. The idea is, 'If I become a Buddha, then at that time I will help those with whom I have formed a relationship.'"[8]

To only try to help others after you become a Buddha yourself is definitely lacking in compassion.

Endo: The passage describing the vow states that they will help other people when they "have attained supreme perfect enlightenment." This is talking specifically about helping those who neither seek nor believe in the Lotus Sutra.

Saito: Fundamentally, a bodhisattva is one who maintains the ardent vow: "I will not attain Buddhahood until I have done everything I can to lead all other people to happiness."

Endo: Those practicing in this way are certainly our fellow SGI members carrying out a great practice far surpassing the vow of the "Peaceful Practices" chapter. During the pioneering stage of our movement, members — no matter how poor they were and no matter how difficult their own lives — would earnestly go about teaching others the Law.

Saito: Even though they would assure people that through this faith they could definitely become happy, they faced being ridiculed, mocked and driven away: "The day you become rich, I'll give it a try!" Undeterred, they never ceased proclaiming the truth.

Ikeda: The nobility of such efforts is beyond words. Members, setting aside their own worries and concerns, wholeheartedly devoted themselves to helping those who were suffering. People burned with a keen sense of pride in carrying out the practice of true bodhisattvas, embodying the spirit of Bodhisattvas of the Earth.

As a result, even if they were poor, in their hearts they were wealthy. In their state of life they possessed immense riches. By fully devoting themselves to the compassionate practice of *shakubuku*, they experienced fundamental peace and happiness even greater than that of the people to whom they were talking.

Saito: The great SGI organization of today has been built by the dedicated bodhisattva practice of these members.

Ikeda: The French author Romain Rolland declared: "Preoccupation with salvation postpones salvation. If you want to save yourself, then the best thing is to forget yourself among others. Then all things will come to you."[9]

This is precisely what we, the Bodhisattvas of the Earth, are doing. Soka Gakkai members in the early days of our movement, though widely reviled as a gathering of the poor and the sick, possessed noble hearts. The truth is that while fundamentally Buddhas, they took on this guise (of sickness and poverty) to prove the Mystic Law.

Not social status, or academic background or wealth in itself counts for anything in the world of the Soka Gakkai, a world where human greatness is pursued.

Endo: In the SGI it is not uncommon to find people of little formal education confidently lecturing university professors on Buddhism.

Suda: Most people rate others as great or unimportant on the basis of education, fame or wealth. Particularly in Japan, the tendency to rank people on the basis of such externals has in recent years become quite pronounced.

Endo: The same psychology would seem to be at work in Japanese politicians who make disparaging and arrogant statements about developing countries.

Ikeda: Among children, that kind of discriminatory attitude manifests as bullying, which casts a dark shadow over many young people's lives.

Suda: The Soka Gakkai's movement has begun to fundamentally change the entrenched hierarchical character of society.

Saito: One scholar cites the Japanese people's deep-seated irreligiousness as one reason for the emergence of a rigid social structure in which so much depends on educational background. He postulates that the present hierarchical society would not have developed if Japan had had a religious tradition in which all people were seen as equal before, for example, a deity.

Endo: That's a profound insight into the social significance of religion.

Ikeda: The human being is the central concern of Buddhism. Buddhism focuses on the heart and on life.

From the perspective of the Buddha and the Law, there are people who, even though they are not Buddhists, manifest the state of life of a bodhisattva. On the other hand, among Buddhists there are those who qualify as "non-Buddhists"; who on the surface appear to have faith but whose hearts are in the world of hunger or animality. Buddhism does not ask "What religion does this person follow?" but "What is this person's state of life?"

Buddhism exists to enable all people to cultivate and manifest the world of Buddhahood in their lives. Society is a realm of discrimination and distinctions. But Buddhism transcends all superficial differences and focuses directly on life.

RELIGIOUS DIALOGUE
FOR TRUE PEACE AND HAPPINESS

Saito: Shouldn't it be possible for any two religions to surmount their differences and carry on a dialogue based on their common humanity?

Ikeda: I believe so. The nucleus of the Buddhist philosophy of peace lies in a recognition of the commonality that all people share. As long as religion keeps people from respecting one another's dignity and from carrying on dialogue as human beings, it will only cause people misery.

Saito: The SGI Charter reads, "SGI shall, based on the Buddhist spirit of tolerance, respect other religions, engage in dialogue and work together with them toward the resolution of fundamental issues concerning humanity." This expresses that fundamental spirit. Of course, the overarching premise is that those participating in such dialogue are not motivated by private interests or the desire for self-promotion, but that, as human beings, they are sincerely pursuing the happiness of humankind.

Ikeda: The founders of the various world religions were all fundamentally individuals of towering humanity. Mahatma Gandhi said: "The greatest men of the world have always stood alone. Take the great prophets, Zoroaster, Buddha, Jesus, Mohammed — they all stood alone."[10] All of them, including Gandhi himself, resolutely stood up for the peace and happiness of humankind. They waged a struggle of great sincerity.

President Toda said: "If the founders of the great religions of the world all got together and held a conference, they would very quickly move beyond any differences. Since they were all earnestly concerned with helping all people become happy, they would immediately see eye to eye."[11] With this spirit, I am doing everything I can to promote inter-civilizational dialogue.

Suda: It is sad that religion is frequently used as a pawn in political struggles.

Endo: In Japan, certain elements have branded the Soka Gakkai as self-righteous and exclusivist and, acting in collusion with powerful politicians, are threatening people's basic religious freedom. While preaching tolerance, they are supporting religious oppression, a form of supreme intolerance. This is an appalling contradiction.

Saito: That's symptomatic of most Japanese people's extremely shallow view of religion. When religious figures become involved in conspiracies or violence, they are committing religious suicide; such actions betray an utterly bankrupt humanity.

Suda: Superiority or inferiority in matters of religion, while fundamentally a question of the profundity of the teaching, ought to be reflected in the actions and character of the religion's practitioners. The extent to which they actually prize human rights, protect life and encourage humanity will increasingly become the focus. As the Daishonin says, "even more valuable than reason and documentary proof is the proof of actual fact" (WND-I, 599).

Ikeda: President Makiguchi predicted that the age of military, political and economic conflict would eventually give way to an age of humanitarian competition. In other words, he foresaw the arrival of a time when more importance would be placed on the power of spirit and character than on military, political and economic power. Increasingly, conditions in the world make any alternative to such a course less and less tenable.

Suda: One cannot help feeling awed by President Makiguchi's tremendous foresight.

Ikeda: He was our predecessor. We should take pride in having had such a person as our founder. The names of presidents Makiguchi and Toda will doubtless come to shine with increasing brilliance; and, in fact, it is the mission of a disciple to see that they do. Toward that end, we need to show splendid actual proof by producing many humanitarian and global-minded individuals.

At any rate, the key point is to transcend factionalism and ideology and work to bring all people to a state of peace and happiness. To do this, we have at our disposal the wisdom of the Lotus Sutra.

Our efforts to achieve peace must be based on dialogue. Ours is a great movement to fundamentally transform the destiny of humankind, which has experienced endless strife. Taking pride in this great mission, let us progress with our heads held high.

Turning the "Wheel of the Law" of Dialogue

Endo: The final passage of "Peaceful Practices" explains the parable of the priceless gem in the topknot. It goes as follows: There is a wheel-turning sage king who rewards soldiers who have won distinction in battle by giving them arms, fields, houses, treasures and various other things. He does not give away to anyone the bright jewel that he keeps in his topknot, however. That's because "this one jewel exists only on the top of the king's head, and if he were to give it away, his followers would be certain to express great consternation and alarm" (LSOC, 245). When the wheel-turning king sees someone who has gained truly great distinction, however, he is delighted and gives the person the brilliant jewel in his topknot, something he would never do recklessly.

Shakyamuni explains that the Buddha is like this wheel-turning sage king and has long concealed the foremost teaching of the Lotus Sutra in his heart, never imparting it to anyone. "Through the long night I have guarded and protected it and have never recklessly propagated it. But today for the first time I expound it for your sake" (LSOC, 247).

Suda: Wheel-turning sage kings are ideal rulers in Indian mythology. This parable explains just how great and rare the Lotus Sutra is. Just as the wheel-turning sage king had never before bestowed the bright jewel on anyone, Shakyamuni had never expounded the true teaching but had all along continued to expound provisional teachings.

Ikeda: A wheel-turning sage king possessed a wheel made of jewels.

Saito: Yes. He was said to destroy evil and govern the world by turning this wheel. The treasure wheel was also supposed to be a weapon, like the wheels of war chariots or something one would hurl at enemy forces.

Ikeda: Just as the king turns the treasure wheel, the Buddha turns the wheel of the Law. If the king's treasure wheel may be likened to hard power, we can say that the Buddha's wheel of the Law is soft power effected through discussion and dialogue.

Saito: The Buddha's preaching is termed "turning the wheel of the Law."

Ikeda: Buddhism is fundamentally a religion of vigorous and free dialogue. We have to "fight" for peace with the "weapons" of dialogue and discussion.

Nichiren Daishonin says, "The wheel-turning king can travel throughout the entirety of the four continents in an instant" (WND-1, 507). Time and again the Buddha turns the wheel of the Law from one friend to another, from here to there, from one country to the next. At the same time he bravely fights to refute evil. This is the Buddha's struggle.

Dr. Johan Galtung, the founder of peace studies, once compared Buddhist philosophy to a wheel. He observed that from the beginning Buddhism has been an open religion and—like a wheel that rolls ever forward—has throughout its history generated new insights and wisdom and addressed the current problems of society.

Endo: This certainly describes the movement of the SGI.

Ikeda: The teaching of Buddhism is certainly not stiff and rigid. It is free of narrow dogmatism and is open to society. Dr. Galtung places great emphasis on this point.

Suda: Buddhism is a religion that pulses vibrantly in society.

Ikeda: Our fellow SGI members put this into practice daily. Turning the wheel of the Law of discussion, day in and day out they engage in the work of creating peace in society. This is most noble.

They tirelessly go from house to house encouraging members. They talk with one friend after another about Buddhism. Such activities certainly amount to 'turning the wheel of the Law.' This is the action of wheel-turning sage kings of kosen-rufu who are "turning" and expanding the flow of the Mystic Law throughout the world. In the process they are accumulating eternal good fortune.

The Record of the Orally Transmitted Teachings says, "To go round and round unendingly in the cycle of birth and death, birth and death, throughout the three existences of past, present, and future, is what is called being a wheel-turning sage king" (OTT, 76). To the extent that we take action in the present, in our next lives and the next and the ones after that, we will be reborn as great leaders of society, as great scientists, great writers, people of wealth, great scholars, as anonymous champions of the people. Assuming all kinds of appearances, we will lead people to enlightenment based on the Mystic Law.

The Daishonin says, "With these peaceful practices, let us proceed to the Pure Land of Holy Eagle Peak with ease" (OTT, 232). Both while we're alive and after we die, we can make our way filled with joy to the pure land of Eagle Peak. It is a state in which being alive is itself a joy; in which life as well as death is a joy.

To realize such an existence, we must achieve a state of life in which we enjoy chanting daimoku to the Gohonzon and telling friends about Buddhism. If doing gongyo is a painful ordeal for you, then you are not in that state of life yet. Unless we really adore and cherish the Gohonzon from the bottom of our hearts, our faith is not genuine.

Saito: When we possess such joy in faith, we truly experience boundless peace and happiness.

Endo: The Daishonin's teaching that encountering difficulties is itself peaceful is the noble way to construct a great state of life that will endure throughout eternity.

Ikeda: By fighting to overcome great difficulties, we can thoroughly polish our lives and create a towering self. Therein lies true peace and happiness.

In the *Divine Comedy*, which describes the transformation of Dante's state of life, we find the lines:

> *This Mount is not like others: at the start*
> *it is most difficult to climb, but then,*
> *the more one climbs the easier it becomes;*

> *and when the slope feels gentle to the point*
> *that climbing up would be as effortless*
> *as floating down a river in a boat*—[12]

He is crying out: "At the crucial moment, climb! Be a hero!" When we climb a mountain, our state of life expands. Descending into a valley might be easy, but when we reach the bottom, our lives will be filled with misery.

The curtain is rising on the brilliant century of Soka. I hope all members, without exception, will follow the unsurpassed path in life and scale the mountain of kosen-rufu, attaining the brilliant state of life of unshakable peace and happiness. This is my ardent prayer.

NOTES

1. T'ien-t'ai, *The Words and Phrases of the Lotus Sutra*, vol. 8.

2. *Shoju:* Propagating Buddhism by gradually leading a person to the supreme Buddhist teaching without refuting his or her attachment to lower or erroneous teachings. *Shoju* was generally employed during the Former and Middle Days of the Law.

3. Middle Day of the Law: The second thousand-year period following Shakyamuni's death.

4. This indicates a country populated with people who conceive no desire to seek the Buddhist way.

5. *Nichijun Shonin zenshu* (Collected Writings of Nichijun Shonin) (Tokyo: Nichiren Shoshu Bussho Kankokai, 1960), part 2, p. 1620.

6. See *The Words and Phrases of the Lotus Sutra*, vol. 8.

7. *The Daibyakurenge*, November 1957, pp. 18–19.

8. Ibid., p. 18.

9. Romain Rolland, *Le Voyage Intérieur* (Voyage Within) (Paris: Éditions Albin Michel, 1959), p. 366.

10. *The Collected Works of Mahatma Gandhi* (New Delhi: The Publication Division, Ministry of Information and Broadcasting, Government of India, 1970), vol. 41 (June–October 1929), p. 465.

11. *Toda Josei zenshu* (Collected Writings of Josei Toda) (Tokyo: Seikyo Shimbunsha, 1983), vol. 3, p. 289.

12. Dante Alighieri, *The Divine Comedy,* Purgatory, trans. Mark Musa (New York: Penguin Books, 1985), vol. 2, p. 43.

PART V

"Emerging from the Earth" Chapter

7 "Upsetting Attachments and Arousing Doubts": Inducing a Revolutionary Leap in Consciousness

Saito: We now turn to the latter half of the sutra, or the essential teaching.

Endo: The transition from the theoretical teaching (first half of the Lotus Sutra) to the essential teaching (latter half) represents a dramatic revolution. That's because as we enter the essential teaching, the way of thinking that prevails in the theoretical teaching is completely overturned. The Bodhisattvas of the Earth both symbolize and are the catalyst of this revolution in awareness.

Suda: When the Bodhisattvas of the Earth appear, the other bodhisattvas and beings taking part in the Ceremony in the Air are so startled that they begin to have doubts about what Shakyamuni has been preaching up to this point—that he attained enlightenment in this lifetime. This illustrates the principle of "upsetting attachments and arousing doubts," or causing uncertainty in people's minds about the ideas to which they have been attached. Having doubt cast on the correctness of their current beliefs allows them to open their eyes to a higher plane of awareness.

Ikeda: Their surprise, shock and doubt represent the reaction of all those believing in the pre-Lotus Sutra teachings, as well as the Lotus Sutra's theoretical teaching. "Upsetting attachments and arousing doubts" indicates a sudden overturning of the beliefs and convictions that people have held up to that point. It is a decisive blow to the foundation of an existing worldview. Through this dramatic overturning of familiar and comfortable values, Shakyamuni reveals his true identity, his true state of life.

Suda: Philosophy has been described as "the product of wonder."[1] The French philosopher Henri Bergson writes, "The spirit marches from surprise to surprise."[2] In that sense, we could perhaps say that this "upsetting attachments and arousing doubts" in the Lotus Sutra sparks an important development in Buddhist thought.

Ikeda: On a deeper level, it amounts to a spiritual revolution, a complete transformation of people's views of life and living, society and the world. Implicit in the "Emerging from the Earth" and "Life Span" chapters is a potent treatment for the ills of modern civilization, which now stands at a crossroads.

COUNTLESS BODHISATTVAS EMERGE FROM THE EARTH

> *When the Buddha spoke these words, the earth of all the billion lands of the saha world all trembled and split open, and out of it emerged at the same instant immeasurable thousands, ten thousands, millions of bodhisattvas mahasattva.[3] The bodies of these bodhisattvas were all golden in hue, with the thirty-two features and an immeasurable brightness. Previously they had all been dwelling in the world of empty space underneath the saha world. But when these bodhisattvas heard the voice of Shakyamuni Buddha speaking, they came up from below.*
>
> *Each one of these bodhisattvas was the leader of his own great assembly, and each brought with him a retinue equal in number to the sands of sixty thousand Ganges Rivers.* (LSOC, 252–53)

"The Thus Come One wishes now to summon forth and declare the wisdom of the Buddhas, the freely exercised transcendental power of the Buddhas, the power of the Buddhas that has the lion's ferocity, the fierce and greatly forceful power of the Buddhas." (LSOC, 258)

Saito: Let us now consider the flow of the text.

Suda: The title "Emerging from the Earth" refers to the appearance of those bodhisattvas who will spread the Mystic Law after Shakyamuni's death. They are called Bodhisattvas of the Earth because they emerge from within the ground.

Ikeda: The time after the Buddha's passing means the ten thousand years and more of the Latter Day of the Law; that is, the eternal future. Pervading the Lotus Sutra is the Buddha's immense sense of responsibility to lead all people in every age throughout eternity to happiness. The Bodhisattvas of the Earth embody this responsibility, compassion and wisdom. They are great benefactors who work to elevate the spiritual state of humankind. And we are at the forefront. This is truly amazing. Our mission is tremendous.

Endo: The Bodhisattvas of the Earth appear at the start of the "Emerging from the Earth" chapter. Until this point, from " The Teacher of the Law" (tenth) chapter through the "Peaceful Practices" (fourteenth) chapter, the central theme of the sutra has been the question of whom Shakyamuni can entrust with the task of propagating the teaching after his death. The voice-hearers, even though they have received specific prophecies that they will become Buddhas in the future, aspire to spread the teaching not in the strife-ridden *saha* world but in other worlds.

By contrast, in the "Encouraging Devotion" chapter, the bodhisattvas vow to spread the teaching in the *saha* world, even if it means having to endure the attacks of the three powerful enemies. The theoretical teaching thus ends in such a way as to give the clear impression that the baton of propagation of the Mystic Law will be passed to these bodhisattvas.

Suda: Then, at the start of the "Emerging from the Earth" chapter, the bodhisattvas who had joined the assembly from other worlds vow to spread the Mystic Law in the *saha* world after Shakyamuni's passing. This is the pledge of these bodhisattvas of high attainment gathered from throughout the universe. From the way things develop, one feels sure that Shakyamuni will entrust them with this great mission.

Saito: Shakyamuni's first statement in the essential teaching therefore comes as a complete surprise: "Leave off, good men!" he tells them. "There is no need for you to protect and embrace this sutra" (LSOC, 252). When he said this, the entire assembly must have recoiled in shock. Everyone doubted their ears at these words; they must have felt as though their hearts had stopped beating. But Shakyamuni's next words surprise them even more.

Suda: Yes. He then says: "Why? Because in this saha world of mine there are bodhisattvas . . . who are as numerous as the sands of sixty thousand Ganges Rivers" (LSOC, 252). He explains that these bodhisattvas will spread the sutra. Next, the earth trembles and splits open and countless Bodhisattvas of the Earth come forth. They are described as "golden in hue, with the thirty-two features and an immeasurable brightness" (LSOC, 252).

Ikeda: It's a momentous scene. Their entry is most dramatic. The earth splits open and countless bodhisattvas appear in unison. Moreover, each emits a golden light. Nowhere in any sutra are there bodhisattvas as brilliant as these Bodhisattvas of the Earth. Even the bodhisattvas of the provisional teachings and the bodhisattvas gathered from other lands are struck with admiration.

Comparing the two groups, Nichiren Daishonin says that the bodhisattvas already present at the assembly "seemed like a pack of apes or monkeys, with the new bodhisattvas appearing among them like so many Shakras" (WND-1, 252). The sutra explains just how noble the Bodhisattvas of the Earth are.

Suda: Yes. It describes them as follows:

> Firm in the power of will and concentration,
> with constant diligence seeking wisdom,
> they expound various wonderful doctrines
> and their minds are without fear. (LSOC, 260)

It also says that they are:

> skillfully learning the bodhisattva way,
> unsoiled by worldly things
> like the lotus flower in the water. (LSOC, 263)

And:

> They are clever at difficult questions and answers,
> their minds know no fear.
> They have firmly cultivated persevering minds,
> upright in dignity and virtue. (LSOC, 263)

Endo: It's like a description of the Buddha.

Saito: In a sense, they might have been even more magnificent than the Buddha himself. If we compare Shakyamuni to a youth of twenty-five years, then the Bodhisattvas of the Earth are in appearance like great elders with a hundred years of rich life experience.
The Daishonin describes them in the following manner:

> Solemn, dignified, they were beings of great and lofty stature. Aside from Shakyamuni, Many Treasures, and the emanations of Shakyamuni from the ten directions,

they were worthy of being good friends upon whom all beings could rely. (WND-1, 253)

Ikeda: In other words, they towered over others like great mountains over small hills and were genuine, reliable leaders.

Suda: Each bodhisattva is also the leader of a great assembly. The sutra describes them as having brought with them a "retinue equal in number to the sands of sixty thousand Ganges Rivers" or followers "equal to the sands of fifty thousand, forty thousand, thirty thousand, twenty thousand, or ten thousand Ganges Rivers" or "only one thousand, one hundred, or ten" followers (LSOC, 253).

The sands of one Ganges indicates the number of grains of sand lining the Ganges River of India. Since sixty thousand Ganges Rivers means sixty thousand times this truly enormous number, the figures here are utterly beyond reckoning.

Endo: Retinue in a broad sense indicates all who receive a Buddha's teaching.

Ikeda: That's right. And the appearance of the Bodhisattvas of the Earth is in no way disorderly or confused. They are vital, energetic and free; but at the same time they are united and harmonious. In a sense, they are the image of an ideal organization.

Saito: We often say that the SGI is an organization that exists and is advancing in accord with the Buddha's will, but I think we need to carefully consider what this means.

Suda: The first thing the Bodhisattvas of the Earth do is bow to the Buddhas Shakyamuni and Many Treasures who are seated within the treasure tower. Then they go around to the innumerable Buddhas gathered from the worlds in the ten directions and praise them in various ways. For countless Bodhisattvas of the Earth to greet countless Buddhas takes time, a long period the sutra describes as "fifty small kalpas"[4] (LSOC, 253). Nevertheless, Shakyamuni uses his supernatural powers to make it seem to those in the assembly like only half a day.

Endo: It must have been tremendously engrossing. By contrast, when we are bored, even an hour can seem like an eternity.

THE MAGNIFICENT RELATIONSHIP OF MENTOR AND DISCIPLE

Ikeda: In praising these Buddhas with utmost respect, the Bodhisattvas of the Earth are actually praising the eternal oneness of mentor and disciple. A Buddha lives each moment with the greatest sense of fulfillment, fully awakened to the truth that the present moment is itself eternity. The Bodhisattvas of the Earth are in fact also Buddhas whose lives are illuminated by the awareness that the present moment is one with eternity. This, in other words, is a meeting between Buddhas. Therefore it is joyful. Accordingly even fifty small kalpas does not seem like a long time.

Representing all the Bodhisattvas of the Earth, the four great leaders—Superior Practices, Boundless Practices, Pure Practices and Firmly Established Practices—begin conversing with Shakyamuni about the great objective of leading all people to enlightenment.

Suda: Yes. They press their palms together and say to Shakyamuni, "World-Honored One, are your illnesses few, are your worries few, are your practices proceeding comfortably?" (LSOC, 254).

Saito: That's a standard way of greeting the Buddha. The Buddhas of the worlds in the ten directions extend Shakyamuni the same greeting on their arrival. But the four bodhisattvas then follow by asking: "Do those whom you propose to save readily receive instruction? Does the effort not cause the World-Honored One to become weary and spent?" (LSOC, 254)

Ikeda: This shows their heartfelt concern for Shakyamuni's well-being. Their attitude is completely different from that of the voice-hearers who, in their state of abject dependence, sometimes express doubts or complaints.

Although on a different level, I was always concerned about the health of my mentor, Josei Toda. Whenever I saw him, I tried to get a sense of whether he was tired, how he was feeling. President Toda was even more concerned about my health. If I was perspiring, he would say to me: "Dai, you should change shirts right away. Otherwise you'll catch cold." He was truly a wonderful mentor.

From the conversation between the Bodhisattvas of the Earth and Shakyamuni, we sense a profound heart-to-heart exchange. It's like a work of art.

Suda: Shakyamuni says in reply: "The Thus Come One is well and happy, with few ills and few worries. The living beings are readily converted and saved and I am not weary or spent. Why? Because for age after age in the past the living beings have constantly received my instruction ... So when these living beings see me for the first time and listen to my preaching, they all immediately believe and accept it, entering into the wisdom of a Thus Come One ..." (LSOC, 254–55).

"I'm all right," he says in effect. "You don't need to worry. I will lead all people to happiness without fail."

The Bodhisattvas of the Earth praise Shakyamuni: "Excellent, excellent / great hero, World-Honored One! ... / We are accordingly overjoyed" (LSOC, 215). And Shakyamuni in turn praises the Bodhisattvas of the Earth for having aroused in their hearts a spirit of rejoicing.

Endo: Shakyamuni's disciples who have been at the assembly of the Lotus Sutra all along are quite surprised by this exchange. A succession of events totally inexplicable to them has unfolded. First there was the appearance of the treasure tower, then the gathering of the Buddhas from the worlds in the ten directions, and the opening of the Ceremony in the Air. All of this was unprecedented; yet they have somehow managed to understand and believe. Now there is the additional surprise of the appearance of the Bodhisattvas of the Earth. It is easy to imagine that anyone at the scene would be completely dumbfounded at this point.

Saito: Giving expression to the wonderment felt by all in the great assembly, Bodhisattva Maitreya (also known as Ajita) asks Shakyamuni:

> Immeasurable thousands, ten thousands, millions,
> a great host of bodhisattvas
> such as was never seen in the past —
> I beg the most honored of two-legged beings to explain
> where they have come from,
> what causes and conditions bring them together!
> (LSOC, 255–56)

Ikeda: This is the famous question of Maitreya that prompts Shakyamuni to expound the "Life Span" chapter, his quintessential teaching. Questions are very important. Shakyamuni therefore praises him saying, "Excellent, excellent, Ajita, that you should question the Buddha about this great affair" (LSOC, 258).

Saito: The attendants serving the Buddhas who are Shakyamuni's emanations from other lands ask their respective teachers the same question that Maitreya has asked: "World-Honored One, this great multitude of immeasurable, boundless asamkhyas of bodhisattvas — where did they come from?" (LSOC, 258).

The Buddhas reply:

> "Good men, wait a moment. There is a bodhisattva mahasattva named Maitreya who has received a prophecy

from Shakyamuni Buddha that he will be the next here-
after to become a Buddha. He has already inquired
about this matter and the Buddha is now about to
answer him. You should take this opportunity to listen
to what he says." (LSOC, 258)

Ikeda: This phrasing is very interesting. Among the vast number
of bodhisattvas and voice-hearers who have a profound connection with Shakyamuni, it is significant that Maitreya is the one to
ask this question.

Saito: Maitreya is known as the bodhisattva who will become the
next Buddha after Shakyamuni. He enjoys high standing even
among Shakyamuni's most senior disciples. Maitreya's question
raises an important issue not resolved in the theoretical teaching
(first half) of the Lotus Sutra.

Ikeda: Yes. Even though they understand that all people have the
Buddha nature and have received specific prophecies that they
will attain enlightenment in the future, this alone is insufficient.
That's because without the clarification in the "Life Span" chapter that Shakyamuni actually attained enlightenment in the remote
past, the path for all beings to attain Buddhahood has no more substance than, for example, a picture of food in a painting.

I will discuss this in detail later, but for the time being suffice it
to say that the emergence of the Bodhisattvas of the Earth is indispensable for clarifying the eternity of Shakyamuni's life. And it is
in response to Maitreya's question that Shakyamuni expounds his
true teaching.

Suda: Shakyamuni's reply is more surprising still. He reveals that
he has been instructing the Bodhisattvas of the Earth since the
remote past in this *saha* world.

Endo: That's the line where he says,

> Ever since the long distant past
> I have been teaching and converting this multitude.
> (LSOC, 261)

The Great Teacher T'ien-t'ai of China interprets this passage as constituting the "abbreviated opening of the near and the revelation of the distant" (where "near" means the teaching that Shakyamuni first attained Buddhahood in his present lifetime in India, and "distant" means the teaching that he actually attained enlightenment in the remote past).[5] He calls it this because it explains in summary the "opening of the near and the revelation of the distant" expounded more completely in the "Life Span" chapter, which follows.

Suda: This comes as a great shock. Up to that point, Maitreya and the others in the assembly had all believed that Shakyamuni attained enlightenment in his present lifetime when he sat in meditation beneath the bodhi tree. They all supposed he had attained Buddhahood for the first time in his present existence as a result of an arduous practice carried out over many previous existences. This view is known as Shakyamuni's "attaining enlightenment during his lifetime in India."

Saito: The teaching of his "actual attainment of enlightenment in the remote past" has not yet been spelled out in its entirety. Still, Shakyamuni's statements here decidedly contradict the view that he first attained enlightenment in his present lifetime in India.

Suda: The assembly members are utterly baffled at seeing for the first time these countless legions of Shakyamuni's disciples, the Bodhisattvas of the Earth. Everything they had believed up to this point about Shakyamuni now rings hollow. It all comes crashing down. It is as shocking as if the ground on which they stand were to suddenly flip over and switch places with the sky.

Saito: This illustrates the principle of "upsetting attachments and arousing doubts." Their attachments crumble and they are filled with great doubt. Maitreya, again voicing the thoughts on everyone's mind, then asks:

> "World-Honored One, when the Thus Come One was crown prince, you left the palace of the Shakyas and sat in the place of enlightenment not far from the city of Gaya, and there attained supreme perfect enlightenment. Barely forty years or more have passed since then. World-Honored One, how in that short time could you have accomplished so much work as a Buddha? ...
>
> "Suppose, for example, that a young man of twenty-five, with ruddy complexion and hair still black, should point to someone who was a hundred years old and say, 'This is my son!' ... This would be hard to believe, and so too is what the Buddha says ...
>
> "We ourselves have faith in the Buddha, believing that he preaches in accordance with what is appropriate, that the words spoken by the Buddha are never false, and that the Buddha's knowledge is in all cases penetrating and comprehensive. Nevertheless, in the period after the Buddha has entered extinction, if bodhisattvas who have just begun to aspire to enlightenment should hear these words, they will perhaps not believe or accept them but will be led to commit the crime of rejecting the Law. Therefore, World-Honored One, we beg you to explain so we may put aside our doubts, and so that, in future ages when good men hear of this matter, they will not entertain doubts!" (LSOC, 261–62)

The "Emerging from the Earth" chapter closes with this question from Maitreya.

PERCEPTION OF THE BUDDHA TRANSFORMED

Suda: Maitreya's very candid question illustrates the great turmoil in the hearts of the disciples.

Ikeda: Nichiren Daishonin says: "This present doubt was the greatest doubt of all"; and "If the Buddha had failed to dispel Maitreya's doubts, the sacred teachings of his entire lifetime would have amounted to no more than froth on the water, and all living beings would have remained tangled in the snare of doubt" (WND-1, 255). It could be said that this is the fundamental question on which the enlightenment of all people hinges.

Suda: First, the assembly is surprised at the countless Bodhisattvas of the Earth—bodhisattvas whom they, including even the most experienced Maitreya, had never seen or heard of—who in the "Emerging from the Earth" chapter suddenly bound forth from within the earth.

Endo: While the Bodhisattvas of the Earth are frequently described as "equal in number to sixty thousand Ganges Rivers," this is in fact but a mere fraction of their total number. If their followers and retinues are included, their number is truly "immeasurable, boundless, beyond anything that can be known through calculation, simile, or parable" (LSOC, 253). Their number far surpasses human comprehension.

Saito: In appearance, moreover, unbelievable as it may seem, they are even more splendid than Shakyamuni. Nevertheless, their attitude in greeting Shakyamuni is most humble and respectful. They are filled with great respect for their mentor.

Endo: On that point, the bodhisattvas of the theoretical teaching may still have been lacking somewhat in respect for their teacher. They might have taken him for granted.

Ikeda: Maitreya knew of Shakyamuni's practices in his previous lives. What's more, he was a person of great wisdom who had grasped the principle Shakyamuni revealed in the theoretical teaching that all people can attain Buddhahood.

But with the appearance of the Bodhisattvas of the Earth, the very foundation of what Maitreya believed up to that time was demolished. "Just who is this person Shakyamuni that he is being reverently greeted by this multitude of great bodhisattvas?" he must have wondered. Seeing for himself these mysterious disciples from the remote past — the Bodhisattvas of the Earth — causes him to wonder, "What is the truth about my mentor?" "What is my mentor's true identity?" In other words, the appearance of the Bodhisattvas of the Earth brings on a great transformation in how people view the Buddha.

Saito: They must have thought: "We were mistaken about the identity of the World-Honored One. He may be a much greater Buddha than we had imagined. Have we ever really known our mentor's true greatness?"

Ikeda: That's right. This is the condition Shakyamuni describes in the "Life Span" chapter where he says that living beings "do not see me even when close by" (LSOC, 271). At the very least, Maitreya senses this and reflects what it means to live his life as a disciple of so great a Buddha.

An important aspect of the essential teaching is that it guides people to seek out their own inherent brilliance. The appearance of countless Bodhisattvas of the Earth in the "Emerging from the Earth" chapter points all people to the greatness of their lives.

Suda: The appearance of these disciples—the Bodhisattvas of the Earth, en masse—is dazzling. "If our mentor's disciples are this splendid," the others muse, "then he must truly be amazing." I think this appearance of the Bodhisattvas of the Earth in response to Shakyamuni's call well illustrates the real nature of the relationship of mentor and disciple.

Endo: I may be presumptuous in making this comparison, but I heard the following account from someone in the Kansai area in Japan. He told me that when you, President Ikeda, took the lead in that region's activities, everyone was really moved by your earnestness. You displayed all the more thoroughness and seriousness, however, in matters pertaining to your mentor, Josei Toda. Your spirit to serve your mentor left a truly inspiring impression on all. The complete earnestness of your actions and words toward President Toda displayed a dedication that gave people a feeling of momentousness. Observing your behavior allowed everyone to understand what an outstanding person President Toda was.

Saito: The transition to the essential teaching thus begins with all of Shakyamuni's disciples past and present assembled before him.

Looking back on the course followed in the theoretical teaching, we see that the teaching of the true aspect of all phenomena in the "Expedient Means" chapter clarifies that all people possess the Buddha nature. The disciples who hear this teaching dance for joy and resolve to set their sights on attaining the same state as the Buddha and to undertake the actions of the bodhisattva. They say they have well understood the Buddha's intent.

But when we come to the essential teaching and the vow of the disciples present to spread the teaching after Shakyamuni's passing, they are adamantly rejected. It is as though Shakyamuni himself overturns all he has taught up to this point.

Endo: "Why should he say such a thing now after we've resolved to do what he's asked of us?" they might have wondered, somewhat crestfallen.

Ikeda: Again, when we come to the essential teaching, everything Shakyamuni has taught up to that point is fundamentally overturned. The theoretical teaching reveals a series of important doctrines; these include the true aspect of life (or true aspect of all phenomena), the enlightenment of the people of the two vehicles (the voice-hearers and cause-awakened ones), the enlightenment of women, and the enlightenment of evil people. In addition, predictions of future enlightenment were given to Shariputra, the disciple reputed to be foremost in wisdom, and Shakyamuni's other disciples who had comprehended these doctrines.

In an instant, however, all of this becomes meaningless. The very foundation of these teachings, the premise upon which they were based, has fallen apart.

Saito: In "The Opening of the Eyes," the Daishonin says:

> When we come to the essential teaching of the Lotus Sutra, then the belief that Shakyamuni first obtained Buddhahood during his present lifetime is demolished, and the effects of the four teachings are likewise demolished. When the effects of the four teachings are demolished, the causes of the four teachings are likewise demolished. (WND-1, 235)

In other words, Shakyamuni himself rejects his earlier teaching about the causes leading to the effect of his Buddhahood based on the premise that he first attained enlightenment in his present existence.

Ikeda: That's right. His denial of the "effect of Buddhahood" expounded in these teachings amounts to a denial of the "cause of Buddhahood" undertaken with that aim. He thus completely refutes people's understanding of the causes and effects of his enlightenment. It is a revolution with Copernican implications.

Endo: Speaking of Copernicus, the revolution in thought for which he is credited—from a geocentric (earth-centered) to a heliocentric (sun-centered) view—entailed tremendous "upsetting of attachments and arousing of doubts" among his contemporaries.

In a speech, Mr. Ikeda, you once described the final events in the life of the sixteenth-century Italian Renaissance philosopher Giordano Bruno. Bruno adopted the heliocentric theory and developed a new view of the world based on the idea that the universe is boundless. This overturned the common view of his contemporaries, who believed that the Earth was the center of the universe and could not possibly be in motion.

Suda: We cannot fathom the extent to which people's thinking was constrained by traditional views of the world. Reportedly, many reacted to the idea that the Earth revolved around the sun with disbelief. They did not want to believe it even if it were true.

Ikeda: That was probably the honest sentiment of many. "Even if I am called ignorant for not accepting this," they might have thought, "I prefer ignorance to having my world, as I know it, destroyed." To have one's common knowledge—the basic assumptions upon which one has relied—overturned is extremely painful. It is very hard to accept.

The doctrine expressed in the essential teaching came as perhaps even more of a shock. The essential teaching reveals for the first time the ever-present existence of the Buddha. That's a dramatic revelation, one that fundamentally overturns Shakyamuni's previous teaching. It is a revolution in how people view the Buddha.

A Movement That Shakes Up
Existing Value Systems

Saito: Seen from that perspective, we might call the Daishonin's practice of *shakubuku* a great attempt to "upset attachments and arouse doubts" in the people of his day. Wasn't it a struggle to shake up the existing Buddhist establishment?

Ikeda: His impact was not limited to the world of Buddhism. He also upset attachments and aroused doubts in the minds of those in power in the Kamakura government, those allied with the government, and in general throughout the populace.

He essentially refuted mistaken views of religion and faith that had prevailed up to that time. Beliefs about life, society and the people were entirely overturned. The strong reaction against the Daishonin was only natural. It is inconceivable that he could have avoided such difficulties.

Endo: SGI members are spreading Buddhism just as the Daishonin taught. Consequently, they, too, upset attachments and arouse doubts in society.

Saito: In Japan, certainly, most people tend to suppose that religion concerns only people who are "different" or, conversely, that it makes no difference what religion people believe in. In this environment, Soka Gakkai members seriously discuss the truth and falsehood of religions and assert the correctness of Nichiren Buddhism. There is no doubt that their efforts often have an earth-shaking effect.

Suda: More than just a matter of surprise, many people have become livid. To begin with, in Japan's cultural climate, the spirit of propagation, the very life of religion, has been lost. The spirit to determine through dialogue what is true and what is false in matters of religion is itself lacking. The disposition expressed in the saying "Yield to the powerful" has deep roots indeed.

Japanese people seek solace in ambiguity and tend to dislike anything that clarifies matters in black-and-white terms. Perhaps it is only natural, therefore, that the conviction of Soka Gakkai members who don't mince words in religious matters has aroused a negative reaction. Moreover, because the existing order is shaken by this Soka Gakkai movement to open people's eyes to the correctness of Buddhism, it has unavoidably invited suppression by those in power.

Ikeda: The greater the degree to which attachments are upset and doubt aroused, the greater the difficulties that will arise. Since we are upsetting attachments and arousing doubts in order to fundamentally improve the lives of all people, it is impossible for us not to face tremendous obstacles.

Also, our efforts have the world as their focus. We are implementing the principle of upsetting attachments and arousing doubts on the global stage. While spreading peace, culture, education and friendship, we are steadily changing people's views about Buddhism and about what it means to be human.

Saito: This reminds me of something we talked about at the start of this series. At that time, you said that all human endeavor is ultimately inspired by the questions: "Where do we come from?" "Where are we going?" and "Why are we here?" It would seem that the view of the Buddha as eternal, which develops in the "Emerging from the Earth" and "Life Span" chapters, certainly offers a reply to those questions.

Suda: Petrarch writes, "Often have I wondered with much curiosity as to our coming into this world and what will follow our departure."[6] He asked why we had been born, where we came from and where we went after death. For Petrarch, to speculate about mundane concerns without the spirit to pursue answers to such fundamental questions testifies to humankind's nonchalance about life.

Ikeda: That's exactly right. Never before have people been so oblivious to their own existence, nor have they looked down on themselves as so inconsequential and insignificant as they do now. Within the immense systems of modern society, a sense of powerlessness shrouds people's hearts; they feel: "My own ability is trifling. Nothing I do will change the world. All I can manage is simply to try to keep up with society."

Saito: This is the fundamental cause for the sense of helplessness in the world today. Convinced of their own insignificance, people have ceased even to question things. They live complacently, unquestioning. Such spiritual sterility makes people smaller still. The teaching of the Lotus Sutra, however, breaks down the petty limitations that people set on their lives.

Ikeda: Yes. The "Emerging from the Earth" chapter breaks through the frozen earth of resignation, the sense that "this is the way it has to be." It is a struggle to reveal before the entire world the underlying power and towering dignity of humanity and of the people.

Suda: Dr. Margarita I. Vorobyova-Desyatovskaya of the Institute of Oriental Studies, Russian Academy of Science, said she felt the "Life Span" chapter explained the state in which the individual fuses with the Buddha. She suggested that in this state the energy of the universe becomes one's own energy and that one experiences the eternal.

Ikeda: That was very insightful of her. Don't the Bodhisattvas of the Earth embody this state of fusion with the Buddha, of oneness with the universe? Though we speak of them as bodhisattvas, they are in fact Buddhas.

Where have the Bodhisattvas of the Earth come from? The Great Teacher T'ien-t'ai says that they dwell in the "utmost depth of the essential nature of phenomena and the ultimate of profound Buddhist principles."[7] In other words, they represent the truth that exists in the depths of life, the fundamental Law of Nam-myoho-renge-kyo.

Nam-myoho-renge-kyo is the wellspring of the universe and the fundamental power of life. It is the ultimate expression of wisdom and the foundation of all laws and principles. The Bodhisattvas of the Earth embody that fundamental energy. Moreover, they are committed to the bodhisattva ideal.

Bodhisattva is not a stage of completion (the effect of Buddhahood) but of incompleteness (the cause of Buddhahood). Bodhisattvas, while incomplete, display the state of completion (the effect of Buddhahood). Put another way, while partaking of a state of life of boundless joy and completion (the effect of Buddhahood), a bodhisattva at the same time takes action to advance, to ascend ever higher, and to lead still more people to enlightenment. In other words, it is a state of "incomplete completeness."

The Bodhisattvas of the Earth are eternal activists who base themselves on the Mystic Law; theirs are lives of eternal progress. Our summoning forth the boundless energy of these bodhisattvas constitutes the "emergence of the Bodhisattvas of the Earth" within our own beings. When we do this, we can break through the shell of the lesser self that has constrained us.

Saito: Certainly, if we were not practicing Buddhism, it would be all we could manage simply to take care of ourselves. In all likelihood, we wouldn't have the latitude to try to help people who are miserable. The thought of trying to change the country or the destiny of humankind would probably never occur to us.

Endo: Through the SGI, we have learned about the Gohonzon and led incomparably greater lives than we might have otherwise. As

Nichiren Daishonin says, "A blue fly, if it clings to the tail of a thoroughbred horse, can travel ten thousand miles . . ." (WND-1, 17). This fills me with immense gratitude.

Ikeda: It comes down to people revolutionizing their states of life. From a broad perspective, our efforts to cause countless Bodhisattvas of the Earth to emerge — to help many people revolutionize their lives — amount to a struggle to change the state of life of society at large. It is a struggle to elevate the state of all humankind. Isn't this the transformation that "breaking through the earth" symbolizes?

Saito: In that sense, the preconception held by those in the assembly of the Lotus Sutra — that Shakyamuni first attained enlightenment during his lifetime in India — indicates their confusion about the origin of their own lives. They don't understand the eternal energy of life that is the foundation and wellspring of their own existence. The situation is similar today.

Ikeda: That's right. Failing to comprehend the greatness of their own lives, people become attached to unimportant details. The power of the Bodhisattvas of the Earth is the essential power we human beings possess to break through all differences — ethnicity, race, gender or social standing — and lead people to happiness. We are ordinary people, plain and unadorned. We are thoroughly human and infinitely courageous. This is the pride of the Bodhisattvas of the Earth.

The appearance of the Bodhisattvas of the Earth is an earth-shaking event attesting to the great underlying power of life. We have to convey this to people throughout the world. The essential teaching transforms how people perceive the Buddha, which amounts to a fundamental transformation in how people perceive themselves.

Endo: Yes. The Nobel laureate Dr. John Eccles [who received the prize for medicine and physiology in 1963] comments on super-stition in the present age as follows:

> It takes no deep philosophical insight to recognize the connection between what a person does and what a person thinks he is, between what others expect of us and what they think of us. So close is this connection that much of social and political history can be understood in just these terms. Whether one takes human beings to be "children of God," "tools of production," "matter in motion," or "a species of primate" has consequences.[8]

He says that modern people are shrouded by the darkness of what he terms the "superstitions" of materialism and environmental determinism and argues that they should question those superstitions. He also says:

> One need only consider such phrases as "the divine right of kings" or "the African is a slave by nature" or "Pharaoh is the living god" to recall how entire epochs have been colored and shaped by eccentric theories about ourselves and others.
>
> But every epoch is generally far more uncritical about its own perspective than about those embraced by an earlier age.[9]

Saito: Later generations may consider as greatly distorted the view of humanity that people today hold as self-evident.

Suda: The ideas that Dr. Eccles terms the *superstitions of the present age* limit the parameters of human existence. For instance, although people today generally suppose the mind to reside only within the brain, Buddhism teaches that it in fact permeates and encompasses all time and space.

Endo: This is a case where it is necessary to upset attachments and arouse doubts. A society informed by such a limited view of human beings will inevitably become spiritually desolate and bereft of hope.

Ikeda: This process of upsetting attachments and arousing doubts will be initiated by the voices and actions of the Bodhisattvas of the Earth. They will do this in the same manner that they upset attachments and arouse doubts through their grand entrance. In any event, we can take the emergence of the Bodhisattvas of the Earth today as an overture, setting the stage for the global revolution of thought and spirit that will continue over the course of the twenty-first, twenty-second and twenty-third centuries, and throughout eternity.

The Daishonin calls out to his followers: "Since great slander already exists in our land, the great correct Law will spread without fail. What could any of you have to lament? Even if you are not the Venerable Mahakashyapa, you should all perform a dance. Even if you are not Shariputra, you should leap up and dance. When Bodhisattva Superior Practices emerged from the earth, did he not emerge dancing?" (WND-I, 1119).

Do not lament! he is telling us. Because great evil exists, great good is sure to follow. Advance, dancing joyfully and in high spirits, just as the bodhisattvas leapt forth dancing from the earth. We are the Bodhisattvas of the Earth. Therefore, let us vigorously dance forth from the "great earth" of the people.

NOTES

1. *Bloomsbury Thematic Dictionary of Quotations* (London: Bloomsbury Publishing Limited, 1988), p. 291.

2. Henri Bergson, *La pensée et le mouvant* (Geneva: Editions Albert Skira, Paris: Presses universitaires de France, 1946), p. 91.

3. *Mahasattva:* A great being, another term for a bodhisattva.

4. *Kalpa:* An extremely long period of time deriving from ancient Indian tradition. There are various explanations of a *kalpa*, but all of them, except one, are metaphoric and defy exact computation. According to the one exception, a *kalpa* is 15,998,000 or approximately 16 million years long. A hundred *kalpas,* then, is about 1.6 billion years.

5. T'ien-t'ai, *The Words and Phrases of the Lotus Sutra,* vol. 9.

6. Petrarch's *Secret,* trans. William H. Draper (London: Chatto & Windus, 1911), author's preface.

7. *The Words and Phrases of the Lotus Sutra,* vol. 9.

8. Sir John Eccles and Daniel N. Robinson, *The Wonder of Being Human: Our Brain and Our Mind* (New York: The Free Press, a division of Macmillan, Inc., 1984), p. 1.

9. Ibid., p. 3.

8 *A Cultural History of the Lotus Flower*

Saito: The "Emerging from the Earth" chapter is the one in which, by way of praise, the Bodhisattvas of the Earth are compared with lotus flowers. In the sutra they are said to be "like the lotus flower in the water" (LSOC, 263). I'd like to suggest, as a way to deepen our understanding of "Emerging from the Earth," that we narrow the focus of our discussion to an examination of the lotus flower.

Ikeda: That sounds fine. The lotus is indeed a mysterious flower. In the Buddhist canon it has deep significance. If we were to focus solely on a discussion of the various doctrines that pertain to the lotus flower we could fill dozens of volumes. That would mean that this series of conversations would never end.

   Therefore, I propose we begin by taking a look at how people in different parts of the world have viewed the lotus flower throughout history—a sort of cultural history of the lotus. Let us save for another occasion a more detailed study of the profound principles of Buddhism as they relate to the lotus flower.

Saito: I agree. Culturally people in different places and ages certainly must have viewed the lotus flower very differently. To begin with, I suspect quite a few young people these days have never actually seen one.

Suda: In Japan, the lotus is associated with funerals and the annual Festival of Lanterns.[1] On the other hand, however, since ancient times the lotus has been taken to symbolize nobility. In China, for example, it was known as the flower of nobility.

Endo: In modern Japanese, there is an expression comparing a beautiful woman to a cotton rose; originally, however, the word for the flower in this expression meant the lotus. Similarly, I understand that in India there is an expression comparing the beauty of a woman's eyes to the lotus flower.

Saito: In Japan today it would be rare to associate a woman's beauty with that of the lotus flower. But even if someone did, few women would consider it a compliment.

Ikeda: India and Japan are two different cultures. That brings to mind something that happened during my first visit to Portugal. I went to a flower shop to buy some chrysanthemums to present to a guest, but the local people there discouraged me from doing so. In Japan, chrysanthemums are symbols of elegance and refinement, but in Portugal they are used primarily at funerals and are taken as a sign of sadness and grief. People's perceptions of flowers vary widely from one country or culture to the next.

THE LOTUS AND THE WATERLILY

Ikeda: Why don't we conduct a little quiz? The Japanese term *renge* (lotus flower) refers to two general varieties of flowers: the lotus and the waterlily. What is the relation between these two?

Endo: All right. In terms of its botanical classification, *renge* refers to the waterlily (Nymphaeaceae) family, which includes the lotus (*Nelumbo*) genus and waterlily (*Nymphaea*) genus. The Chinese characters for the waterlily genus, by the way, mean "sleeping lotus." Among such waterlilies, some bloom during the day and some bloom at night. They are called sleeping lotuses because, in either case, when the proper time arrives, they fold up their petals as though falling asleep.

Saito: There is also a type of waterlily native to Japan called ram grass (pygmy waterlily). This species is so called because it opens its petals at the time known in Japanese chronology as the hour of the ram, which is around 2:00 p.m.

Endo: Such day-blooming lilies close up and "go to sleep" when the sun sets.

Suda: It seems that the plants of the lotus genus also open their petals around dawn and close in the afternoon.

Ikeda: While the lotus and waterlily seem similar, they differ in a number of ways. What about their appearance?

Suda: In the case of the lotus, both the stem and the rhizome, or root, are hollow. The rhizome has joints, and from these joints the leaves and flower emerge. The stem grows out over the water's surface, and the bud blossoms atop it. It then produces seeds from this position suspended above the water.

By contrast, neither the stem nor the roots of the waterlily are hollow. Its roots are solid like those of a potato. The flowers float on the surface of the water and there they bloom. When the flowers wither, they sink down and then seed underwater.

Saito: In the general Buddhist canon, *renge* may refer to either the lotus or the waterlily. But in the Lotus Sutra, it refers to only the lotus, and to the white lotus in particular.

Ikeda: How many varieties of lotus and waterlily are there?

Endo: From a botanical viewpoint, there are only two kinds of lotus. There is the strain that is prevalent in Asia and Oceania, and there is the American lotus or water chinquapin of North America.

As for the waterlily, there are approximately forty strains throughout the world. While most of these are tropical, there are temperate varieties. Included among them are Japan's ram grass and the white waterlily originally from the Mediterranean region (which has spread widely across the Eurasian continent).

Suda: In South America's Amazon basin, there is a strain of waterlily called the water platter or Victoria lily. This plant is so large that its floating pad can support the weight of a small child on the water.

Ikeda: I recall hearing about that. By the way, do you suppose there are lotus flowers or waterlilies in Europe?

Endo: The white waterlily that I mentioned is native to the Mediterranean region and grows wild in Europe. It seems, however, that there are no wild lotus plants, although there are lotus fossils from the region.

Ikeda: As I recall, lotus plants have been traced back as far as the Cretaceous period (or about 135 million years ago). It seems they flourished immediately after the appearance of seed plants or spermatophytes.

Suda: In Europe, the white waterlily is a symbol of chastity. In the language of flowers, the waterlily signifies inner purity and faithfulness.

Ikeda: Speaking of European waterlilies, the paintings of waterlilies by the French Impressionist Claude Monet are well known. The Tokyo Fuji Art Museum has one in its collection. What about in Africa then?

Saito: There are waterlilies in Egypt. The waterlily is in fact Egypt's national flower. Many grow along the banks of the Nile River.

These include both night-blooming white waterlilies and day-blooming blue waterlilies, with the latter the more numerous.

Ikeda: The clusters of blue and white waterlilies floating on the Nile make a beautiful scene. I think it was the Greek historian Herodotus of the fifth century BCE who wrote that parts of the lotus plant were used for food in ancient Egypt.

Endo: That's right. In his *History*, Herodotus refers to the lotus as a type of lily.[2] The lotus is also known as the waterlily in English.

Suda: Another type of lily is the lily of the valley *(Convallaria majalis)*, which leads me to wonder if the name "lily" itself has any special significance.

Endo: It seems that lily is a generic term given to flowers that are especially fresh and beautiful. Lilies have long been regarded as symbols of purity.

Saito: The white lily, appropriately, is the symbol of the Soka Gakkai women's division.

Ikeda: How about lotus plants? Or did ancient Egypt only have waterlilies?

Endo: There are indications that lotus plants did grow in ancient Egypt. A source mentions a type of lily resembling a rose, but little is known of the details.

SIMULTANEOUS PRODUCTION OF FLOWERS AND FRUIT

Ikeda: Why do you suppose the lotus is called *hasu* in Japanese? What is the derivation of this word?

Saito: In olden times, lotuses (the *Lotus* genus) were called *hachisu* in Japan, which is short for *hachi-no-su*, or "wasp's nest."

When a lotus flower opens, a fruit shaped like an inverted shower-head appears. Because of its resemblance to a wasp's nest, this part of the plant was called *hachi-no-su*, which was later shortened to simply *hasu*. It is this part of the plant that is referred to by the Chinese character *ren* (of *renge*).

Ikeda: That's right. Technically, this part is known as the receptacle. The lotus seeds are found inside the holes of this "wasp's nest" (to which the petals, stamen, pistils and other parts attach).

Suda: Because it contains the seeds, we can think of this part of the plant as the fruit.

Endo: A unique feature of the lotus flower is that its fruit (the receptacle) develops even before the flower blooms. In most plants, the flower blooms first and the fruit appears some time later. If we associate this with cause and effect, flowers represent the cause and fruit the effect. Ordinarily, the cause comes first and the effect later. But in the case of the lotus flower, the flowers (cause) and the fruit (effect) develop at the same time. That's why the lotus flower is used as a metaphor for the Lotus Sutra's doctrine of the simultaneity of cause and effect.[3]

THE BODHISATTVAS OF THE EARTH SIGNIFY ETERNAL ADVANCE

> *In this manner these sons*
> *study and practice my teaching of the way.*
> *And in order that day and night with constant diligence*
> *they may seek the Buddha way,*
> *in this saha world*
> *they have been dwelling in the empty space in its lower part.*
> *Firm in the power of will and concentration,*

with constant diligence seeking wisdom,
they expound various wonderful doctrines
and their minds are without fear.
(LSOC, 260)

Ikeda: The simultaneity of cause and effect is an extremely profound doctrine. I propose that we discuss it in detail another time.

For the time being, I'd just like to point out that the causality referred to here specifically indicates the causes and effects pertaining to the attainment of Buddhahood. The state of Buddhahood is the effect, and the practice to attain that state is the cause. The idea that these two could coincide seems counterintuitive; the usual assumption is that by carrying out Buddhist practice (the cause), a person later attains Buddhahood (the effect).

But when we practice Nam-myoho-renge-kyo (the true cause for attaining Buddhahood), our practice already encompasses the world of Buddhahood (the true effect). Nam-myoho-renge-kyo is at once the true cause and the true effect of attaining Buddhahood. This marvelous teaching of the Mystic Law embodying the simultaneity of cause and effect is compared to the lotus flower. The important point here is that the Bodhisattvas of the Earth manifest this simultaneity of cause and effect in their lives.

Saito: Because outwardly they are bodhisattvas, they are still in the process of making causes to attain Buddhahood. But in terms of their inner lives, they are Buddhas, that is, they have already gained the effect of Buddhahood.

Ikeda: Buddhahood is not a fixed or static condition. Just as the fruit and flowers of the lotus mature at the same time, the effect, or the world of Buddhahood, develops in our lives simultaneously as we carry out our Buddhist practice for the spread of the Law. In that sense, the Bodhisattvas of the Earth signify eternal progress and eternal growth. Conversely, if a person ceases to advance in faith, he or she is no longer a Bodhisattva of the Earth.

THE THOUSAND-PETALED LOTUS

Ikeda: Why don't we continue our discussion of the cultural history of the lotus flower? What is the history of the lotus in Asia? Let's look first at Japan and then at China and India.

Suda: Japanese have had fond associations with the lotus since olden times. References can be found in such early Japanese works as the *Nihon Shoki*[4] and *Man'yoshu*,[5] which date from the eighth century. As Buddhism spread, many splendid varieties of lotus flowers were brought here from China for people to admire.

Endo: It seems that lotus flowers have grown in many areas of Japan since ancient times. Indeed, many place names are related to the lotus.

Ikeda: That's right. According to one explanation, Chiba, the modern name of the region where Nichiren Daishonin was born, comes from the term *thousand-petaled lotus.*

Saito: According to a classical literary source, there was once a body of water called Ikeda Pond in which thousand-petaled lotus flowers bloomed. This is reportedly the origin of the name Chiba.
    [The *Myoken jitsuroku senshuki* (Thousandfold Collection of Mysteries Seen and Factually Recorded) says: "The Ikeda Pond is a pure and clear pond. In this pond there bloomed thousand-petaled lotus flowers."]

Suda: I wonder, President Ikeda, if there is some relation to your name.

Ikeda: I'm not really very clear on the matter, but someone has suggested that my family has its roots in the Ikeda area of Chiba Prefecture. Also, I have heard that the Chiba prefectural office roughly marks the spot where this Ikeda Pond once stood.

Saito: I understand that "thousand" in thousand-petaled lotus does not simply mean "many" but is to be taken literally.

Endo: I wonder whether lotus flowers with a thousand petals have actually existed. The "Devadatta" chapter of the Lotus Sutra also mentions a thousand-petaled lotus.

Ikeda: Bodhisattva Manjushri is described as being "seated on a thousand-petaled lotus blossom big as a carriage wheel" (LSOC, 224).

I understand that lotus flowers usually have between twenty and twenty-five petals. Flowers with a single set of such petals are usually referred to as "one-layer bloomers." But there are lotus flowers with multiple layers, some with enough to have a hundred or even as many as three hundred petals per flower. Also, there is a variety called the many-headed lotus, so called because the receptacle puts forth multiple flowers — one after another. I understand that the number of petals on these may range from three thousand to five thousand.

While I have never seen a thousand-petaled lotus, I will always remember the lotus pond near a house where I lived as a child. I think it was when I was in the fifth year of elementary school (1938). The Sino–Japanese War had begun shortly before (in 1937), and my older brothers were drafted. Also, my father's health had declined. As a result, we had to vacate the large house where we had lived until then, and we moved to this house, right next door to a lotus pond. There must have been easily several hundred lotuses there. I cannot forget the scene as their flowers bloomed here and there one after another. We would eagerly look forward to that season each year.

We were eventually forced to evacuate that house, too [due to the intensifying air raids on Tokyo]. It seems that the pond no longer exists today. Everything around us changes with the passage of time.

Getting back to our discussion, what about lotus flowers in China?

Suda: As for writings in praise of lotus flowers in China, there is the famous *Ai lian shuo* (On Love for the Lotus) by the Song dynasty (960–1127) author Zhou Dunyi. In it, the author cites a number of reasons for people's fondness for the lotus flower. These can be summarized as follows: (1) They emerge from a swamp but are not stained by the muddy water, reminding us of the description in the sutra, "unsoiled by worldly things / like the lotus flower" (LSOC, 263); (2) they are cleansed by pure wavelets and are free of anything unpleasant; (3) their stalks are hollow on the inside, and perfectly straight on the outside, having neither tendrils nor branches; (4) their fragrance carries long distances and becomes more refreshing at greater distances; (5) they grow in an upright and orderly arrangement and thus should be enjoyed from afar rather than from close by.

He further praises the lotus for its purity as the flower of nobility.[6]

Ikeda: I see. So the lotus flower represents all that is pure. In Buddhism, too, the lotus represents purity.

Incidentally, why aren't lotus flowers discolored by the muddy water in which they grow?

Saito: According to the Japanese botanist Dr. Tomitaro Makino, it's apparently because the fine hairlike filaments on its leaves repel water.

Endo: It seems that it was due to the influence of Buddhism that lotus flowers came to be associated with purity in China. Before Buddhism came to that country, the lotus was a symbol of fertility and prosperity. Also, we may attribute the reason for lotus flowers having come to symbolize love and affection to the similarity between the pronunciation of the character for lotus and such words as *love* and *pity*.[7]

Also, in China parts of the lotus plant are used as food or medicine.

Ikeda: People have indeed had a close relationship with the lotus since ancient times.

Endo: Lotus roots, leaves and stamens are used to stop bleeding. In China, these have been combined with other herbal remedies and used to treat gastric ulcers, uterine bleeding, hemorrhoids and other conditions.

Suda: I hear that in India people eat lotus seeds raw and may pickle or fry the root. In Indian medicine, too, the lotus has long been put to various uses.

THE ROBUST VITALITY OF LOTUS SEEDS

Endo: In China, lotus seeds are regarded both as having nutritional value and as medicine for restoring health and strength. They are extolled for increasing vigor and curing ills of all kinds, and if taken consistently over time are thought to retard the aging process and increase longevity. Since they are as hard as rock, they are referred to in Chinese as "rock lotus seeds."

Saito: Speaking of hardness, the scientific name of lotus is *Nelumbo nucifera*. *Nucifera* means "having hard fruit." The seed has an extremely hard shell. (*Nelumbo* means "lotus" in Sri Lankan.)

Ikeda: Because they are so very hard, lotus seeds can withstand harsh conditions and still bud and produce flowers. The famous Oga Lotus sprouted from a seed that had lain dormant for at least two thousand years; some scientists estimated the period of dormancy at more than three thousand years. That is phenomenal.

There are now lotus plants descended from the Oga Lotus growing at the Kansai and Tokyo Soka Junior and Senior High Schools and at Soka University.

Endo: According to Dr. Oga, lotus seeds can remain viable after so long a time because of their hard and thick shell. Moreover, because the seeds respire extremely slowly with very little exchange of moisture or gases, it takes an extremely long time before they are smothered by the carbon dioxide that they produce.

Ikeda: This gives us a sense of the lotus flower's awesome life force.

The Lotus Sutra is the "seed" for attaining Buddhahood. The Lotus Sutra is great because it contains the seed of Buddhahood enabling all people to become Buddhas. This seed of Buddhahood is compared to a diamond; like a diamond, it cannot be damaged or broken. It will not be destroyed even if one should fall into the hell or any of the evil paths.

The Bodhisattvas of the Earth have the virtue of never losing the seed of Buddhahood. That's because, since the remote past, they have been inwardly embracing and outwardly practicing Nam-myoho-renge-kyo, the seed of Buddhahood, which is the Lotus Sutra's essence.

Suda: The fact that this teaching is named the law of the lotus reflects the wisdom to discern that the seed of the lotus flower is strong and long-lived.

Endo: The Oga Lotus bloomed in 1952, an auspicious year marking the seven-hundredth anniversary of Nichiren Daishonin's establishment of his teaching. Moreover, its seeds were discovered in Chiba Prefecture, Nichiren Daishonin's birthplace.

Ikeda: That's right. Also, I recall that around the same time there were reports in the news that in a national park in Washington, D.C.,[8] a big pale crimson flower bloomed from a lotus seed that had lain dormant for tens of thousands of years in Manchuria. Thus, in the year marking the seven-hundredth anniversary of the founding of Nichiren Buddhism, lotus flower seeds thousands and tens of thousands of years old bloomed in both East and West. Josei Toda, the second Soka Gakkai president, interpreted this as a wonderful sign portending the revival of the Great Pure Law.

[On September 30, 1952, President Toda said: "The single great desire of people who are wallowing in the muddy swamp of suffering is for the appearance of the one great Buddhist teaching. Now is the time when this great Buddhism—sublime and true, clearly elucidating reward and punishment and worthy of anyone's trust—has to appear. Lotus flowers have now bloomed in both East and West, sprouting from the mud to put forth beautiful blossoms, having awakened from a slumber of thousands or tens of thousands of years. Now, in the swamp of the Japanese people, the supreme Buddhism of the original Buddha of the Latter Day has suddenly burst into bloom, breaking the slumber that has prevailed from the distant past and, more recently, for the past seven-hundred years. If these lotus flowers blooming in both East and West are not a sign that the teaching of the original Buddha of the Latter Day is about to gloriously blossom, then what are they?"][9]

I was twenty-four at the time. It helped me solidify my determination to dedicate myself to spreading the supreme law of the lotus in Asia, the United States and throughout the world.

THE LOTUS FLOWERS OF THE LOTUS SUTRA

Ikeda: And so we come at last to India. In India, lotus flowers have been widely known since ancient times and occupy an important place in the Hindu canon.

Suda: That's right. Lotus flowers are mentioned in the *Rigveda*, India's oldest extant religious text.

Ikeda: Just what kinds of lotus appear in the Lotus Sutra?

Saito: A line in the "Benefits of the Teacher of the Law" chapter mentions "red lotus flowers, blue lotus flowers, white lotus flowers" (LSOC, 296).

When we look at the corresponding terms in the Sanskrit text of the sutra, we find that "red lotus flowers" is a translation of *padma.* This is a white waterlily, but it seems there are pink varieties, too. "Blue lotus flowers" is a translation of *utpala (nilotpala),* a blue waterlily. And "white lotus flowers" is a translation of *pundarika,* the white lotus. The term *pundarika* is used in the sutra's Sanskrit title.

Ikeda: I understand that in the Sanskrit text, lotus flowers are usually mentioned in the order of blue, yellow, red and white. The white lotus flower, which is mentioned last, is accorded the highest value and reverence. Because the Lotus Sutra is the highest teaching, its Sanskrit title is the *Saddharma-pundarika* sutra, or, literally, "Sutra of the White Lotus of the Wonderful Law."

Suda: The Lotus Sutra in addition mentions a night-blooming white or red waterlily called the *kumuda.* Also, the term *flower* in Pure Flower Constellation King Wisdom, the title of the Buddha in the world to the east where Bodhisattva Wonderful Sound dwells, is a red lotus called the *kamala.*

Ikeda: That's a lot of detail. What about yellow lotus flowers?

Suda: Chinese translations of the Lotus Sutra other than Kumarajiva's *Miaofa lianhua jing* (Myoho-renge-kyo) mention a yellow lotus. [Yellow lotus flowers are mentioned, for example, in the eighteenth and the twenty-fourth chapters of Dharmaraksha's *Zhengfahua jing* (Jpn *Sho-hokke-kyo*).[10]]

In reality, however, it seems that there are no yellow lotuses or waterlilies in India.

Endo: Yellow lotuses do apparently exist; for example, the American lotus or water chinquapin found in the Mississippi basin in the United States.

Suda: The so-called esoteric teachings of Buddhism describe an imaginary black lotus in addition to red, white, blue and yellow lotus flowers.

Saito: That's a little hard to visualize.

Ikeda: Buddhist texts describe lotus flowers of various colors. In one text, Shakyamuni reminisces about the blue, red and white lotus flowers that grew in the garden of the palace where he grew up.[11]

Lotus flowers give a sense of cool respite from the heat of summer. Since the summer heat in India is so severe, that association may have been even stronger.

Saito: Lotus flowers are described as growing in Anavatapta Lake (literally, "Heat-Free Lake"), which appears in Buddhist literature and was supposed to be part of an ideal land. The Daishonin in fact refers to this lake in his writings (WND-1, 262). A lotus pond was apparently an indispensable feature of such a place. The Pure Land of Perfect Bliss of Amida Buddha is also described as filled with lotus flowers.

Suda: It seems that the importance early Indians accorded to lotus flowers is part of a tradition that can be traced back to the civilization of the Indus Valley (which existed through 1500 BCE). A statue resembling an earth goddess with a lotus flower on her head has been unearthed from the famous ruins of Mohenjo-Daro in southern Pakistan.

Ikeda: The ruins of Mohenjo-Daro are thought to be more than three or four thousand years old. That the lotus flower was important so long ago is very interesting. I am also intrigued by the connection between the lotus flower and the earth goddess. Like the statue of the earth goddess, the Bodhisattvas of the Earth appearing in the Lotus Sutra also emerge from the ground as human lotus flowers. It occurs to me that this image of emerging from the earth — irrespective of its profound meaning in Buddhism — may have resonated strongly with Indian cultural traditions. While nothing definite can be said, I look forward to what further research may reveal in this area.

Saito: We find the concept of an "earth mother" in many different cultures, and India is no exception. Many cultures have traditions that revere the earth as the mother or goddess that gives life to all things.

Endo: Perhaps we can say that the earth mother is the womb that gives birth to the Bodhisattvas of the Earth.

Ikeda: Their emergence suggests an image of lotus flowers emerging from the water stretching out as far as the eye can see. More precisely, the sutra describes the Bodhisattvas of the Earth as having existed in the "empty space in the lower part" of the earth. Let's think about this a moment. Doubtless some will wonder what the sutra means by the empty space beneath the earth.

The "Empty Space" Beneath the Earth Is the Ultimate Origin

Endo: Ancient Indian cosmology describes the world's underground structure in the following way: The ground on which we dwell is the surface of the earth wheel. Beneath that, there is a gold wheel, and below that, a water wheel. The border between the gold wheel and the water wheel is termed the "edge of the gold wheel." Beneath the water wheel there is a wind wheel, and this wind wheel is said to float above empty space.

Saito: From the time of the *Rigveda*, Indians have considered the question of the origin of all things in various ways. According to one philosophical poem, the creating deity, upon making the world, "placed water as a womb in the vastness of space." This suggests that space is more fundamental even than water. In later commentaries, space comes to be revered as Brahma, the ultimate origin of all beings.[12] Viewed in light of this cultural tradition, the "empty space in the lower part" where the Bodhisattvas of the Earth are said to have dwelled formerly would seem to indicate the most primary realm of all and, hence, the origin of origins.

Endo: The idea that they were born from the "origin of origins" seems very close to what the Daishonin terms the "the utmost depth of the essential nature of phenomena" or "the ultimate of profound Buddhist principles" (WND-2, 843). This association is of course far from conclusive.

Ikeda: The Bodhisattvas of the Earth are the disciples from the remote past of the Buddha described in the "Life Span" chapter. These disciples from the remote past are born from the ultimate ground of existence. The "the utmost depth of the essential nature of phenomena" and "the ultimate of profound Buddhist principles," of course, refer to the ultimate truth, or the Law of Nam-myoho-renge-kyo.

Based on that recognition, the statement in the "Emerging from the Earth" chapter that these bodhisattvas emerge from "the world of empty space underneath the saha world" (LSOC, 252 53) may reveal their origin in terms of space, while Shakyamuni's remark that he has been teaching and converting them "ever since the long distant past" (LSOC, 261) may reveal their origin in terms of time.

The emergence of the Bodhisattvas of the Earth is a great drama of life and the universe. It suggests that the ultimate Law contained in the depths of the essential teaching (second half) of the Lotus Sutra is the ultimate principle governing the universe.

The Silk Road Is a "Lotus Road"

Saito: Looking at things this way, I am impressed anew at how important a symbol the lotus has been throughout the world.

Suda: The Egyptian hieroglyph of the lotus flower and the existence in Egyptian shrines of pillars carved with a lotus at the crown suggest that Egyptian civilization was a great center of lotus culture.

Endo: We could say the same of Greek civilization, which inherited a great deal from Egypt. For example, lotus flowers are seen in an arabesque pattern in the temple at Olympus.

Ikeda: Alexander the Great brought Greek civilization to India. Alexander's expedition resulted in a melding together of the Greek civilization of the West with Asian civilization. The encounter of Indian and Western civilizations eventually gave birth to the brilliant Buddhist art of Gandhara,[13] which spread throughout Asia by way of China, eventually reaching as far as the Korean Peninsula and even Japan. While it is difficult to prove anything about the specific influence of the lotus, it is clear that in a sense the entire Eurasian continent was united by a grand Lotus Road.

Saito: The Silk Road was therefore also a Lotus Road.

Ikeda: The camel, known as the "ship of the desert," was one of the principal means for traveling that road. Chang Shuhong, the late honorary director of China's Dunhuang Relics Research Institute, observed that the hoofprints of camels resemble lotus flowers.[14]

Endo: So the Lotus Road was actually marked with a pattern of lotus flowers!

Suda: That's a wonderful image.

Ikeda: Fragrant lotus flowers of human happiness similarly mark the road of kosen-rufu that we are now forging. And our lives likewise become a beautiful Lotus Road of value creation.

Last, why don't we discuss the relation between the sun and the lotus flower? This is an extremely important point in that it relates to Nichiren Daishonin's name.

The Sun Is the Lotus Flower of the Heavens, the Lotus Is the Sun of the Earth

Endo: Well, to begin with, in Egypt the lotus flower is also associated with the sun. Because of the way its petals open out from the center, it was probably thought to resemble the rays of the sun. It seems the fact that many lotus flowers open in the morning and close by evening reinforced this connection with the sun.

Suda: According to Egyptian myth, at night the corolla of the lotus flower becomes the "cradle of the sun." And at dawn it supposedly imparts new life to the sun.

Ikeda: The sun is regarded everywhere as a symbol of boundless vitality. Also, since it sets only to rise again the following morning, it is taken as a symbol of rebirth and eternal life.

Saito: Lotus flowers were placed atop mummies or used in funerals to express the wish for eternal life or rebirth. An Egyptian legend reportedly suggests that when a lotus born from primal waters bloomed, the newborn sun, represented as a beautiful child, appeared and created the world.

Suda: Also, the people of ancient Persia thought of lotus flowers as incarnations of the sun. There are depictions of the sun god wearing a robe of light and a crown of lotus flowers.

Ikeda: In the ancient Orient, the lotus flower seems to have been regarded as an earthly sun, and the sun as a heavenly lotus. The lotus flower was thought to give birth to, or contain, something sacred. It must have been looked upon as a divine plant.

Saito: In India, likewise, from ancient times the lotus was thought to give birth to the sacred. The thousand-petaled lotus mentioned in the Lotus Sutra that we talked about earlier exemplifies this.

An early legend describes the creation of the universe as follows: In the beginning there was only water. From within this water a lotus flower floated to the surface, and then a thousand-petaled lotus shining with a golden light like that of the sun came forth. Within that lotus flower, which is described as a golden womb, Brahma, the creator of the universe, was born.

Suda: The golden womb is the origin of all things mentioned in the ancient Hindu text, the *Rigveda.* It contains within it all things in embryonic form and brings all things into being.

Endo: The receptacle of the lotus plant in Sanskrit is called the *garbha,* which literally means womb or uterus; this is probably because it produces the seeds. Also, the golden lotus is used to symbolize the sun.

Saito: The image of a thousand-petaled golden lotus also appears in Buddhist texts. In a miraculous account of occurrences at Shravasti,[15] the dragon kings Nanda and Upananda make a thousand-petaled golden lotus as large as a chariot wheel and with a stem of jewels, and they present this to Shakyamuni.[16]

The Buddha Is the Sun and the Lotus

Ikeda: Shakyamuni is addressed as "Sun of wisdom, great sage and venerable one" (LSOC, 60). The image is that of a sun radiating the light of wisdom. In other words, Shakyamuni, the teacher who expounds the Law for all people, is the sun and the lotus. This is extremely important.

Saito: In *The Treatise on the Great Perfection of Wisdom*, there are comments elucidating the connection between the "thousand-petaled lotus" and the "light of wisdom." It says that when Shakyamuni is in *samadhi,* or profound meditation, he emits a great light. Each of the rays of this light, it says, becomes a "thousand-petaled lotus" made of jewels, and on top of each of these lotus flowers a Buddha is born.

Ikeda: The Buddha's wisdom and compassion are both compared to light. The Buddha's wisdom is called "wisdom light" and the Buddha's compassion, "mercy light." This suggests that the light of the Buddha's wisdom and compassion is the mother that gives birth to all Buddhas.

We have to shed light on people, to give people light. We must also bathe ourselves in light. We must never remain in darkness, nor must we allow others to remain in the dark. Flowers will not bloom, the lotus will not blossom, in darkness. We have to send the light of the Mystic Law to all those with whom we share a bond. Doing so also increases our own light.

Countless Buddhas being born atop countless thousand-petaled lotus flowers — this is a magnificent image. The Lotus Sutra describes similar scenes. During the Ceremony in the Air, the two Buddhas Shakyamuni and Many Treasures sit side by side in the treasure tower. And around the treasure tower gather the Buddhas of the worlds in the ten directions who are Shakyamuni's emanations.

Suda: Yes. This congregation of Buddhas is likened to a multitude of lotus flowers.

All Teachings Arise
From the Lotus Flower

Ikeda: Along the same lines, without going into a detailed discussion, the Flower Garland Sutra develops the idea that all beings are born from lotus flowers through the concept of the Lotus Treasury World.

Nichiren Daishonin says regarding the single character *ren* (or lotus):

> Then the source of all phenomena, the threefold contemplation in a single mind, the three thousand realms in a single moment of life, the three truths, the six stages of practice, the unification of reality and wisdom, the ultimate meaning of the essential teaching and theoretical teaching—all these teachings have their origin in and arise from the single character *ren*. (WND-2, 904)

He also says, "All teachings arise from the two characters *ren* [lotus] and *ge* [flower]" (GZ, 809). The lotus flower that produces all teachings is ultimately Nam-myoho-renge-kyo.

We have not finished our discussion on the connection between the lotus flower and the sun, but I wonder if there are any similar concepts.

Saito: There is a concept called the "lotus flower in the breast." According to one explanation, this refers to the heart. The heart is at the same time likened to the sun.

Ikeda: The heart is probably compared to the lotus flower because its shape resembles that of a closed lotus flower. Moreover, the muscle striations in the heart give it the appearance of being divided into eight sections. Consequently, the heart is called the "eight-petaled lotus."

Endo: Ancient Indians viewed the human body as the palace of

Brahma, the place in which Brahma (the fundamental principle of the universe) dwells. They conceived of the heart as the "small palace of the white lotus flower" within the palace of the body.

Ikeda: We have seen that the heart is likened to a lotus flower. But we still need to explain how it also represents the sun.

Saito: Both the human heart and the sun were thought to be held together by fine capillaries. The light of the sun provided nourishment for the activity of the *atman*, or self, within the heart.

Suda: In short, the implication is that the vital energy that gives life and causes the heart to beat comes from the sun.

Ikeda: From that standpoint, it accords nicely with the view of modern science. If we trace the food chain from its source, we find that the sun is the origin of all energy on the planet. The sun is the mother of all life on earth, and all human activities also ultimately depend on the beneficent rays of the sun.

In short, both the sun and the lotus flower represent the source of universal energy. At the core the essence of both is Nam-myoho-renge-kyo; the Mystic Law is both the sun and the lotus flower. In human terms, the Daishonin is the sun and the lotus flower.

The Daishonin Is the Sun and Moon and the Lotus Flower

Saito: The "Supernatural Powers of the Thus Come One" chapter, compares the Bodhisattvas of the Earth to the sun. It says:

> As the light of the sun and moon
> can banish all obscurity and gloom,
> so this person as he advances through the world
> can wipe out the darkness of living beings . . .
> (LSOC, 318)

And so the Bodhisattvas of the Earth, like Shakyamuni Buddha, are compared to lotus flowers and to the sun.

Ikeda: That's right. The Daishonin says that this "Supernatural Powers" passage "means that the first five hundred years of the Latter Day of the Law will witness the advent of Bodhisattva Superior Practices, who will illuminate the darkness of ignorance and earthly desires . . ." (WND-1, 993). The Daishonin, who spread Nam-myoho-renge-kyo—the essence of the Lotus Sutra—in the Latter Day of the Law, thus suggests that he himself is the incarnation of Bodhisattva Superior Practices.

He also says: "Names are important for all things . . . Giving myself the name Nichiren (Sun Lotus) derives from my own enlightenment regarding the Buddha vehicle" (WND-1, 993).

Suda: The Daishonin is the Buddha who attained the state of Buddhahood on his own, and the name *Nichiren* expresses his enlightenment.

Endo: In a letter to Shijo Kingo's wife, the Daishonin says: "The Lotus Sutra is the sun and moon and the lotus flower. Therefore it is called the Lotus Sutra of the Wonderful Law. Nichiren, too, is like the sun and moon and the lotus flower" (WND-1, 186).

Ikeda: His taking the name Nichiren, the Daishonin says, signifies that he embodies the essence of the Lotus Sutra. The Daishonin reveals that he is at one with the sun eternally illuminating the lives of all people in the Latter Day, and the pure lotus flower—or white lotus—giving life to all Buddhas.

There are various profound teachings concerning the name Nichiren. The twenty-sixth high priest, Nichikan, sums these up in his "On the Two Characters in the Name Nichiren." He observes in his conclusion that the Daishonin, by taking the name Nichiren, strongly declares that he is the votary of the Lotus Sutra in the Latter Day of the Law and in fact the original Buddha.[17]

Saito: This means that we who are the Daishonin's followers also have to become "suns" and "lotus flowers" in our own right.

Ikeda: When we become suns, all darkness is banished from our lives. Each day is filled with light, and we can brightly illuminate the lives of others, too. When we become lotuses, we can change the muddy swamp of earthly desires into joyous enlightenment.

The "Emerging from the Earth" chapter describes the Bodhisattvas of the Earth as being "like the lotus flower in the water" (LSOC, 263). As Bodhisattvas of the Earth, we dwell in the "swamp" of society; we certainly do not seek to escape from reality. And what's more, our lives are in no way stained or tainted by society. Why is this? It is because we never forget our mission.

The Daishonin says of the Bodhisattvas of the Earth, "Their fundamental mission is to propagate Nam-myoho-renge-kyo, the one great reason for the Buddha's appearance in this world" (GZ, 833). It's a matter of dedicating one's life to kosen-rufu. It's a matter of possessing the spirit to help others become happy through the Mystic Law of Nam-myoho-renge-kyo. The spirit of the Bodhisattvas of the Earth is found in the faith to dedicate oneself wholeheartedly to kosen-rufu. If people lose this spirit, then no matter how splendid their appearance, their hearts will be tainted by worldly affairs and concerns.

Suda: The Daishonin also says, "'[Untainted by] the things of the world' indicates not being swayed even though one may receive lands or a court rank from the sovereign or a minister" (GZ, 833). This means that no matter what powerful people may do to entice them with wealth or status, the Bodhisattvas of the Earth absolutely never allow their faith to bend.

Ikeda: And they absolutely never betray their comrades. A treacherous individual is sure to meet a pitiful end. This is as true now as it was in the past.

The essence of the Lotus Sutra that Nichiren Daishonin

revealed with his life is found in the spirit to treasure kosen-rufu even more highly than one's life. When we advance with such a lofty spirit, the sun of the "greatest of all joys" rises in our hearts, and our lives, like a golden lotus or a thousand-petaled lotus, blossom as fragrant flowers of happiness.

Kosen-rufu is a movement to cause the sun of compassion to rise and the lotus flower of happiness to bloom in society.

NOTES

1. Festival of Lanterns: A traditional festival for the deceased, held in midsummer. Also called the Bon Festival.

2. Technically, lilies belong to a different family, but the term is used in a generic sense to include all flowers resembling lilies.

3. This is called the "figurative *renge*." In *The Profound Meaning of the Lotus Sutra*), Great Teacher T'ien-t'ai of China interprets *renge* of Myoho-renge-kyo in two ways: as the figurative *renge* symbolizing the Law, and as the entity of the Law itself.

4. *Nihon shoki* (Chronicle of Japan): The oldest history of Japan.

5. *Man'yoshu* (Collection of Ten Thousand Leaves): The earliest extant collection of Japanese poetry.

6. *Hasu no bunkashi* (Cultural History of the Lotus), ed. Kodai Miura (Koshigaya, Japan: Kado Sobo, 1994), pp. 167–68.

7. Ibid., p. 97.

8. "Lotus Blooms From Seed Centuries Old." New York Times Associated Press Wirephoto 1 July 1952: 26. In Washington, D.C.'s National Capital Park, a plant grew from a seed tens of thousands of years old found in geologic deposits in Manchuria in 1950. The blossom measuring six inches in diameter opened in the summer of 1952. Also, *Tokyo Shimbun,* 11 July 1952.

9. *Toda Josei zenshu* (Collected Works of Josei Toda) (Tokyo: Seikyo Shimbunsha, 1981), vol. 1, pp. 86–87.

10. Dharmaraksha's *Zhengfahua jing*: The earliest Chinese translation of the Lotus Sutra, or the Saddharma-pundarika-sutra, consisting of twenty-seven chapters in ten volumes. This translation (dated CE 286) corresponds with Kumarajiva's *Miaofa lianhua jing* (CE 406) in most respects, except that it contains several parables, which the latter omits.

11. Hajime Nakamura, "Gotama Budda" (Gautama Buddha), bk. 1, *Nakamura Hajime senshu* (Selected Writings of Hajime Nakamura), vol. 11 (Tokyo: Shunjusha, 1992), p. 155.

12. Hajime Nakamura, "Upanishaddo no Shiso" (Upanishad Thought), *Nakamura Hajime senshu* (Selected Writings of Hajime Nakamura), vol. 9 (Tokyo: Shunjusha, 1990), p. 95.

13. Gandhara: An ancient country in northern India, located north of Punjab and northeast of Kashmir.

14. Chang Shuhong and Daisaku Ikeda, *Tonko no kosai* (The Brilliance of Dunhuang) (Tokyo: Tokuma Shoten, 1990), p. 56.

15. Shravasti: The capital of the Kosala Kingdom of ancient India, located to the east of present-day Delhi. The Buddha is said to have made Shravasti his base of activities during the rainy season for twenty-five years, and to have converted many people there including King Prasenajit.

16. Akira Miyaji, *Gandara—Hotoke no fushigi* (Gandhara—Wonders of the Buddha) (Tokyo: Kodansha, 1996), p. 252.

17. *Fujishugaku yoshu* (Selected Works of the Fuji School), vol. 3, pp. 255–58.

9 "I Am a Bodhisattva of the Earth": The Discovery of the Eternal Self

Ikeda: It has been fifty years since I took faith in Nichiren Buddhism, fifty years of fierce struggle amid gale-force winds. During those fifty years, I have run tirelessly together with President Toda.

In everything, President Toda has been my source of inspiration. Through this unity with him, I have won. President Toda once said: "We have to bring about a great revolution. It's a revolution that will be accomplished not through force or arms. We have to bring about a human revolution, a bloodless, peaceful revolution. This is true revolution."

We of the Soka Gakkai, who were scorned as a gathering of the poor and the sick, have accomplished a revolution of the people, by the people and for the people. And we have done this without relying on power or wealth. We have embraced individuals and provided each with encouragement and the means to become prosperous and healthy. Today, more than ten million friends around the world are advancing along this path of human revolution.

Endo: The fact that the Soka Gakkai was vilified as a gathering of the poor and the sick is proof that the light of the Soka Gakkai has reached those suffering the most. Dr. Dong-Hoon Kim, director of the Asia-Pacific Human Rights Information Center in Osaka, commented that for a religious body working to help people, to be called a "gathering of the poor and the sick" is the highest honor.

Saito: He commented that this attests to the merit of the Soka movement.

Suda: To me, this type of gathering seems to match the image of bodhisattvas emerging from below the earth. Of course, "below" doesn't mean the underside of society; rather, it indicates the well-spring of life itself, the Mystic Law.

Saito: I'm not sure that these two can be entirely separated. So many of the members in the early days of our movement had nothing on which to rely. Starting literally from zero, they had no recourse other than to tap their inherent strength and ability. For precisely this reason, they were quick to realize the greatness of faith in the Lotus Sutra, which enabled them to transform the state of their lives.

Ikeda: They had neither the armor of authority, the shield of learning, nor the sword of wealth or status. No avenue was available to them other than that of struggling to summon forth their inherent strength. They had no alternative but to stand on their own two feet and forge a solidarity of humanism.

The SGI Is a Gathering of Bodhisattvas

Endo: I recall an address that Professor Su Dongtian of Shenzhen University in China gave at a meeting sponsored by the SGI of Hong Kong. [Titled "The Twenty-first Century and Buddhism —SGI President Ikeda's Buddhist Thought and the Civilization of the Twenty-first Century," it was held at the Hong Kong Culture Centre in September 1996.]

Characterizing the present as a time when most people are controlled by cravings and desires, Professor Su asserted that the "conscientious wisdom" of people such as yourself, Mr. Ikeda, is a bright light guiding humankind toward the future. He credited you with having created many "gatherings of bodhisattvas," mentioning the members of the Soka Gakkai in Japan and of the SGI of Hong Kong.

Professor Su further noted that the SGI is a unique organization in that its members are, in their activities, not motivated by concern for profit or by ideology nor are they bound by a set of rules or a contract. Instead, ties of the heart and friendship, entirely free of any coercion or external pressure, form the basis of members' association.

Ikeda: He really sees things very clearly.

Everything comes from the self-directed power of the people themselves. We have succeeded in helping people cultivate their own "inner power." This is a remarkable achievement. And therein lies the SGI's underlying strength. So many people would never carry on such vigorous activities over such a long time merely on the directive of some authority figure. The SGI's success in facilitating the empowerment of the people is truly the actualization of the Lotus Sutra's teaching of "emerging from the earth."

Suda: The Bodhisattvas of the Earth do not descend from the heaven like gods. Rather, they dance forth from the earth. This gives us a sense of the importance that the Lotus Sutra places on human beings.

A GATHERING OF BODHISATTVAS WHO DANCE FORTH

> *I beg the most honored of two-legged beings to explain*
> *where they have come from,*
> *what causes and conditions bring them together!*
> *Huge in body, with great transcendental powers,*
> *unfathomable in wisdom,*
> *firm in their intent and thought,*
> *with the power of great perseverance,*
> *the kind living beings delight to see —*

where have they come from? (LSOC, 256)

. . .

These great bodhisattvas
for countless kalpas
have practiced the Buddha wisdom.
All have been converted by me;
I caused them to set their minds on the great way.
These are my sons,
they dwell in this world . . . (LSOC, 260)

Endo: Speaking of dancing forth from the earth, Nichiren Dai-shonin says, "When Bodhisattva Superior Practices emerged from the earth, did he not emerge dancing?" (WND-1, 1119).

There are transcriptions of the Lotus Sutra, even of Kumarajiva's Chinese translation, in which the "Emerging from the Earth" chapter is titled "Dancing Forth from the Earth." This variation is found even in copies of the Lotus Sutra included in the *Taisho shinshu daizo kyo* (New Compilation of the Buddhist Canon in the Taisho Era [1912–26]), a collection of virtually all the sutras that have been translated into Chinese. A copy of the Lotus Sutra unearthed at Dunhuang in China also reads "dance forth" instead of "emerge."

Ikeda: I see. It seems that "dancing forth" is a fitting image for the appearance of the Bodhisattvas of the Earth. After all they do appear on the scene fully aware of their mission to spread the Mystic Law. They don't come forth reluctantly because Shakya-muni told them to; rather, the Bodhisattvas of the Earth leap forth and dance exuberantly with the sense: "Our time has come at last!"

Saito: There are several places in Nichiren's writings, too, where he uses "dance forth" in place of "emerge," both terms in Japanese being pronounced the same.

Ikeda: By practicing with the self-motivated faith to "dance forth," we can attain eternal happiness.

President Toda explained the supreme benefit of faith as follows:

> Attaining Buddhahood means achieving the state in which we are always reborn overflowing with abundant and powerful life force; we can take action to our heart's content based on a profound sense of mission; we can achieve all our goals; and we possess good fortune that no one can destroy. Because we can live tens, hundreds, thousands, tens of millions of lives in this way, our happiness truly knows no bounds. Someone who does not aspire for such a life of happiness, and who instead greedily seeks out minuscule joys, is truly pitiful.[1]

The purpose of faith is to realize a state of eternal happiness. This existence is as fleeting as a dream. We practice faith to awaken from this dream and firmly establish a state of eternal happiness in the depths of our lives during this lifetime. That is what it means to "attain Buddhahood in this lifetime." And that's why, as I always say, we must exert ourselves to the utmost in faith.

What, then, is necessary to achieve Buddhahood? Nichiren Daishonin says, "If you are of the same mind as Nichiren, you must be a Bodhisattva of the Earth" (WND-1, 385). Those who struggle for kosen-rufu with the same spirit as the Daishonin are the true Bodhisattvas of the Earth. Everything in the cosmos moves along its own path in exquisite harmony. Just as the Earth naturally follows its own orbit, so too is kosen-rufu like the revolution of a planet around the sun. In the same manner, our individual human revolution is like the rotation of a planet on its axis. These two motions are inseparable.

The SGI represents the function of the Buddha. It is only natural, therefore, that we are attacked by devilish functions. For, as the Daishonin says, "The Buddha and Devadatta are like a form and its shadow—in lifetime after lifetime, they are never separated"

(WND-1, 278). We have to search out and win over negative forces. This is the spirit of sharing and teaching others about Nichiren Buddhism.

When we are "of the same mind as Nichiren," what can we possibly have to fear? Tsunesaburo Makiguchi and Josei Toda, the first and second Soka Gakkai presidents, never retreated a single step, even when under attack by the militarist authorities during the war. They continued advancing straight ahead with the spirit of the lion king, which is the spirit of Nichiren Daishonin.

Endo: That was where the Soka Gakkai and the Nichiren Shoshu priesthood decisively parted ways. Priests, far from being "of the same mind as Nichiren," trampled the Daishonin's spirit underfoot out of fear of persecution.

ENDURING HARDSHIP ON ACCOUNT OF FAITH EQUALS ATTAINING BUDDHAHOOD

Ikeda: It was in prison that President Toda attained his enlightenment, which has become the origin of our movement. This is a key point. He was imprisoned on account of his faith in the Lotus Sutra. In light of the Daishonin's writing, "The Four Debts of Gratitude,"[2] this is comparable to reading the Lotus Sutra with one's life constantly throughout each day without a moment's rest.

During his imprisonment, President Toda had the instantaneous realization: "I am a Bodhisattva of the Earth!" He carried out his human revolution while undergoing great persecution. Enduring difficulties on account of faith equals attaining enlightenment.

In truth, he proved with his life the golden words, "If you are of the same mind as Nichiren, you must be a Bodhisattva of the Earth." Strictly speaking, unless we encounter difficulties we cannot genuinely be "of the same mind as Nichiren."

President Toda's enlightenment in prison is our eternal starting point. At that moment, the Lotus Sutra was revived, and the sun of human revolution dawned on the modern age. Although in the deep darkness of the time no one realized it, dawn had already broken in President Toda's life.

Saito: President Toda left behind various statements about the enlightenment he experienced while imprisoned. It was during the early winter of 1944. At the time, he was continually pondering the Lotus Sutra while chanting earnest daimoku in an effort to grasp the sutra's essential principles.

Endo: He would walk about in his solitary cell saying to himself, "I have to know! I simply must understand!" Whether asleep or awake, he continued to seriously grapple with the sutra's text. That is how President Toda describes the process leading to his enlightenment in his book *The Human Revolution.*

He goes on to relate how one morning, as he was on the verge of reaching 1,800,000 daimoku since the start of the year, he had a mystic experience while chanting daimoku in quiet concentration that seemed to refresh him in both body and mind. As he describes it in the narrative [in the third person]:

> It was neither a dream nor an illusion . . . In terms of time, it may have lasted for several seconds or for several minutes, or even for several hours . . . He [Toda] really had no way of knowing. He discovered himself at the Ceremony in the Air among a great multitude of beings incalculable in number, reverently bowing to the Dai-Gohonzon that shone before him with a brilliant golden hue . . .
>
> When he tried to cry out, "This isn't a lie! I am here right now!" he found himself seated in a chair in his solitary cell. The morning sun shone fresh and bright.[3]

From this we can conclude that he perceived himself to be present at the Ceremony in the Air described in the "Emerging from the Earth" chapter.

Ikeda: President Toda's enlightenment at that moment has become the starting point of world kosen-rufu. President Toda's great conviction, "I am a Bodhisattva of the Earth!" is the spring at the source of the great river of kosen-rufu.

Suda: He also wrote:

> The Lotus Sutra that I see now is the same Lotus Sutra that until recently I found impenetrable to my understanding no matter how I exerted myself. Now I can read it, however, and draw forth its meaning as easily and accurately as if I were looking at something in the palm of my hand. Sensing the wonder of this, I am filled with immense gratitude; it is as though I have recollected a teaching that I learned in the distant past.[4]

And he made this determination: "My future has been decided. I will devote the remainder of my existence to spreading this most exalted of teachings — the Lotus Sutra!"

Ikeda: It was a truly mystic revelation. Yet, for President Toda, it was an unmistakable experience. He read with his life T'ien-tai's words, "The assembly at Eagle Peak which continues in solemn state and has not yet dispersed." [5]

Saito: High Priest Nichijun praised President Toda as the "vanguard of the Bodhisattvas of the Earth" and credited him with having called into appearance in the world the Bodhisattvas of the Earth making up the Soka Gakkai's membership of 750,000 households. He also recognized the number 750,000 as significant because of its association with the phrase "the seven characters or five characters" of Nam-myoho-renge-kyo.[6]

The "Emerging from the Earth" chapter could therefore truly be called the lifeblood of the SGI.

We Can "Enter the Treasure Tower" Through Faith

Suda: What is the relationship of President Toda's awakening as a Bodhisattva of the Earth and his earlier revelation that "the Buddha is life"?

Saito: President Toda attained his revelation that the Buddha is life in early March 1944, when he had been contemplating passages from the Immeasurable Meanings Sutra. Specifically, he had been pondering the matter of the real nature of the Buddha that transcends the so-called thirty-four negations: "His body neither existing nor not existing, neither caused nor conditioned, neither self nor other . . ."[7]

He had his revelation as to his identity as a Bodhisattva of the Earth in November of that same year, or about eight months later. During that interval, President Toda continued chanting daimoku and pondering the sutras.

Endo: It seems to me his realization that the Buddha is life has something of an intellectual flavor to it. His awakening to his identity as a Bodhisattva of the Earth seems to represent a deepening of this earlier awakening—such that he experienced it, not intellectually, but at the very core of his being. In that sense, I think we can see a link between his revelation that the Buddha is life and his revelation eight months later that he is a Bodhisattva of the Earth.

Ikeda: While the total content of President Toda's enlightenment is beyond words, it is a fact that he was thrown into prison because of his belief in the Lotus Sutra and that he maintained his belief while enduring persecution. This in itself amounts to reading the Lotus Sutra with one's life—with the totality of one's being.

Enduring hardships on account of faith equals attaining Buddhahood. Because he struggled against extreme difficulties based on faith in the Mystic Law, a great transformation occurred in his life. This is just as the Daishonin indicates where he says, "Although I and my disciples may encounter various difficulties, if we do not harbor doubts in our hearts, we will as a matter of course attain Buddhahood" (WND-1, 283).

Enlightenment is not simply a matter of recognition or awareness of eternal life. This is very important. The eternity of life is not something to be recognized intellectually; it is something that we have to experience with our own lives. And only if we practice a correct teaching can we do so.

The difficulty is that even if one consciously makes an effort to become aware of the eternity of life, ultimately it is life that supports the self that is trying to achieve this awareness. One cannot comprehend what is large with what is small; a wave cannot comprehend the ocean over whose surface it passes. What, then, are we to do?

The only way to awaken to life's eternity is to cause the greater, eternal self to "emerge" within the small self. And to do this, we need to undertake the task of self-purification wholeheartedly, with our entire being. This is the purpose of Buddhist practice.

Originally our lives are in harmony with the Mystic Law. But because we live in a strife-ridden world, we tend to base ourselves on egoism. As a result, our hearts become clouded by illusion and karma, and we grow befuddled and confused. This prevents the brilliant light of the eternal world of Buddhahood from illuminating our lives.

Endo: The "Life Span" chapter states that befuddled living beings cannot see the Buddha even when he is nearby (see LSOC, 271). It also describes befuddled people as drowning in a sea of suffering (see LSOC, 271).

[Shakyamuni says: "I make it so that living beings in their befuddlement / do not see me even when close by" and "When I look at living beings / I see them drowned in a sea of suffering."]

Ikeda: That's right. I'd like to go into this in more detail later when we discuss the "Life Span" chapter, but for now suffice it to say that the Buddha this refers to is Shakyamuni as the original Buddha enlightened since the remote past. The Buddha is called the "Thus Come One," indicating the state of life of one in whom the Mystic Law naturally manifests at each moment.

This eternal pulsing dynamism of the Mystic Law is itself eternal life. It is the true identity of the Buddha—the original Buddha. Furthermore, it is the wellspring of the benefit that all Buddhas enjoy. Just as President Toda realized, the Buddha is life itself. In addition, this original Buddha is the very wellspring of our lives. In this sense, the sutra speaks of the original Buddha as being nearby. Befuddled, however, people fail to perceive this Buddha.

By struggling against difficulties, we polish our clouded hearts and fuse with eternal life. We might think of it as gaining self-mastery. It's a matter of harmonizing one's life, as though tuning a musical instrument, with the eternal rhythm of the Mystic Law. It is a matter of fusing one's entire being with the eternal life of the cosmos. This is what it means to be a Bodhisattva of the Earth.

Nichiren Daishonin says, "These great bodhisattvas [who emerged from the earth] are particularly suited to bring benefit to people in the Latter Day of the Law, like fish who are at home in the water or birds that move freely through the sky" (WND-2, 551). The Bodhisattvas of the Earth have earnestly practiced the Mystic Law since the distant past. They have tempered their lives with the Mystic Law based on faith. That's why the Daishonin says, "these bodhisattvas are the ones who had thoroughly forged their resolve" (WND-1, 953).

Because the Bodhisattvas of the Earth have such strong faith—that is, because in the depths of their lives they dwell in the world of Buddhahood—they can spread the Mystic Law in this strife-ridden *saha* world even while undergoing great persecution.

Suda: This is how they differ from the bodhisattvas of the theoretical teaching.

Ikeda: That's right. The bodhisattvas of the theoretical teaching and bodhisattvas from other lands all aspire to become Buddhas. For this reason, they cannot endure the difficulties of spreading the teaching in the *saha* world. It is the Bodhisattvas of the Earth of the essential teaching, who are thoroughly versed in and have mastered the eternal Mystic Law, who can endure the hardships incumbent upon those undertaking this great task.

President Makiguchi said: "Although it is said that particles of dust collect to form mountains, there are in fact no mountains that are formed from accumulated particles of dust. At the most all they can form is a small hill. Real mountains are formed by great shifts in the earth's crust. By the same token, no matter how much minor good you accumulate, it will never amount to major good."[8]

The bodhisattvas of the provisional teachings are like those trying to attain Buddhahood by accumulating minor good. In contrast, the bodhisattvas of the essential teaching cause the great vitality of Buddhahood to issue forth from the depths of their lives —from the fundamental nature of the Law, which is to say the very wellspring of their being—with explosive force like a volcanic eruption.

The Bodhisattvas of the Earth constantly practice the Mystic Law and at each moment live in harmony with eternal life. While they are bodhisattvas in their appearance as practitioners, in terms of their state of life they are Buddhas.

President Toda's experience of being present at the Ceremony in the Air as a Bodhisattva of the Earth signifies his entry into the realm of eternal life, the world of truth of the original Buddha.

Endo: His realization that "the Buddha is life itself" thus closely relates to his awareness that he was a Bodhisattva of the Earth.

Ikeda: That's right. President Toda wrote:

> *Awakening*
> *to the life of the Buddha,*

I take pride
in having been a Bodhisattva of the Earth
since the remote past.[9]

He composed this verse in 1951, the year he became the Soka Gakkai's second president.

Saito: The Ceremony in the Air is a cosmic scene that crystallizes the eternity of life. The Bodhisattvas of the Earth reveal in themselves the eternity of life. And the Gohonzon, set within the eternal realm of the Ceremony in the Air, embodies the life of Nichiren Daishonin, which is one with the eternal Mystic Law.

In that sense, President Toda's experience signifies his having entered the realm of the Gohonzon. When he returned to his home in 1945 after his release from prison, President Toda immediately sat upright before the Gohonzon and carefully examined the writing on it, thereby confirming the truth of the enlightenment he had attained.

Endo: In your book *The Human Revolution*, President Ikeda, you describe this moment as follows:

> He removed his glasses and scrutinized each character, bending so close it seemed his face would touch the scroll.
>
> "It was just like this. No mistake. Exactly, just as I saw it . . ."
>
> Murmuring silently, he satisfied himself that the solemn and mysterious Ceremony in the Air he had witnessed in his cell was indeed inscribed on the Gohonzon. Profound delight surged through him and tears streamed down his face . . . He cried out from the depths of his being: "Gohonzon! Daishonin! I, Toda, will accomplish kosen-rufu!"[10]

Ikeda: In a well-known passage, the Daishonin says: "Never seek this Gohonzon outside yourself. The Gohonzon exists only within the mortal flesh of us ordinary people who embrace the Lotus Sutra and chant Nam-myoho-renge-kyo" (WND-1, 832). President Toda vividly felt the truth of these lines. Just as the Daishonin teaches when he says that through faith one can "enter the treasure tower of the Gohonzon" (WND-1, 832), he "entered" the treasure tower and took his place at the Ceremony in the Air.

The Gohonzon is itself the treasure tower, and the treasure tower is none other than one's own life. President Toda grasped this truth with his entire being.

THE LOTUS SUTRA PORTRAYS THE DRAMA IN ALL PEOPLE'S LIVES

Saito: President Toda attained that enlightenment in his heart. Had someone been there with him while he had this experience in prison, that person, of course, could not have seen the Ceremony in the Air.

Ikeda: It's something that he perceived within his own life. President Toda explained that the Lotus Sutra itself is a teaching that came out of Shakyamuni's very own life. What was foreshadowed in the "Introduction" and "Supernatural Powers of the Thus Come One" chapters, as well as Shakyamuni's exchanges with the voice-hearers and bodhisattvas, the astonishing appearance of the treasure tower, the emergence of the Bodhisattvas of the Earth — we can interpret all of these as dramas taking place in Shakyamuni's own life.

Suda: When I visited Eagle Peak in India, the setting of Shakyamuni's preaching of the Lotus Sutra, there was someone in our party who purportedly went around trying to find a chasm of some kind in the earth from which the Bodhisattvas of the Earth might have emerged. But this and other events in the sutra shall be taken as dramas occurring within Shakyamuni's life; they are not to be interpreted literally.

Ikeda: While not historically factual, the events described in the sutra do express truths about life and the nature of existence.

Saito: For purposes of convenience, we have at times discussed the events of the Lotus Sutra as though they really happened. That is because they can be thought of as expressing the truth of life.

Endo: If we say that the Lotus Sutra is a teaching arising from Shakyamuni's own life, then Shakyamuni's identity becomes an issue. That is to say, the Shakyamuni appearing in the Lotus Sutra becomes "Shakyamuni in Shakyamuni's own life."

Ikeda: Shakyamuni's appearance in the Lotus Sutra represents Shakyamuni's true self. In a sense, the reason for the development from the theoretical teaching (or first half) of the Lotus Sutra to the essential teaching (or second half) is to enable Shakyamuni to reveal his true self. The other figures who appear and the various events that occur all function to assist in this revelation.

Saito: The original Buddha of the "Life Span" chapter, who has been enlightened since the remote past, corresponds to Shakyamuni's true self.

Ikeda: That's right. The original Buddha enlightened since the remote past is the eternal self that is one with the eternal Mystic Law.

Suda: The Bodhisattvas of the Earth must also exist in Shakyamuni's life.

Ikeda: They are eternal bodhisattvas representing an aspect of Shakyamuni's eternal self. *The Record of the Orally Transmitted*

Teachings says, "In order first of all to reveal the identity of the Buddha of the original state who is eternally endowed with the three bodies, the Buddha summons forth the disciples of the essential teaching whom Shakyamuni taught in his original state" (OTT, 232).

This is not only true for Shakyamuni. The Daishonin says, "A single individual has been used as an example, but the same thing applies equally to all living beings" (WND-2, 844). Shakyamuni's eternal self is the eternal self of all living beings. In a broad sense, all beings are original Buddhas. The Bodhisattvas of the Earth are therefore eternal bodhisattvas existing in the lives of all people. The Daishonin explains this, saying: "Shakyamuni Buddha, who has attained perfect enlightenment, is our own flesh and blood. His practices and the resulting virtues are our bones and marrow" (WND-1, 365); "The Shakyamuni Buddha within our lives is the eternal Buddha since time without beginning" (WND-1, 365); and, "The bodhisattvas Superior Practices, Boundless Practices, Pure Practices, and Firmly Established Practices[11] represent the world of the bodhisattva within ourselves" (WND-1, 366).

Endo: The drama of the Lotus Sutra takes place in the lives of all people. The same can be said of the Gohonzon, which is the Lotus Sutra of Nichiren Daishonin.

Ikeda: Based on the Ceremony in the Air described in the Lotus Sutra, Nichiren Daishonin manifested his eternal self in the form of the Gohonzon. The Daishonin's eternal self, needless to say, is Nam-myoho-renge-kyo; accordingly, down the middle of the Gohonzon are inscribed the characters "Nam-myoho-renge-kyo Nichiren."

Saito: In Nichiren's writings, he says, "I, Nichiren, have inscribed my life in sumi[12] ink ... the soul of Nichiren is nothing other than Nam-myoho-renge-kyo" (WND-1, 412).

Ikeda: We can think of President Toda's enlightenment in prison as the moment in which he connected with his eternal self as the leader of the movement to propagate the Mystic Law. That was the meaning of his presence at the Ceremony in the Air. What he awakened to in that instant was the unmistakable truth of life, the fundamental transcendent reality. Therefore, President Toda talked about the Ceremony in the Air as a fact. And he said that Soka Gakkai members were also all present there.

Endo: He once humorously remarked that those who have difficulty grasping Buddhist concepts are the ones who, during the Ceremony in the Air, were dozing off in spite of themselves at the back of the crowd.[13]

Saito: Again, President Toda once said: "The Gohonzon exists within our own lives. The quintessence of faith in Nichiren Buddhism is to believe that our own lives and the Gohonzon enshrined in the altar are one and the same."[14] I think this was his way of expressing what he had realized while in prison.

Suda: President Toda stated that the vision of the Ceremony in the Air he had while in prison did not differ in the least from the appearance of the Gohonzon that the Daishonin inscribed. This seems to me evidence that President Toda truly entered the Gohonzon.

Ikeda: President Toda fought the devilish nature of power head-on. And through his faith to wage such a struggle he attained an immense state of life. This is the principle of attaining enlightenment through faith. He could then read and comprehend the Lotus Sutra. That's because he grasped with his life that the Lotus Sutra explains the eternal Mystic Law, or Nam-myoho-renge-kyo. That's why he often said, "It's simply impossible to read the Lotus Sutra without faith in the Gohonzon."

Suda: While in prison, President Toda grappled with the Lotus Sutra as he struggled to chant daimoku and ponder its meaning. But at the same time, it was a struggle to dig into the depths of his life.

Ikeda: Through thoroughly pursuing the question "What is the Buddha?" he came to realize that the Buddha is none other than the self and the great life of the universe; that these two — the self and the universe — are in fact one.

Just as the saying, "Start digging right where you are, for there lies the source!" implies, when we dig into the inner reaches of our own being, the common foundation of life that all people share comes into view. This foundation is none other than the eternal life of the universe. President Toda became enlightened not only to the wellspring at the core of his own being, but also to the foundation of life that all people share. He realized that, as he put it, "in essence, all people are in fact Bodhisattvas of the Earth."

With that conviction President Toda racked his brain to find a way to enable all members to share that same profound level of confidence in their lives. Sometimes in urging the members to work together to accomplish the goal of kosen-rufu, he would address them as "fellow Bodhisattvas of the Earth." President Toda wholeheartedly sought to teach us the nobility and strength we can attain by basing ourselves on an awareness of the truth as the wellspring of our being. He showed actual proof of this truth through his own life. Because of his conviction, the members of the SGI now share this awareness of the common "homeland of life."

The power of one person is truly immense. Such power and strength cannot fail to be activated in those who awaken to their mission as Bodhisattvas of the Earth. Such confidence is the starting point for everything. The very wellspring of our lives is free of all impurity and as vast as the universe. Accomplishing human revolution means realizing and showing actual proof of the existence of this life.

"The Universe Is Itself Compassion"

Saito: Regarding these Bodhisattvas of the Earth, *The Record of the Orally Transmitted Teachings* says, "All the thousand plants and ten thousand trees in the world, there are none that are not in essence bodhisattvas who emerge from the earth" (OTT, 119). This is a little difficult to understand, because we tend to have an image of the Bodhisattvas of the Earth as people.

Endo: The Bodhisattvas of the Earth can perhaps be thought of more in terms of a function that brings living beings benefit. That passage in *The Record of the Orally Transmitted Teachings* continues, "Thus we may say that the bodhisattvas who emerge from the earth are the bodhisattvas of the essential teaching. The word 'essential' or 'original' represents the merits handed down from the past of numberless major world system dust particle kalpas ago, the merits that are without beginning and without end"[15] (OTT, 119).

Ikeda: I think we might find a guideline for interpreting these passages in President Toda's essay "On Compassion."[16] In conclusion, he says, "The universe is itself an entity of compassion." The universe gives life to all things, causing them to come into being, to change, and to repeatedly undergo the cycle of birth and death. The great life that is this universe is itself the entity of the Buddha. It is the entity of the Buddha eternally possessing the three enlightened bodies — Law, wisdom and action.

The compassion of the universe is the function of the Buddha. It is also the function of the inherent world of Bodhisattva, the power of the Bodhisattvas of the Earth. Therefore, in a general sense, all living things in the universe are sacred Bodhisattvas of the Earth; whereas in a specific sense, Bodhisattvas of the Earth refers to those awakened to this law of life.

The path of the bodhisattva lies in supremely humane action. Such action, fundamentally, is at one with the function of the universe's compassion. When we pray, speak out and take action for the happiness of a friend, the eternal life of the universe manifests through our thoughts, words and deeds.

Endo: I feel I have gained a clear sense of Buddhist humanism, which is as vast as the universe. Moreover [in contrast to secular humanism], this humanism is respectful of the sanctity of all things, including even mountains and rivers, plants and trees.

Saito: The Bodhisattvas of the Earth appearing in the Lotus Sutra are described as "filling the sky over immeasurable hundreds, thousands, ten thousands, and millions of lands" (LSOC, 254). This is truly universal in scale; they completely occupy all space.

Suda: This is a depiction of a gathering of countless beings who manifest the principle that the universe is itself compassion. How solemn! What a grand drama! When we open our eyes to the teaching of the "Emerging from the Earth" chapter, it becomes only too obvious how truly petty and insignificant are the discrimination and egoism rampant in society.

Saito: I recall the poem "The Sun of *Jiyu* Over a New Land," which you presented to friends in Los Angeles, President Ikeda. In that poem, you describe the Bodhisattvas of the Earth as "roots" that cut through all differences. You write:

> *As each group seeks their separate*
> *roots and origins,*
> *society fractures along a thousand fissure lines.*
> *When neighbors distance themselves*
> *from neighbors, continue your*
> *uncompromising quest*
> *for your truer roots*
> *in the deepest regions of your life.*
> *Seek out the primordial "roots" of humankind.*

Then you will without fail discover
the stately expanse of Jiyu
unfolding in the depths of your life.

Here is the home, the dwelling place
to which humankind traces
its original existence—
beyond all borders,
beyond all diVerences of gender and race.
Here is a world oVering true proof
of our humanity.

If one reaches back to these fundamental roots,
all become friends and comrades.
To realize this is to "emerge from the earth."[17]

Suda: Everyone is sacred. Everyone is an irreplaceable and unique existence. Moreover, everyone is a child of the great earth of life. This is what the "Emerging from the Earth" chapter teaches.

Endo: Only one year before you composed this poem, tragedy had visited Los Angeles. A group of white police officers were on trial for brutally beating an African American man whom they had apprehended for a traffic violation. When an all-white jury handed down a verdict of "not guilty," racial tensions exploded, resulting in widespread civil unrest [in 1992].

Ikeda: Discrimination is absolutely evil. Those whose minds are clouded by discrimination injure the lives of others as well as themselves. To try to locate the roots of one's identity in a particular racial or ethnic group is an illusion. It is like a mirage in the desert. Such a sense of identity, far from serving as a common "homeland of life" that can be shared by all, only heightens distinctions between oneself and others and becomes an underlying cause of conflict and strife.

Today we need a transformation in how society views the human being. When people's view of the human being changes, everything will change. "You must not yoke yourself to nationality or to ethnicity. You must not think of yourself as powerless or as 'no more than a collection of matter.' You must not regard yourself as a slave to your genes. Fundamentally, you have limitless and immense potential. Fundamentally, the human being is one with the universe! Such is the immense power of one person!" This is the message of the Lotus Sutra.

Endo: That is why it is called the sutra of hope.

THE MIND IS NOT MERELY A FUNCTION OF THE BRAIN

Suda: The tendency to view people as machines made of living matter and to see the spirit as no more than a function of the brain is emblematic of the modern age. The assumption seems to be that advances in the neurosciences will eventually fully elucidate all phenomena of the spirit.

Saito: There is no time to go into a detailed discussion here, but contrary to this idea is also the view that "the more we discover about the brain, the more clearly do we distinguish between the brain events and the mental phenomena, and the more wonderful do both the brain events and the mental phenomena become."[18]

Ikeda: There is also a view of the brain as a tool of the mind and as a venue where spiritual phenomena are worked out. It may be true that without the functioning of the brain, the mind would have no means to express itself. Still, I believe, as current research about the brain and the mind seems to indicate, that the two are in no sense identical.

In modern terms, we may say that the brain is like a wonderful computer; yet, it is ultimately a tool. What uses this tool is the subjective entity called the mind. The mind cannot be a locally defined entity contained within the body or the brain, although many people today seem to suppose so. Scientific research is making this increasingly clear. The mind is more vast and expansive; it has a breadth that transcends material restrictions.

For instance, the American clinical physician Larry Dossey says: "There is good evidence that the mind cannot be localized. It displays its nonlocal character in a million ways, showing us that it is free in space and time, that it bridges consciousness between persons, and that it does not die with the body."[19]

The mind that transcends time and space is an entity whose dimensions are not locally circumscribed; the mind possesses the potential to transcend the small self. Dr. Dossey also writes: "If nonlocal mind is a reality, the world becomes a place of interaction and connection, not one of isolation and disjunction. And if humanity really believed that nonlocal mind were real, an entirely new foundation for ethical and moral behavior would enter, which would hold at least the possibility of a radical departure from the insane ways human beings and nation-states have chronically behaved toward each other."[20]

Endo: The infinite expanse of the mind—this is what the doctrine of the three thousand realms in a single moment of life explains.

Saito: In "On Attaining Buddhahood in This Lifetime," there is the famous passage, "Life at each moment permeates the entire realm of phenomena and is revealed in all phenomena" (WND-1, 3). One senses from passages like this that science is approaching the view of life of Buddhism.

The Lotus Sutra Teaches the True Way of Humanity

Ikeda: Dr. Dossey further states: "If we continue in the ways in which we have conceptualized ourselves for hundreds of years, it is no longer certain that we will have a future on this Earth. If we are to survive, a sacred regard for the Earth and all things in it must arise once more."[21]

Buddhism greatly transforms "the ways in which we have conceptualized ourselves." This is not merely an intellectual transformation; it manifests in the practice of compassion; that is, in altered patterns of behavior. It could be termed a transformation of people's fundamental state of life. And the appearance of the Bodhisattvas of the Earth could be thought of as its grand prelude. Simply put, to have faith in the Lotus Sutra is to have faith in humanity. This is what President Toda said.

Saito: In other words, the human being is truly great. Ralph Waldo Emerson, the flag-bearer of the American renaissance, makes a very interesting comment to the same effect. He says: "The Belief in Christianity that now prevails is the Unbelief of men. They will have Christ for a lord & not for a brother. Christ preaches the greatness of Man but we hear only the greatness of Christ."[22]

Ikeda: Such insight is typical of Emerson. He's right of course. Neither the state nor ideology is sacred, nor is any superhuman Buddha or deity.

The Bodhisattvas of the Earth are in fact Buddhas. But the term *Buddha* is inevitably taken to mean a being somehow transcendental or superior to ordinary human beings. The Bodhisattvas of the Earth thoroughly devote themselves to the way of bodhisattvas as people who carry out Buddhist practice. They thoroughly devote themselves to the way of human beings. This point is tremendously significant.

The restoration of trust and belief in humanity will be the key to religion in the twenty-first century, which is the theme of our discussions.

Suda: The teaching of the Lotus Sutra does indeed stand on the forefront of the age.

Ikeda: For instance, one could argue that the collapse of the Soviet Union — a major change of the latter half of this century — fundamentally arose from an inner thirst in human beings.

Endo: Shimon Peres, the former prime minister of Israel [and Nobel Peace Prize laureate], said: "The Communist Party was not beaten by another party opposing it. The Communist Party was beaten by its own children and not by its rivals. The Soviet Union did not come apart under the impact of American pressure, European intervention, or a Chinese threat. The pressure did not come from without, it sprang from within. This gigantic change in human organization occurred without the army's guns, without political parties' banners, and without superpower threats."[23]

Endo: Peres, looking back on the circumstances of the time, recalled a particularly poignant scene: "One of the most captivating images during the attempted coup against Mikhail Gorbachev was that of a battalion of Red Army soldiers in front of the Russian Parliament, Moscow's 'White House.' The soldiers were indifferent, with a 'who cares' attitude, when suddenly an old Russian woman, a babouchka, went up to them and said: 'Children, what are you doing here? Go home!' It was almost as if the babouchka were the sole commander of the Red Army."[24]

Saito: Given the tenseness of the situation, this was a really courageous woman. Peres' description reminds me of the women of the Many Treasure Group who have steadfastly fought for kosen-rufu since the early days of the Soka Gakkai.

Ikeda: At the crucial moment, ordinary people are the strongest. The thoroughly polished core humanity of the ordinary people shines the brightest. Faith in the Mystic Law enables us to bring out the full brilliance of this essential human core.

Nichiren Daishonin declares, "Nichiren alone took the lead in carrying out the task of the Bodhisattvas of the Earth" (WND-1,

385). Reading this line fills me with profound emotion. The great struggle of the human revolution is the dawn of life that humankind has eagerly awaited. It is the dawn of a new history. The human revolution is a liberation of the human being on the most fundamental level of life, on a dimension ranging over eternity. Nichiren Daishonin stood up alone to enable all people to accomplish this liberation.

We who have gathered beneath the banner of the Law borne by the Bodhisattvas of the Earth share a mystic connection from the distant past. The famous Gakkai song "Doshi no Uta" (Song of Comrades) refers to this with the line: "I now receive the Buddha's decree . . ."

When we understand this, we can see our marvelous mission. It is as though the gears of our lives mesh with a million-horse-power engine. Tremendous energy wells forth, and we develop a self of awesome vitality and strength.

NOTES

1. *Toda Josei zenshu* (Collected Writings of Josei Toda) (Tokyo: Seikyo Shimbunsha, 1983), vol. 3, p. 171.

2. The Daishonin states in his writings, "In this latter age, there cannot be anyone else who upholds the Lotus Sutra twenty-four hours of the day and night without making a deliberate effort to do so" (WND-1, 43).

3. *Toda Josei zenshu* (Tokyo: Seikyo Shimbunsha, 1988), vol. 8, pp. 517–18.

4. Ibid., p. 519.

5. T'ien-t'ai, *The Words and Phrases of the Lotus Sutra.*

6. *Nichijun Shonin zenshu* (Collected Writings of Nichijun Shonin) (Fujinomiya: Nichiren Shoshu Fukyokai, 1960), p. 357. Nam-myoho-renge-kyo consists of seven Chinese characters; Myoho-renge-kyo consists of five.

7. The "thirty-four negations" describing the entity of the Buddha appear in the "Virtuous Practices" (Jpn Tokugyo, or the first) chapter of the Immeasurable Meanings Sutra. President Toda read the sutra with his whole life and finally perceived that the Buddha is life itself.

8. *Makiguchi Tsunesaburo shingenshu* (Collection of Tsunesaburo Makiguchi's Sayings), ed. Takehisa Tsuji (Tokyo: Daisan Bummeisha, 1979), p. 23.

9. *Toda Josei zenshu* (Tokyo: Seikyo Shimbunsha, 1981), vol. 1, p. 416.

10. Daisaku Ikeda, *The Human Revolution* (Santa Monica, California: World Tribune Press, 2004), p. 20.

11. The four bodhisattvas: Superior Practices, Boundless Practices, Pure Practices and Firmly Established Practices.

12. Sumi: Black Chinese ink.

13. *Toda Josei zenshu* (Tokyo: Seikyo Shimbunsha, 1982), vol. 2, p. 39.

14. *Toda Josei zenshu*, vol. 5, p. 283.

15. Numberless major world system dust particle *kalpas*: An immensely long period of time described in the "Life Span" chapter of the Lotus Sutra, which indicates how much time has elapsed since Shakyamuni's original enlightenment.

16. *Toda Josei zenshu*, vol. 3, pp. 44–45.

17. Daisaku Ikeda, *Songs for America* (Santa Monica, Calif.: World Tribune Press, 2000), pp. 38–39.

18. Sir John Eccles and Daniel N. Robinson, *The Wonder of Being Human: Our Brain and Our Mind* (New York: The Free Press, a division of Macmillan, Inc., 1984), p. 36.

19. Larry Dossey, *Recovering the Soul—A Scientific and Spiritual Search* (New York: Bantam Books, 1989), p. 2.

20. Ibid., p. 7.

21. Ibid., p. 11.

22. *The Journals and Miscellaneous Notebooks of Ralph Waldo Emerson*, vol. 5, ed. Merton M. Sealts, Jr. (Cambridge, MA: The Belknap Press of Harvard University Press, 1965), p. 459.

23. *At Century's End*, ed. Nathan P. Gardels (La Jolla, CA: Alti Publishers, 1995), p. 301.

24. Ibid.

Glossary

benefit   (Jpn *kudoku*) *Ku* means to extinguish evil and *doku* means to bring forth good.

bodhisattva   A being who aspires to attain Buddhahood and carries out altruistic practices to achieve that goal. Compassion predominates in bodhisattvas, who postpone their own entry into nirvana in order to lead others toward enlightenment.

Bodhisattvas of the Earth   Those who chant and propagate Nam-myoho-renge-kyo. *Earth* indicates the enlightened nature of all people. The term describes the innumerable bodhisattvas who appear in the "Emerging from the Earth" chapter of the Lotus Sutra and are entrusted by Shakyamuni with the task of propagating the Law after his passing. In several of his writings, Nichiren Daishonin identifies his own role with that of their leader, Bodhisattva Superior Practices.

Buddhahood   The state a Buddha has attained. The ultimate goal of Buddhist practice. The highest of the Ten Worlds. The word *enlightenment* is often interchangeable with Buddhahood.

consistency from beginning to end   The last of the ten factors mentioned in the "Expedient Means" chapter of the Lotus Sutra. It is the integrating factor that unifies the other nine in every moment of life.

conspicuous benefit   Benefit that appears in clearly recognizable form.

daimoku   Literally, "title." (1) The title of a sutra, in particular the title of the Lotus Sutra, Myoho-renge-kyo. (2) The invocation of Nam-myoho-renge-kyo in Nichiren Buddhism.

Daishonin   Literally, "great sage." In particular, this honorific title is applied to Nichiren to show reverence for him as the Buddha who appears in the Latter Day of the Law to save all humankind.

Devadatta   A disciple of Shakyamuni Buddha who later turned against him.

devil king of the sixth heaven   The king of devils, who dwells in the highest of the six heavens of the world of desire. He works to obstruct Buddhist practice and delights in sapping the life force of other beings. He is also regarded as the manifestation of the fundamental darkness inherent in life. Also called the heavenly devil.

Eagle Peak   (Skt Gridhrakuta) Also, Vulture Peak. A mountain located to the northeast of Rajagriha, the capital of Magadha in ancient India, where Shakyamuni is said to have expounded the Lotus Sutra. Eagle Peak also symbolizes the Buddha land or the state of Buddhahood. In this sense, the "pure land of Eagle Peak" is often used.

essential teachings   (1) The teaching expounded by Shakyamuni from the perspective of his true identity as the Buddha who attained enlightenment numberless major world system dust particle *kalpas* ago. T'ien-t'ai classifies the last fourteen chapters of the Lotus Sutra as the essential teaching. (2) The essential teaching of the Latter Day of the Law, that is, the teaching of Nam-myoho-renge-kyo.

five components   Also, the five components of life and the five aggregates. The constituent elements of form, perception, conception, volition and consciousness that unite temporarily to form an individual living being. The five components also constitute the first of the three realms of existence.

Four Peaceful Practices, The   A work by Nan-yüeh. The formal title is *On the Peaceful Practices of the Lotus Sutra*. It explains practices set forth in the Lotus Sutra, particularly those mentioned in the "Peaceful Practices" chapter. The four peaceful practices are those of deeds, words, thoughts and vows set forth in that chapter.

four sufferings   The four universal sufferings of birth, old age, sickness and death. Shakyamuni's quest for enlightenment is said to have been motivated by a desire to find a solution to these four sufferings.

fundamental darkness   Also, fundamental ignorance. The most deeply rooted illusion inherent in life, which gives rise to all other illusions and earthly desires.

Gohonzon   *Go* means "worthy of honor" and *honzon* means "object of fundamental respect." The object of devotion in Nichiren Buddhism and the embodiment of the Mystic Law permeating all phenomena. It takes the form of a mandala inscribed on paper or on wood with the characters representing the Mystic Law as well as the Ten Worlds, including Buddhahood. Nichiren Buddhism holds that all people possess the Buddha nature and can attain Buddhahood through faith in the Gohonzon.

gongyo Literally, "assiduous practice." In Nichiren Buddhism, it means to chant Nam-myoho-renge-kyo and recite portions of the "Expedient Means" and "Life Span" chapters of the Lotus Sutra. It is performed morning and evening.

Hinayana The teaching that aims at attaining the state of *arhat*. Hinayana, literally "lesser vehicle," was originally a pejorative term used by Mahayana Buddhists, who regarded the practitioners of these teachings as preoccupied solely with achieving personal emancipation and indifferent to the salvation of others. Hinayana teachings are represented by the doctrines of the four noble truths and the twelve-linked chain of causation. They regard earthly desires as the cause of suffering and assert that suffering is eliminated only by eradicating earthly desires.

human revolution A concept coined by the Soka Gakkai's second president, Josei Toda, to indicate the self-reformation of an individual — the strengthening of life force and the establishment of Buddhahood — that is the goal of Buddhist practice.

inconspicuous benefit Benefit that accumulates over a period of time and is not immediately recognizable.

jiyu Literally, "emerging from the earth."

kalpa An extremely long period of time. Sutras and treatises differ in their definitions, but *kalpas* fall into two major categories, those of measurable and immeasurable duration. There are three kinds of measurable *kalpas*: small, medium and major. One explanation sets the length of a small *kalpa* at approximately sixteen million years. According to Buddhist cosmology, a world repeatedly undergoes four stages: formation, continuance, decline and disintegration. Each of these four stages lasts for twenty small *kalpas* and is equal to one medium *kalpa*. Finally, one complete cycle forms a major *kalpa*.

karma Potential energies residing in the inner realm of life, which manifest themselves as various results in the future. In Buddhism, karma is interpreted as meaning mental, verbal and physical action, that is, thoughts, words and deeds.

kosen-rufu   Literally, to "widely declare and spread [Buddhism]." Nichiren Daishonin defines Nam-myoho-renge-kyo of the Three Great Secret Laws as the law to be widely declared and spread during the Latter Day. There are two aspects of kosen-rufu: the kosen-rufu of the entity of the Law, or the establishment of the Dai-Gohonzon, which is the basis of the Three Great Secret Laws; and the kosen-rufu of substantiation, the widespread acceptance of faith in the Dai-Gohonzon among the people.

ku   A fundamental Buddhist concept, variously translated as nonsubstantiality, emptiness, void, latency, relativity, etc. The concept that entities have no fixed or independent nature.

Latter Day of the Law   Also, the Latter Day. The last of the three periods following Shakyamuni Buddha's death when Buddhism falls into confusion and Shakyamuni's teachings lose the power to lead people to enlightenment. A time when the essence of the Lotus Sutra will be propagated to save all humankind.

Lotus Sutra   The highest teaching of Shakyamuni Buddha, it reveals that all people can attain enlightenment and declares that his former teachings should be regarded as preparatory.

mahasattva   A "great being." Another term for bodhisattva.

Mahayana Buddhism   The teachings which expound the bodhisattva practice as the means toward the enlightenment of both oneself and others, in contrast to Hinayana Buddhism, or the teaching of the Agon period, which aims only at personal salvation. Mahayana literally means "greater vehicle."

mentor–and–disciple relationship   See *oneness of mentor and disciple*.

Miao-lo   The sixth patriarch in the lineage of the T'ien-t'ai school in China, counting from the Great Teacher T'ien-t'ai. Miao-lo reasserted the supremacy of the Lotus Sutra and wrote commentaries on T'ien-t'ai's three major works, thus bringing about a revival of interest in T'ien-t'ai Buddhism. He is revered as the restorer of the school.

Middle Day of the Law   Also, the period of the Counterfeit Law. The second of the three periods following a Buddha's death. During this time the Buddha's teaching gradually becomes formalized, the people's connection to it weakens, and progressively fewer people are able to gain enlightenment through its practice. Some sources define the Middle Day of the Law of Shakyamuni as lasting a thousand years, while others define it as five hundred years.

mutual possession of the Ten Worlds   The principle that each of the Ten Worlds contains all the other nine as potential within itself. This is taken to mean that an individual's state of life can be changed, and that all beings of the nine worlds possess the potential for Buddhahood. See also *Ten Worlds*.

Mystic Law   The ultimate law of life and the universe. The law of Nam-myoho-renge-kyo.

Nam-myoho-renge-kyo   The ultimate law of the true aspect of life permeating all phenomena in the universe. The invocation established by Nichiren Daishonin on April 28, 1253. Nichiren Daishonin teaches that this phrase encompasses all laws and teachings within itself, and that the benefit of chanting Nam-myoho-renge-kyo includes the benefit of conducting all virtuous practices. *Nam* means "devotion to"; *myoho* means "Mystic Law"; *renge* refers to the lotus flower, which simultaneously blooms and seeds, indicating the simultaneity of cause and effect; *kyo* means sutra, the teaching of a Buddha.

Nichiren Daishonin   The thirteenth-century Japanese Buddhist teacher and reformer who taught that all people have the potential for enlightenment. He defined the universal law as Nam-myoho-renge-kyo and established the Gohonzon as the object of devotion for all people to attain Buddhahood. Daishonin is an honorific title that means "great sage."

nonsubstantiality   One of the three truths. The truth of nonsubstantiality means that all phenomena are nonsubstantial and in a state transcending the concepts of existence and nonexistence.

oneness of body and mind   A principle explaining that the two seemingly distinct phenomena of body, or the physical aspect of life, and mind, or its spiritual aspect, are two integral phases of the same entity.

oneness of life and environment   The principle stating that the self and its environment are two integral phases of the same entity.

oneness of mentor and disciple   This is a philosophical as well as a practical concept. Disciples reach the same state of Buddhahood as their master by practicing the teachings of the latter. In Nichiren Buddhism, this is the direct way to enlightenment, that is, to believe in the Gohonzon and practice according to the Daishonin's teachings.

seven kinds of treasures   Also, the seven treasures. Seven precious substances. The list differs among the Buddhist scriptures. In the Lotus Sutra, the seven are gold, silver, lapis lazuli, seashell, agate, pearl and carnelian.

shakubuku   A method of propagating Buddhism by refuting another's attachment to heretical views and thus leading him or her to the correct Buddhist teaching.

Shakyamuni   Also, Siddhartha Gautama. Born in India (present-day southern Nepal) about three thousand years ago, he is the first recorded Buddha and founder of Buddhism. For fifty years, he expounded various sutras (teachings), culminating in the Lotus Sutra.

six difficult and nine easy acts   Comparisons expounded in the "Treasure Tower" chapter of the Lotus Sutra to teach people how difficult it would be to embrace and propagate the sutra in the Latter Day of the Law. The six difficult acts are to propagate the Lotus Sutra widely, to copy it or cause someone else to copy it, to recite it even for a short while, to teach it even to one person, to hear of and accept the Lotus Sutra and inquire about its meaning, and to maintain faith in it. The nine easy acts include such feats as teaching innumerable sutras other than the Lotus Sutra, walking across a burning prairie carrying a bundle of hay on one's back without being burned, and kicking a major world system into a different quarter.

Soka   Literally, "value creation."

Ten Worlds   Ten life-conditions that a single entity of life manifests. Originally the Ten Worlds were viewed as distinct physical places, each with its own particular inhabitants. In light of the Lotus Sutra, they are interpreted as potential conditions of life inherent in each individual. The ten are: (1) hell, (2) hunger, (3) animality, (4) anger, (5) humanity or tranquillity, (6) rapture, (7) voice-hearers or learning, (8) cause-awakened ones or realization, (9) bodhisattva and (10) Buddhahood.

theoretical teachings   The first fourteen chapters of the twenty-eight chapter Lotus Sutra, as classified by T'ien-t'ai. In contrast to the essential teaching—the latter fourteen chapters of the sutra, which represent preaching by Shakyamuni as the Buddha who attained enlightenment in the remote past, the theoretical teaching represents preaching by the historical Shakyamuni, who first attained enlightenment during his lifetime in India. The core of the theoretical teaching is the "Expedient Means" chapter, which teaches that all phenomena manifest the true aspect and that all phenomena are endowed with the ten factors.

Theravada "Teaching of the Elders." One of two main branches of Buddhism, together with Mahayana. It teaches that since Buddhahood is almost impossible to attain, one should aim for the lesser goal of *arhat*, or worthy. Emphasizes a strict adherence to discipline and a literal interpretation of doctrine.

three assemblies in two places A division of the Lotus Sutra according to the location and sequence of the events described in it. The three assemblies are the first assembly on Eagle Peak, the Ceremony in the Air and the second assembly on Eagle Peak. The two places are on Eagle Peak and in the air.

three existences Past, present and future. The dimension of time. The three aspects of the eternity of life, linked inseparably by the law of cause and effect. "Throughout the three existences" means throughout eternity.

Three Great Secret Laws The object of devotion of Buddhism, the invocation or daimoku of Buddhism and the high sanctuary of Buddhism. These three constitute the core of Nichiren Buddhism.

three obstacles and four devils Various obstacles and hindrances to the practice of Buddhism. The three obstacles are: 1) the obstacle of earthly desires; 2) the obstacle of karma, which may also refer to opposition from one's spouse or children; and 3) the obstacle of retribution, also obstacles caused by one's superiors, such as rulers or parents. The four devils are: 1) the hindrance of the five components; 2) the hindrance of earthly desires; 3) the hindrance of death, because untimely death obstructs one's practice of Buddhism or because the premature death of another practitioner causes doubts; and 4) the hindrance of the devil king.

three poisons Greed, anger and foolishness. The fundamental evils inherent in life that give rise to human suffering.

three powerful enemies   Also, the three types of enemies. Three types of people who persecute those who propagate the Lotus Sutra after the Buddha's passing, as described in the "Encouraging Devotion" chapter of the sutra. They are: (1) lay people ignorant of Buddhism who denounce the votaries of the Lotus Sutra and attack them with swords or staves; (2) arrogant and cunning priests who slander the votaries; and (3) priests respected by the general public who, fearing the loss of fame or profit, induce the secular authorities to persecute the sutra's votaries.

three thousand realms in a single moment of life   A philosophical system set forth by T'ien-t'ai in his *Great Concentration and Insight*, clarifying the mutually inclusive relationship of the ultimate truth and the phenomenal world. This means that the life of Buddhahood is universally inherent in all beings, and the distinction between a common person and a Buddha is a phenomenal one.

Thus Come One   One of the ten honorable titles for a Buddha, meaning one who has arrived from the world of truth. That is, the Buddha appears from the world of enlightenment and, as a person who embodies wisdom and compassion, leads other beings to enlightenment.

T'ien-t'ai   Also called Chih-I. The founder of the T'ien-t'ai school, commonly referred to as the Great Teacher T'ien-t'ai.

treasure tower   A tower adorned with treasures. A treasure tower often appears in Buddhist scriptures. In Nichiren Daishonin's writings, the treasure tower primarily indicates the tower of the Buddha Many Treasures that appears from beneath the earth in the "Treasure Tower" chapter of the Lotus Sutra. He also equated this with the Gohonzon and human life.

voice-hearers   Shakyamuni Buddha's disciples. Those who listen to his preaching and strive to attain enlightenment. In this sense, voice-hearers are also called voice-hearer disciples. Voice-hearers also denote those who hear the teaching of the four noble truths and aim at attaining the state of *arhat*.

Index

"breaking through the earth," symbolizes, 215–16

Bruno, Giordano, 211

Buddha, 57, 81, 201; characteristics of a true, 153; epitome of the, 119; and the existence of the world of hell, 77; narrow view of a, 87; original, 259; struggle of a, 188; three enlightened bodies of the, 267; true, 19; way of life of a, 130; what is a, 266

"Buddha is life," relationship of Toda's awakening as a Bodhisattva of the Earth to his earlier revelation that the, 257–58, 260

Buddhahood, attaining, in one's present form, 69–71; benefit of tapping into our, 38; condition of, 227; consequences if women were incapable of attaining, 101; experiencing, 258; factors preventing the attaining of, 258; manifesting, 18; meaning of attaining, 120; practice for attaining, 168; reason for dragon girl changing into a man to attain, 103–04; seed for attaining, 232; as seen by Josei Toda, 15; way to attain, 84, 253

Buddha nature, 86

Buddhas of the ten directions, 7, 18, 21–22, 29, 50, 241

Buddhism, 3–4, 36–37, 82; central concern of, 182; essence of, 130; equality of sexes in early Japanese, 112–13; equality of sexes in Nichiren Daishonin's, 111–13, 152; false users of, 141; inner struggle in Nichiren, 55; Johan Galtung's observations about the teachings of, 188; living beings viewed in, 104; major shake up in the existing beliefs with the appearance of the Daishonin's, 211–12; and priests, 3–4; teaching of, 68

bullying, 183

Campbell, Joseph, 3

cause and effect, doctrine of the simultaneity of, 227

Ceremony in the Air, 6, 24–25, 62, 241, 265; beginning of the, 7; crystallizes, 261; purpose for the creation of the, 48. *See also* treasure tower

Chang Shuhong, 238

change, 40

Chappell, David W., 3, 28

Chartier, Emile-Auguste, 138

Chih-li, 88

China, 41–42; represents in Japan, 222

Christianity, dominant aspect of, 118

chrysanthemums, represents in Japan, 222; symbolizes in Portugal, 222

civilization, transforming the fabric of modern 123–24

compassion, 3, 38, 54, 58–59, 77, 123, 246, 272; lacking in, 181

concern, for others, 202

Confessions of Nuns, 108

conflicts, underlying causes of, 269

Confucius, 80

conviction, 161

Copernicus, 210

Costa Rica, 68

country, transforming the destiny of a, 45

Cousins, Norman, 34, 59

daimoku (Nam-myoho-renge-kyo), practice of chanting, 25, 78

Dante, 118

"Declaration for the Abolition of Nuclear Weapons," 57

democracy, 28–29

Dengyo, 147

Descartes, 52

Devadatta, 68–70; characteristics of, 141, 152; five severe precepts of, 153; in past existences, 83–84; precepts put forth by, 74–75; reason for Shakyamuni to call, a good friend, 82; and scheme to replace Shakyamuni, 153; as seen by Josei Toda, 76; as seen by Nichiren Daishonin, 119; significance of the enlightenment of, 120, 122

"Devadatta" chapter (Lotus Sutra), 69, 83–84, 86, 96; dragon girl in the, 93–94; importance of the, 69–71; key to understanding the, 77; outline of the, 77–79; purpose of the, 101, 130; significance of the, 120–21; teaches, 84, 119, 121; truly reading the, 90

devil, 57

devil king of the sixth heaven, function of the, 53–54

Dharmaraksha, 234

dialogue, 186, 188; conducting humanistic, 42; factors affecting an openhearted, 43–44; one-to-one, 135

differences, power to break through all, 216

difficulties, 85; encountering, 188–90, 259

Díez-Hochleitner, Ricardo, 42

discrimination, 100, 268–69

Divine Comedy (Dante), 118, 190

Doamidabutsu (priest), 85

Doryu (priest), 81, 85

"Doshi no Uta" (Song of Comrades), 274

Dossey, Larry, 271

dragon girl, 69–71, 93; enlightenment of, 95–96, 99–103; enlightenment signifies, 98–100, 102, 114, 120–24, 134; as seen by Nichiren Daishonin, 119; stands for, 123; vow of, 97

Eagle Peak (India), 262

earth, 17

earth mother, 236

earthly desires, 85

earthly desires are enlightenment,

principle of, 168; signifies, 120

Eccles, John, 216–17

economics, 159–60

egoism, 80, 90, 268

Egypt, 224

"Emergence of the Treasure Tower" chapter, 16, 95, 130; title of the, 11

"Emerging from the Earth" chapter (Lotus Sutra), 196, 221, 245, 255–56; closes with a question, 206; pledge of the Bodhisattvas of the Earth, 198; reveals, 214, 268–69; title refers to, 197; title in Kumarajiva's Chinese translation, 252

Emerson, Ralph Waldo, 272

Emile (Rousseau), 148–49

encouragement, importance of offering specific, 134–35

"Encouragements of the Bodhisattva Universal Worthy" chapter (Lotus Sutra), 171

"Encouraging Devotion" chapter (Lotus Sutra), 110, 171; central theme of the, 197–98; essence of the, 161; spirit of the, 130, 176; title in Sanskrit text, 137

"Entity of the Mystic Law, The" (Nichiren Daishonin), 81

essential teaching, 16, 22, 209–10; bodhisattva of the, 260; important aspect of the, 208, 2211; reason for the development from the theoretical teaching to the, 263

evil, 79–81, 83, 85, 90; conquering inner, 76, 84; enlightenment for people of, 83, 86; recognizing, 150; refuting, 173; root of, 80

evil people, 70, 75; measures to deal with, 73; nature of, 145

"Expedient Means" chapter (Lotus Sutra), 71, 85; clarifies, 209

faith, 18, 22, 26, 98, 262, 273; benefits of having strong, 24; benefits of possessing joy in, 189; genuine,

form of our, 16; wellspring of our, 266

Lives and Times of Archy and Mehitabel, The (Marquis), 60

Los Angeles, 269

lotus flower, in ancient Orient, 240; in ancient Persia, 239; in Chinese medicine, 231; is compared to in India as, 222; in Egyptian history, 238–39; in Greek history, 238; in Indian history, 233–36, 240; in Indian medicine, 231; in Japanese history, 221, 228; Japanese word for, 225–26; as metaphor in the Lotus Sutra, 226; relationship between the sun and the, 239–40, 242–43; relationship between waterlily and, 222–25; scientific name for, 231; Shakyamuni is compared to the sun and the, 240–42, 244; symbolizes in China, 222, 230; thousand-petaled, 229

Lotus Sutra, oneness of the, and the Daishonin's teachings, 23; benefit of believing in the, 23, 53, 55, 61–62; benefit of propagating the, 46; Chinese title of the, 234; copy found in Dunhuang, 252; as described by Nichiren Daishonin, 244; difficulties in spreading the, 51; difficulty to practice the, in the Latter Day of the Law, 49–50; essence of the, 47, 52, 54, 232, 244, 246, 270; fundamental revelation of the, 99; having faith in the, 272; human endeavors can be reoriented by the, 160; key theme of the, 93; in the Latter Day, 50; objective of studying the, 12; meaning of practicing the, 148; Nichiren Daishonin's, 264; non-discriminatory character of the sexes in the, 110; in order to have a completed, 86–87; power of the, 87, 96; practice of the, 54, 81; rarity in preaching the, 187; reason for Shakyamuni expounding the, 29; Sanskrit title for the, 234; as seen by Josei Toda, 262; Shakyamuni's method of expounding the, 105; spirit of the, 122, 133, 141, 148; teachings of the, 110, 152, 214; votaries of the, 52; way to read the, 265; way to transmission of the, 78

Mahakashyapa Bodhisattva, 218

Mahaprajapati (aunt of Shakyamuni), 106, 134–35

Mahayana Buddhism, 103–04; women attaining Buddhahood in, 109

Maitreya Bodhisattva, 203; in awe of Shakyamuni, 208; famous question of, 206–07; view of Shakyamuni's enlightenment believed by, 205–06

Makiguchi, Tsunesaburo, 50, 80–81, 88, 150, 161; foresight of, 186; spirit of, 254

Makuno, Tomitaro, 230

Man's Search for Meaning, an Introduction to Logotherapy (Frankl), 59

Manchuria, 233

Manjushri Bodhisattva, 95–96, 123, 175, 229; introduction of the dragon girl by, 102–03

Many Treasures Buddha, 8, 13, 17–20, 22, 47, 50, 94, 200, 241; condition to see, 6; function of, 21, 29; vow of, 5, 7

Many Treasures Group, 273; function of, 21

Marquis, Don, 60

Masaryk, Tomas, 29

masculinity, negative aspects of, 121; positive aspects of, 121

Maudgalyayana Bodhisattva, 74

Medicine King Bodhisattva, 132

meetings, large, 133–35

mentor and disciple, eternal oneness of, 201, 209

Daisaku Ikeda, 26; in Kumarajiva's Chinese translation of the Lotus Sutra, 35

Shakra (Hindu god), 61, 120–21

shakubuku (propagation), 171; compassionate practice of, 182; practice of, 172–73. *See also shoju*

Shakyamuni, 6, 8, 10, 17–22, 38–40, 44, 47, 50, 70–72, 80, 94, 103, 130–31, 133–34, 137, 152, 187, 200, 240–41; benefit of expounding the Lotus Sutra after the death of, 132; conversation between the Bodhisattvas of the Earth and, 201–202; Devadatta's schemes to kill, 73; difficulty of expounding the Lotus Sutra after the death of, 131; enlightenment of, 104; events of the Lotus Sutra and life of, 262–64; fight against discrimination in society, 105–07; intense struggles in the life of, 68, 76; non-discriminatory character in the teachings of, 107; order of, 75; in past existence, 84; and reason for employing various teaching methods, 104; rejecting the causes for his enlightenment in his present existence, 210; and relationship with Devadatta from the past, 77–78; revealing true identity of, 195–96, 204; victory declarations of, 83

Shariputra Bodhisattva, 74, 86, 93, 105, 114, 218; and the enlightenment of women, 97–98, 100, 101

Shiba Tatsuto, 112

Shijo Kingo, 20

shoju (propagation), practice of, 171–72. *See also shakubuku*

Shrimala (queen of Ayodhya), 107

Shrimala Sutra, 109

Silk Road, 238

sincerity, 108

six difficult and nine easy acts, 48–49; doctrine of, 55; example of the principle of, 42; as seen by Nichiren Daishonin, 47

society, transformation needed in today's, 270; root causes for the ills of modern, 123

Socrates, 16

Soka Gakkai, 21; branded in Japan as, 185, 249; development of the, 168, 249; existing order of events are shaken with the appearance of the, 212–13; Josei Toda's way to share his enlightenment with the members of the, 266; members' faith in the early days of the, 183, 250; movement of the, 183, 251; Nichijun praising the efforts of the, 174; origins for the development of, 24; struggles that strengthened the faith of the, 85

SGI. *See also* Soka Gakkai International

Soka Gakkai International, action of the members of the, 44–45, 50; activities of the, 26; cause for the development of the, 135–36, 182; character, 184; Dong-Hoon Kim's observation of the underlying strength of the, 251; having immense gratitude toward the, 215; importance of doing activities of the, 170; importance of practicing with the, 146–47; in Hong Kong, 252; lifeblood of the, 256; movement of the, 34; represents, 253; women members of the, 123; young women members of the, 123. *See also* Soka Gakkai

Soka Gakkai members, and the Ceremony in the Air, 265; earnest practice of the, 182, 1868–89

Soka movement, spirit of the, 130

Soviet Union, Daisaku Ikeda's visit to the, 42; reason for the collapse of the, 273

space, in Indian cosmology, 236–37